# WIN-WIN NEGOTIATING

# WIN-WIN NEGOTIATING

## TURNING CONFLICT INTO AGREEMENT

**Fred Edmund Jandt**
with the assistance of
**Paul Gillette**

JOHN WILEY & SONS
New York • Chichester • Brisbane • Toronto • Singapore

**Library of Congress Cataloging in Publication Data:**
Jandt, Fred E.
  Win-Win Negotiating.

  Includes index.
  1. Conflict management.   2. Negotiation in business.
I. Gillette, Paul.   II. Title.

HD42.J36      1985      658      84-25673
ISBN 0-471-88207-0

Printed in the United States of America

10  9  8  7  6  5  4  3  2

In memoriam
Delmer M. Hilyard
advisor and friend

# PREFACE

In 1980 I developed and began conducting the professional development seminar "Managing Conflict Productively." The seminar was based on my academic interest in communication and conflict and on my consulting experience with various organizations. Since then, thousands of professional men and women from business and public service groups of all kinds, from Anchorage to San Juan, have attended that seminar. The seminar explains how conflict in organizations can be controlled and used and how managers can become more adept as negotiators within and without their organizations.

This book represents that seminar as it has grown and developed with the suggestions provided by those individuals who have attended and profited from it. New material and extended explanations and examples are presented in the book that couldn't be presented in the time allotted to a training program.

A consummate professional, Paul Gillette, has been instrumental not only in providing new material but also in sharpening the focus of what I had originally developed and putting the ideas into a meaningful and engrossing written style.

The examples we include are true. We have, on occasion, adapted the examples to highlight the points we are making. In these cases if the names of persons or companies bear any similarity to those of actual persons or companies, the similarity is purely fortuitous.

FRED EDMUND JANDT

*San Francisco*
*January 1985*

# CONTENTS

1. I WANT, YOU WANT: OR THE SICILIAN STALEMATE AND HOW TO AVOID IT   1

2. HOW DO *YOU* DEAL WITH CONFLICT?   7

3. BEYOND EVIL AND ILLNESS: OLD AND NEW IDEAS ABOUT CONFLICT WITHIN ORGANIZATIONS   23

4. WHY CONFLICT IS INEVITABLE WITHIN ORGANIZATIONS   29

5. ONE IS NOT ENOUGH: OR IDENTIFYING THE SOURCES OF CONFLICT   63

6. ON THE ESCALATOR: OR HOW SMALL CONFLICTS QUICKLY BECOME LARGE ONES   75

7. DESTRUCTIVE AND PRODUCTIVE USES OF CONFLICT   101

8.   AN EXERCISE IN DEALING WITH CONFLICT        119

9.   GETTING PAST "YES": OR THE THEORETICALLY
     PERFECT RESOLUTION OF ANY CONFLICT          129

10.  NEGOTIATING FROM STRENGTH: OR HOW TO GET
     OTHERS TO GIVE YOU POWER TO RESOLVE A
     CONFLICT                                     155

11.  HOW PROFESSIONAL NEGOTIATORS OPERATE:
     POSITIONAL BARGAINING VERSUS INTEREST
     BARGAINING                                   179

12.  THE MINI-MAX STRATEGY: OR WHAT SHOULD I
     GIVE AND WHAT SHOULD I GET?                  199

13.  DETERMINING YOUR OPPONENT'S MINI-MAX         217

14.  UNPACKING: OR HOW TO FIND MULTIPLE WAYS
     TO HELP YOUR OPPONENTS GET A GOOD DEAL       229

15.  UNDOING, TOKENING, BONE-THROWING, ISSUE
     SUBSTITUTION: AND OTHER PATHS TO
     PACIFICATION                                 249

16.  THE HARDBALL NEGOTIATOR: OR HOW TO FIGHT
     DIRTY WHEN YOU HAVE TO                       263

17.  IT'S NOT ALWAYS EASY: BUT IT'S USUALLY
     POSSIBLE                                     295

     INDEX                                        299

# 1 I WANT, YOU WANT

## OR THE SICILIAN STALEMATE
## AND HOW TO AVOID IT

Let's start with an easy one.

You're in a lounge at an airport when a slobby-looking guy takes the seat next to yours. He lights a cigarette, tunes his industrial-strength portable radio to the local rock station, and turns up the volume.

Immediately there is a conflict. Cigarette smoke bothers you almost as much as rock music (in fact, you regard the term *rock music* a contradiction), and here is this jerk imposing large doses of both on you. Nonetheless, there is no sign nearby proscribing the smoking of cigarettes or the playing of radios. Your antagonist, from his point of view, is merely exercising his rights.

You might argue that the absence of a sign forbidding an activity does not ipso facto legitimize the activity. There are, after all, no signs at the airport proscribing the molestation of children, the inhalation of cocaine, or the detonation of nuclear bombs.

On the other hand, these acts are prohibited by law. In this particular lounge at this particular airport, there is no law or even a posted local policy against smoking or playing a radio.

But, you might argue, there are certain unwritten rules about what constitutes civil behavior. We cannot simply do whatever we feel like whenever we . . .

Stop. The question here is not whether certain conduct is legally permissible and socially acceptable. The conflict extends beyond the boundaries of mere legality and propriety.

The fact is, this fellow *wants* to smoke his cigarette and play his radio, whereas you have a *conflicting desire* for silence and smoke-free air. The wishes of one of you can prevail only if the wishes of the other are frustrated.

Were you to persuade your tormenter—or cajole him, or intimidate him, or otherwise motivate him—to cease and desist, chances are he would feel deprived and maybe also resentful. Likewise, were it possible to convince you that his behavior was both legally and socially correct, the probability is that you would still be annoyed by his cigarette and his radio.

Okay, how should the conflict be resolved? I promised you an easy one, so here goes:

The lounge where you are waiting is very large and also very sparsely populated. You need not remain in the vicinity of the cigarette-smoking rockophile. You can hie yourself to an opposite corner and await your plane in comfort.

You might not like having to move, but that's a small enough price to pay for the restoration of tranquility, is it not? (When the stakes are low, most of us seek the least unpleasant way out of a conflict.)

Now let's make things a bit more difficult. The lounge is crowded, and this guy took the only vacant seat. You don't merely dislike cigarette smoke: you have a medical condition that is likely to be exacerbated by it—especially if you incur prolonged exposure, which you well may, for the airport is fogged in and all flights are late by anywhere from half an hour to an hour and a half.

Obviously, the more onerous your circumstances, the greater your incentive becomes to seek some sort of resolution to the conflict. If you would walk away from your adversary in a crowded lounge, even though doing so would mean having to stand for an hour while waiting for your flight, how would you react if the same fellow sat next to you in the airplane's no smoking section and lit up?

If you would tolerate this, how would your reaction differ if the person imperiled by smoke was your baby son or daughter? What would you do if you asked your adversary to stop smoking and he refused? How would you react if you sought the aid of the flight attendant and were told that nothing could be done?

I think you'll agree that no matter how patiently you might generally bear wrongs a point eventually would be reached at which you would feel compelled to take a stand. I think you'll also agree that, pleasant though the idea may seem of avoiding conflict completely, few if any of us are in a position to do so.

If you want something and I also want it, we're in conflict, whether what we want is the same job, the same seat on a bus, or any of the many millions of other desiderata over which we might compete.

If you want something and I have no interest whatever in it, we may still be in conflict—for example, when what you want (more police and fire protection, let us say) is at odds with what I want (lower taxes).

Conflict need not be interpersonal. Psychologists long ago developed classifications for conflicts that any of us may experience within himself or herself.

In what is called an "approach-approach" conflict, a person must choose between attractive alternatives. Should I wear my favorite red tie today or my favorite blue tie?

In an "avoidance-avoidance" conflict, we must choose between unattractive alternatives. I do not want to give the electric company my money, but neither do I want my lights turned off.

In an "approach-avoidance" conflict, the same action contains desirable and undesirable elements. For example, the young man on the diving board wants to impress another young man sitting at poolside. He believes he will do so if (approach) he executes his most risky dive, a triple gainer. But he knows also that there is a danger that (avoidance) he will execute the dive poorly, make a fool of himself, and perhaps also injure himself.

All of us deal with dozens—if not hundreds or even thousands—of such intrapersonal conflicts each day. However, most of us long ago developed effective techniques for resolving them.

Where we need help is with interpersonal conflicts—and especially with those that arise in the workplace: employer versus employee, salesperson versus customer, public relations executive versus journalist, government liaison officer versus federal or state regulator.

The biggest danger in such conflicts is that we can get locked into a position where we surrender everything—or, in any event, surrender far more than we should—because we have not learned how to deal with conflict productively.

More than a few employees have walked out on jobs that they liked—and needed—because they were unable to manage a relatively minor dispute with a boss. Likewise, more than a few employers have fired valuable subordinates because these employers could find no way to reconcile certain comparatively unimportant differences.

How many salespeople have lost important accounts because they could not overcome personality-related conflicts with customers? How many executives have embarrassed themselves and their companies because they let an antagonistic journalist goad them into making imprudent statements?

The ultimate conflict, of course, is war, and to engage in it—whether on a global or personal scale—is, in effect, to admit to an inability to deal with disagreement. Yet most nations manage to get involved in armed combat at least once or twice in a century, just as most people at least several times in a lifetime get caught up in a controversy that costs them a job or destroys a friendship or a relationship within the family.

Our inability—as individuals and as a species—to resolve conflict is illustrated by a cartoon that is popular in Sicily, a region of Italy whose motorists are not known for their courtesy. The cartoon, titled "The Sicilian Stalemate," depicts four automobiles that have arrived at the same time at an intersection with a malfunctioning traffic light. Each car's progress is blocked by another car, thus:

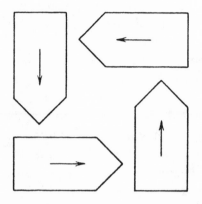

It would, of course, be a relatively simple matter for one of the cars to back up and let another car pass, whereupon all the remaining motorists would have free passage. The point of the cartoon is that we sometimes sacrifice a major interest because we are unwilling to yield on a minor one. Unreasonable though this approach can be seen to be in the context of the cartoon, many of us behave exactly the same way in conflicts at home or on the job.

As a professional negotiator and advisor to governments and major corporations, I've spent most of my adult life dealing with conflict. I've been called in to bargain with terrorists who were holding hostages as well as to mediate between municipal subdivisions with seemingly irreconcilable budgetary differences.

I have conducted seminars on conflict management for executives of General Instrument, GTE Sylvania, Shell Oil Company, State of Georgia Human Resource Department, Blue Cross of California, Seaside Hospital, and California Association of School Business Officials, to name just a few.

My aim in this book is to teach you the same techniques and skills that international diplomats and top corporate managers use when dealing with conflict. For example, I'll tell you how French president François Mitterand persuaded South Korea to withdraw its opposition to France's opening of diplomatic relations with North Korea: He used a technique that I call "unpacking," wherein elements of a conflict are defined separately and concessions on one are repaid with concessions on another.

Also—on the lighter side—I'll tell you how Dwight D. Eisenhower, as president of Columbia University, got students to stop walking on the grass: Assuming that the paths chosen by the students were the most efficient routes from one point on campus to another, he ordered sidewalks installed where the paths were and grass planted where the old sidewalks had been.

The central thesis of this book is that conflict is inevitable but not necessarily bad. Poorly managed conflict can destroy relationships, families, companies, and nations; however, if conflicts are managed skillfully and creatively, the result can be a greater number of benefits for everyone involved.

Moreover, while rampant, uncontrolled conflict can be extremely costly (emotionally as well as financially) for us as individuals as well as for the organizations that we populate, so, too, can be the absence of healthy conflict. Indeed, organizations often become more productive by encouraging certain kinds of conflict and teaching members how to deal with conflict.

This book will focus primarily on on-the-job conflicts. However, the conflict management techniques that it will teach are no less applicable to away-from-the-office disputes. That's right, the same skills that a police psychologist employs to talk a suicide victim down from a window ledge, the same techniques with which a professional mediator brings about harmony between management and a labor union, are applicable whether you are trying to get a refund from a merchant who overcharged you, trying to persuade your boss that you should have a raise, or trying to resolve a squabble between your teenage son and daughter.

A few chapters hence, we'll begin an extensive examination of these techniques and the ways in which they might be applied. First, however, let's look at the ways in which you now deal with conflict.

# ≡2≡HOW DO *YOU* DEAL WITH CONFLICT?

─────────────────────────────

I am going to ask you to respond to seven hypothetical situations. For each situation there are six possible reactions. Choose the one—and only one—reaction that would be closest to your *first* response if you were in that situation.

Please note that I have asked for only *one* reaction. If several of the alternatives seem pertinent, select the one that is *closest* to the way you would react.

You may feel that none of the reactions is pertinent. Or you may feel that while one or more are reasonable, you would be more likely to have yet another reaction. Be that as it may, for the purposes of this exercise please choose one of the six reactions spelled out here.

One or more of the situations—or maybe even the entire self-inventory—may strike you as unrealistic. For the time being, however, please go along with me and respond to every item. Later in this chapter I'll explain why your responses are useful no matter how unreasonable the range of choices may seem.

1. You have reserved a table at a restaurant and have invited important business associates to dine with you. When you arrive, you are told by the head waiter that he has forgotten your reservation and has no table available. You would—

   (a) Wait until a table becomes available.
   (b) Be irritated with yourself for having reserved a table at such a restaurant.
   ✓(c) See the manager and insist that a table be found.
   (d) Forgive the head waiter; it is human to forget.
   (e) Speak sharply to the head waiter about his forgetfulness.
   (f) Go to another restaurant where reservations are not needed.

2. You have to make an urgent telephone call. You are waiting outside a booth that is being used by an elderly man who obviously is in no hurry to finish his conversation. You would—

   (a) Expect the man to notice that you are fidgeting; when he does, he probably will be considerate and terminate the conversation.
   ✓(b) Try to find another telephone.
   (c) Wish you were not dependent on the telephone.
   (d) Bang on the door to demonstrate your impatience.
   (e) Wait patiently; eventually the man will have to stop talking.
   (f) Feel guilty about your hostile feelings toward the old man; his phone call, after all, may be just as important to him as yours is to you.

3. A guest absent-mindedly places a lighted cigarette on your table and burns a hole in the tablecloth. You would—

   (a) Tell him that what he did was stupid.

    (b)   Demand that he pay to have the cloth repaired.

  ✓(c)   Be annoyed with yourself for not having noticed the cigarette before the damage was done.

    (d)   Have the cloth mended without saying anything to your friend.

    (e)   Console your friend by pointing out that this was just an accident of the sort that could happen to anyone.

    (f)   Say nothing; what's done is done, and there is no purpose in saying anything at this time.

4.   Pickets at your favorite supermarket ask you not to buy there because the store is selling vegetables harvested by nonunion laborers. You would—

    (a)   Listen to their arguments and decide whether to take your business elsewhere.

    (b)   Tell them to stop bothering you.

    (c)   Listen to their arguments even though you do not intend to be swayed; the pickets, after all, have a right to express their opinions.

  ✓(d)   Ignore the pickets; this is not something that concerns you; labor disputes eventually get settled, no matter how intensely antagonistic opposing parties may be before the settlement.

    (e)   Apologize to the pickets for not having known about the store's antilabor policies.

    (f)   Tell the pickets that you are not interested because this problem is one for the union and the store's management to work out between themselves.

5.   The Japanese government asks the U.S. to give up certain military bases in Japan. The U.S. should—

    (a)   Refrain from responding; the issue will resolve itself in time.

    (b)   Offer to negotiate.

    (c)   Ask the Japanese to explain how they would defend themselves if the U.S. gave up the bases.

(d)  Recognize that the Japanese government may have been responding to internal political pressures when it made this demand.

(e)  Tell the Japanese that their demand is unwarranted.

✓(f)  Consider what action the U.S. might have taken that caused Japan to make this request.

6.  Chile announces that the price of copper sold to the U.S. will be increased by two hundred percent. The U.S. should—

(a)  Inform Chile that all copper imports will be suspended if the increase is not rescinded.

(b)  Recognize that commodity prices rise and fall with the market; what goes up now is likely to come down in the future.

✓(c)  Call a meeting of U.S. importers of Chilean copper to see why the U.S. has become so dependent on that source.

(d)  Ask Chile to justify the price increase; also, ascertain whether Chile is treating other importing nations the same way.

(e)  Determine whether other sources of copper can be found to meet America's needs.

(f)  Inform all U.S. importers of copper that all prices have risen and that Chile has the right to decide what it will charge.

7.  South Africa complains to the U.S. that the police force in Washington, D.C., has not maintained sufficient control over pickets protesting apartheid in front of the South African embassy. U.S. officials should—

(a)  Inform Washington's police chief of his officers' laxity and threaten sanctions.

(b)  Take no action at present; the situation may soon improve on its own.

✓(c)  Arrange a meeting between Washington's chief of police and an official of the South African embassy to see how the problem might be settled.

(d) Acknowledge receipt of the complaint; the South Africans' concern over the pickets is understandable.

(e) Inform the South African government that its racial policies are the real cause of the problem.

(f) Request that the South African government provide evidence to support its complaint.

Okay, I agree with you, the self-inventory has many flaws. Some of the reactions are extremely naive, others are obviously—and blatantly—counterproductive, and a great many are only partial approaches and not mutually exclusive.

Once again, however, I'll ask you to go along with me. Before I explain why your answers are useful—no matter how unreasonable the choices may seem—please review your responses and make sure that you selected—

1. One reaction to each situation;

2. *Only* one reaction to each situation;

3. The alternative that is closest to the way you *first* would respond in that situation.

Are you satisfied that your responses meet these criteria? Very well, let's continue.

Yes, the self-inventory has many flaws. For example, in Situation 1 you might argue that none of the listed reactions is appropriate because you would not take important clients to a restaurant unless you were certain that your reservations would be honored and service would be impeccable.

I feel the same way. Granted, signals might get crossed under certain circumstances at even the most fastidious of restaurants. All the same, nothing approximating the situation described here has ever befallen me—for the very good reason that I make sure, before taking important clients to dine, that the restaurant is prepared to receive us properly.

Moreover, even if you and I were to assume—for the purposes of argument—that we might find ourselves in this situation, we probably would not react in *only one* of the ways described. We might, for example, initially—and perhaps only fleetingly—be (reaction b) irritated with ourselves for having selected this restaurant, then (c) demand that the manager find a table, and, failing that (f) go elsewhere.

Likewise, in Situation 3 when a friend absent-mindedly burns a hole in the tablecloth, our reaction might well depend chiefly on the importance of the friend in our scheme of things. If he or she were someone on whose good will our business fortunes depended, we probably would be slower to anger (or at least to *visible* anger) than if he or she were a social acquaintance of whom we had never been all that fond anyway.

Also, as in the earlier situation, we might react in more than one of the itemized ways: for example, (c) being annoyed with ourselves for not having noticed the cigarette on the table, (f) saying nothing to the friend, and (d) paying for the mending ourselves rather than asking for reimbursement.

Moving from problems in interpersonal relations to problems in international relations, we might, in Situation 5, simultaneously (d) recognize that the Japanese government may have been responding to internal political pressures when it made its demand; (f) consider what action the United States might have taken that caused Japan to make this demand; (c) ask the Japanese to explain how they would defend themselves if the United States gave up the bases; and (b) offer to negotiate.

Finally, in Situation 6 you and I probably will agree that long before any crisis arose about copper prices the United States should—and almost certainly would—have known (c) why the United States has become so dependent on Chile as a source of copper and (e) whether other sources can be found to meet the United State's needs.

Yet imperfections of the self-inventory notwithstanding, I believe your responses to it can be both significant and revealing. Before we consider why, please perform certain computations on your answers.

In the table on the facing page the seven situations are listed by number in the column at the left. Circle the letter designating your reaction to each situation. [For example, if your choice for Situation 1 was (a) "Wait until a table becomes available," circle the letter *a* under roman numeral VI. Likewise, if your choice in Situation 6 was (a) "Inform Chile that all copper imports will be suspended if the increase is not rescinded," circle the letter *a* under the roman numeral I.]

## TABLE FOR LOGGING RESPONSES TO QUESTIONNAIRE

| Situation | I | II | III | IV | V | VI |
|---|---|---|---|---|---|---|
| 1 | e | c✓ | b | (f) | d | a |
| 2 | d | a | c | (b)✓ | f | e |
| 3 | a | b | c✓ | d | (e) | (f) |
| 4 | (b) | f | e | a | c | d✓ |
| 5 | e | c | f✓ | (b) | d | a |
| 6 | a | d | c✓ | (e) | f | b |
| 7 | e | f | a | (c)✓ | d | b |
| Totals | — | — | — | — | — | — |

Now total the columns. Then transfer the totals to their corresponding boxes in the chart below:

## CHART FOR TOTALS
## FROM THE TABLE

| I | II |
|---|---|
| *1* | (1) |
| III | IV |
| (3) | (2)　5 |
| V | VI |
| 4 | (1)　1 |

Have you done so? Okay, let's proceed.

The seven-situation inventory is adapted from a much larger inventory devised by Norwegian sociologist Bjørn Christiansen and published first in *Attitudes toward Foreign Affairs as a Function of Personality*.* In the quarter of a century since that book first appeared, one version or another of the self-inventory has been administered to hundreds of thousands of managers, lawyers, physicians, engineers, and students. No matter where this was done, people responded in certain patterns that correlated to the sort of work they did and to their circumstances within various organizations.

This is very important. It means that, whatever the self-inventory's flaws, the device has proven itself—empirically—to be a valid evaluative tool. A comparison might be made to psychology's well-known Rorschach test, in which subjects look at a series of inkblots and tell the examiner what images or emotions each of the inkblots invokes. The value of the test does not lie in the character of the inkblots or their ability to provoke certain types of responses. Rather, Hermann Rorschach, the Swiss psychologist who developed the test, observed over a number of years that certain groups of people responded to the same inkblots in the same ways.

For example, psychiatric patients who had been diagnosed as schizophrenic responded in much the same way as each other but dramatically differently from the ways in which other psychiatric patients—depressives, for instance, or paranoids—responded. Likewise, the responses of psychiatric patients as a class were significantly different from the responses of the general population.

Initially, the inkblots were merely the *vehicle* that permitted the responses to be accumulated and classified. However, once the patterns had been established and their validity and reliability demonstrated, it became possible to use the inkblot test as a diagnostic tool. In other words, a person's responses could be used to suggest a hypothetical diagnosis or to help confirm a diagnosis that was based on other evidence.

I repeat, the inkblots initially were only a vehicle. Were it possible to find similar patterns of response when people were asked to

*Oslo: Oslo University Press, 1959.

pick a number between 1 and 10, such a test would be no less use-ful than the inkblot test. And so it is with the Christiansen self-inventory: Though some of the situations may seem unrealistic and many of the reactions may seem silly or inapt, the fact re-mains that a variety of people responding to the self-inventory demonstrated patterns that related closely to the sort of work they did and to their circumstances within various organizations.

Let us look first at the patterns, then at some of the groups whose responses fit these patterns.

The boxes on the left side of the chart that you just filled in—that is, the boxes with odd numbers—all involve assigning blame for the situation.

**Box I.**   We blame someone else. For instance, in the situation (2) involving the elderly man and the telephone, we bang on the door to demonstrate impatience. We are saying, in effect, that *our* trouble is *the man's* fault. Likewise, in the situation (1) at the res-taurant, we blame the head waiter. If *he* had not forgotten our res-ervations, *we* would not have this problem.

**Box III.**   We blame ourselves. We wish that we were not so de-pendent on the telephone. Or we are irritated with ourselves for choosing this restaurant. In both situations, we see the problem as *our* fault.

**Box V.**   We blame someone else by granting absolution. Thus we *forgive* the headwaiter his trespass of forgetting our reserva-tion because "it is human to forget." Likewise, by reminding our-selves that the elderly man's phone call may be just as important to him as ours is to us—and by feeling guilty about our hostile feel-ings toward him—we absolve him of his sin of inconveniencing us.

Of course, a case could be made that the responses might pro-voke action that could solve our problem. For example, the elderly man, because we bang on the door, might end his call sooner than he otherwise would have. Or the head waiter, because we speak sharply to him, might give us a table that was being held for someone else. However, in Christiansen's formulation, the *primary* element in all of these responses is the assignment of blame.

Most of us can think of dozens of examples from everyday life in which people have focused on blame to the exclusion of virtually everything else. Not too long ago I found myself in such a situation.

☐ I discovered an important error in a large printing job and telephoned the printer to make arrangements to have the job redone. The printer replied that he could not understand how the error might have been made and promised to investigate immediately.

☐ I was not interested at the time in learning how or why the error had been made. I needed the material urgently, and my main concern was in getting the job redone as quickly as possible.

☐ I told the printer this, but he was determined to assign responsibility for the error before he would talk about redoing the job. For the better part of a quarter hour, I tried futilely to persuade him that there would be plenty of time to assign blame after the job had been redone. Finally, in desperation, I said that *I* was responsible for the error, and I agreed to pay to have the job redone. I was willing to do so because my need for the material was so urgent. Satisfied, he quickly redid the job correctly.

☐ In a sense, I was the "loser" in the transaction, having paid for an error that was not mine. But I did get what I needed when I needed it. The printer, meanwhile, lost a good customer.

Returning to the chart, please note that the boxes with even numbers—that is, those on the right of the chart—deal with changing the situation rather than assigning blame.

*Box II.* We assume that someone else will bring about the desired change. Thus we expect the elderly man to notice that we are fidgeting and therefore to terminate his conversation. Likewise, in the restaurant, we demand that the manager intervene. In both situations, our attitude is, "We've got a problem, and *you* should do something about it."

*Box IV.* We take action ourselves. We look for another telephone. Or we go to another restaurant. (We've got a problem, and *we* are going to do something about it.)

*Box VI.* We expect the solution to our problem to come about spontaneously. Eventually the elderly man will stop talking. Eventually someone will finish eating and we will get that table. (We've got a problem, and *someone—somewhere—sometime—* is going to do something about it.)

My reaction in the conflict with the printer was of the Box IV variety: I took action (by accepting responsibility for the error) in order to impel him to redo the job.

Very well, these are the six categories of responses to the Christiansen inventory, each category representing a different *style* of dealing with conflicts. The point here is not that one style is superior or inferior but rather, quite simply, that the styles exist.

Do your responses fit one of these patterns? Was there one box on the chart that attracted more of your responses that any other? Did it attract more than half? Did it attract *all* of your responses? The likelihood is that the greater the percentage of your responses a given box attracted, the more fixed you are in that style of problem-solving.

In the course of my own work, I have administered the inventory to thousands of executives. Their responses correlate closely with those of people who have responded to the inventory in other settings throughout the world.

Here are some of the patterns I have observed:

**Midlevel managers and administrators tend toward Box IV responses.**

That is, these executives impose the problem-solving activity on themselves.

This is hardly surprising. In most organizations, midlevel managers spend most of their time resolving conflicts of one sort or another. Indeed, problem-solving may be the typical midlevel manager's principal activity. Accepting the responsibility for solving the problem often means seeing to it personally that the problem does get solved.

**Entrepreneurs, especially in small organizations, tend even more strongly toward Box IV responses.**

And this is hardly surprising. Most entrepreneurs built their businesses by taking personal charge of whatever problems arose. If the entrepreneur did not personally solve the problem, the problem did not get solved.

**Top-level managers tend toward Box II responses or display no pattern.**

These executives—chairpersons, presidents, or senior vice presidents of large organizations—either favor Box II or scatter their responses among the six categories, with no single category drawing a majority (four or more).

The Box II pattern may at first seem surprising. Indeed, we might wonder how a person who rose to the command of a large organization could possibly have done so while leaving all the problem-solving to someone else. Remember, however, that we are not talking about the style of response that the top-level manager employed *on the way up* but rather about his or her *present* style of response. The top-level manager usually, if not always, has at his or her disposal a plethora of Box IV types who are ready, willing, and eager to solve the problems. "Handle it," says the top-level manager—and the problem goes away.

The absence of a pattern is no less understandable. Indeed, on reflection, we may conclude that this "nonstyle" is more logical than any pattern would be.

The nonstyle top-level manager is extremely flexible. Sometimes he or she says, "Handle it." Sometimes, "I'm going to handle this one myself." Sometimes, "Let it sit." Sometimes, "Solving this particular problem is far less important than determining how it arose and ensuring that it won't arise again."

**Other patterns of response are uncommon among managers but prevalent among professionals, students, and other groups of respondents.**

For example, Box I and Box III attract a disproportionately high number of physicians and engineers. In both occupations diagnosis—that is, assigning blame (in the broadest sense)—is a crucial step in developing a solution.

Boxes I and III also attract a disproportionately high number of blue-collar workers, students, and the unemployed—perhaps because these people often see themselves as incapable of exerting much control over their problems and therefore concentrate instead on why the problems arose (in the interest of minimizing the chances that the problems will arise again).

Box VI, interestingly enough—at least to me—does not correlate closely to occupations but does correlate (albeit rather loosely) to location. I've received a disproportionately high percentage of Box VI responses when I've administered the self-inventory in Hawaii. Other investigators had similar results in beach cities of Florida or of countries on the Mediterranean, Aegean, or other tropical or semitropical seas. That attitude is, "Surf's up! Go to the beach!" In other words, "Leave the problem alone. It will still be there when we get back—or maybe it will go away."

None of the above is to say that Box VI people—or possessors of any other pattern—are better or worse equipped to deal with conflict than the rest of us. As I noted earlier, the point of this chapter is not to argue that one style is preferable; rather, the point is simply to demonstrate—and dramatize—the different styles.

In fact, each style can be seen as having both its strengths and its drawbacks. Extreme Box IV people often accomplish their aims at the expense of their own physical and emotional well-being. I have no data to support my conjecture, but I would be willing to wager a very expensive bottle of wine that the percentage of Box IV people undergoing treatment for ulcers is substantially higher than the percentage of people whose responses favor any of the other five boxes.

Even if the Box IV manager pays no physical or emotional price, there may be a price in efficiency. When we assume the responsibility for solving problems, people tend to bring us problems to solve. We then reward them by solving their problems—and, in the process, we encourage them to bring us yet other problems.

Eventually we get involved in virtually every problem that relates even tangentially to our own areas of responsibility, no matter how trivial these problems may be. Does the office need a new typewriter? We are asked for an opinion on the make, the model, and even the color. Are two secretaries quarreling over who should go to lunch first? The Box IV manager is asked to arbitrate.

Extreme Box IV people (hereinafter, EB-IV) may be responsible for situations that hurt the organization rather than help it. For example, EB-IV managers, intent on addressing every detail personally, create staffs whose problem-solving skills go undeveloped. Thus all the problems wind up on the EB-IV manager's desk, and this creates bottlenecks. Work stacks up elsewhere in the office because the EB-IV manager has not found time to pass judgment on problems that subordinates—had they been given the opportunity to develop their skills—could have solved very easily.

Moreover, if the EB-IV manager takes a vacation or becomes ill, virtually nothing gets accomplished because no one knows enough about the EB-IV's job to take over—and, in most offices, subordinates do not dare make decisions that the EB-IV might regard as an encroachment on the EB-IV's personal domain.

Indeed, many EB-IVs (especially entrepreneurs) never take a vacation. Or, if they do take one, they close the business. Their assumption is that nothing can be accomplished if they do not take personal charge of the situation.

What is the principal complaint of the EB-IV? There is never enough time. *Of course* there is never enough time for the manager or administrator who insists on doing everything personally.

Several important lessons can be drawn from the above consideration of styles of responding to situations of conflict.

First—and rather obvious—is that people (*some* people, anyway) behave fairly consistently no matter what type of problem they are facing.

Second, other people may perceive patterns in our behavior even if we ourselves do not. (Chances are that your children know your problem-solving style better than any of your co-workers or social acquaintances—and chances are that your children can, by virtue of this knowledge, exert much greater control over your behavior than anyone else with whom you deal.)

Third, and perhaps most important to your work, being predictable in your style can place you at the mercy of your adversaries. As they learn your patterns, they may gain control over the outcome of any conflict.

For example, in my conflict with the printer, I may have clued him about my Box IV style long before he delivered the job with the major error in it. Indeed, he may have noticed the error and delivered the job anyway, reasoning along these lines: "Well, we goofed up, there's no question about that. But if I call Jandt and tell him what happened, he'll demand that we reprint the stuff immediately at our own expense. Meanwhile, if we deliver the thing the way it is and let him discover the error, he'll go crazy wondering how he can get the job corrected in time to meet his deadline. When he phones about the error, I'll pretend I never noticed it, and then I'll make a big to-do about finding out who is responsible. If I stick to my guns, he eventually will get so frustrated that he'll tell me to reprint the darned thing at his expense."

This is not to say that you should strive deliberately to be unpredictable—although some successful executives have done (successfully) just that. The point is simply that you should be aware that you may indeed have a pattern of response. Your knowledge that the pattern exists can be extremely valuable as you deal with situations of conflict.

# ≡≡≡3≡BEYOND EVIL AND ILLNESS

## OLD AND NEW IDEAS ABOUT CONFLICT WITHIN ORGANIZATIONS

For the longest time, the prevalent view of conflict within organizations was that:

1. Conflict is intrinsically bad. Its presence is evidence that something is wrong within the organization. For the good of the organization, the conflict must be eliminated.
2. The members of the organization who caused the conflict are emotionally disturbed—otherwise they would not cause the conflict.
3. To eliminate the conflict (and thereby solve the problem), it is necessary to fire or get psychiatric help for the responsible employees.

This perspective, which prevailed well into the 1960s—even in organizations that were regarded as extremely enlightened—has since given way to an almost diametrically opposite approach. The modern view is that:

1. Conflict is inevitable and not necessarily harmful.
2. Some kinds of conflict can contribute immeasurably to the health and well-being of the organization—for example, by stimulating productive competition.
3. No matter what the conflict, it can be managed in such a way that losses are minimized and gains maximized.

The old view depended in large part on the assumption that conflict was in some way alien to the behavior of socially well-developed humans. In other words, conflict was seen as a manifestation of ignorance and dyscontrol—rather like bad table manners or public flatulence. One who *knew how* to behave did not behave *that way*.

The new approach regards conflict as inevitable in certain situations that arise within every organization. In other words, you cannot *have* an organization without having conflict. Ergo, not only is conflict not abnormal, it is a phenomenon whose *absence* would be abnormal.

Let us, before proceeding further, make a distinction between certain dictionary definitions of conflict and other definitions that apply specifically to conflict within organizations.

In the most general terms, the noun *conflict* is defined by *The Random House Dictionary of the English Language** as

> *a battle or struggle, especially a prolonged struggle; strife; controversy; a quarrel (conflicts between church and state); . . . discord of action, feeling, or effect; antagonism, as of interests or principles; . . . a striking together; collision; . . . incompatibility or interference, as of one idea, desire, event, activity, etc., with another.*

These definitions, almost without exception, connote that conflict is irresolvable without combat, and they encourage the as-

*The Random House Dictionary of the English Language, The Unabridged Edition, Jess Stein, Editor in Chief (New York: Random House, 1967).

sumption that conflict is malum in se, evil in itself. However, some characterizations provided by psychologists are unburdened by this connotation. Consider the following characterization by Edward J. Murray:*

> *Conflict refers to a situation in which a person is motivated to engage in two or more mutually exclusive activities.... On the overt behavioral level, a tribesman may be motivated both to approach and to avoid the taboo object. On the verbal level, a person may want to speak the truth but fear to offend. On the symbolic level, ideas may clash and produce cognitive dissonance. On the motivational level, the visceral responses involved in fear and digestion are incompatible.*

> *Motives are important in conflict.... Conflict occurs only when the overt, verbal, symbolic, or emotional responses required to fulfill one motive are incompatible with those required to fill another.*

In the same book†, a political scientist's perspective is provided by Robert C. North:

> *A conflict emerges when two or more persons or groups seek to possess the same object, occupy the same space or the same exclusive position, play incompatible roles, maintain incompatible goals, or undertake mutually incompatible means for achieving their purposes.*

Sociologist Lewis Coser has refined these concepts and applied them specifically to conflicts of the sort that we observe most often within organizations. Conflict, as Coser sees it, consists of "a struggle over values . . . [or over] claims to scarce status, power, and resources." The aims of the opponents in this struggle are "to neutralize, injure, or eliminate their rivals."††

For our purposes as students of conflicts within organizations, Coser's formulation is particularly apt. Please note its two distinct parts:

---

*International Encyclopedia of the Social Sciences, Vol. 3 (New York: Macmillan; The Free Press, 1968), p. 220.

†Ibid., p. 226.

††Lewis Coser, The Functions of Social Conflict (New York: The Free Press, 1956), p. 8.

### 1. A struggle over values ... [or over] claims to scarce status, power, and resources.

In other words, the parties in the conflict are *competing*. Their competition may be over whose values will prevail: for example, among members of a museum's board of directors, one faction may advocate innovative programs designed to attract the largest possible audience, whereas another faction may seek to preserve the traditional character of the museum's exhibits. Or competitors may be vying for the vice presidency of a company, the authority to hire people without a senior executive's approval, or such perquisites as a corner office or a computer terminal.

In competitions over values, one ideology cannot prevail except at the expense of another. In other words, it is definitional that the museum cannot both change and remain the same.

When the competition involves status, power, or resources, the competitors may not be seeking something unique or "one of a kind." In other words, there might be more than one vice-presidency over which they are competing, and there may be quite a few corner offices or computer terminals. However, the operative word in Coser's formulation is "scarce." There cannot be an *unlimited* number of vice presidencies, corner offices, or terminals. (If all of us stand on tip-toe, none of us sees any better.)

### 2. The aims of the opponents are "to neutralize, injure, or eliminate their rivals."

In other words, if only one of us can have a certain thing, you and I must do what we can to prevent each other from getting it. Likewise, if 25 of us are competing for three prizes, the victorious trio will comprise those of us who found some way to surpass the 22 losers.

This does *not,* of course, mean that we must kill or maim each other. One can neutralize, injure, or eliminate a competitor simply by building the proverbial better mousetrap. The point, however, is that we are in a struggle over desiderata of which there are not enough to go around. If you get what you want, I and/or some of your other opponents will not get what we want.

The fact that we are competitors does not mean that we must be *enemies*. Rivalries need not be unfriendly. As Coser notes,

> *Conflicts and hostile sentiments, though often associated, are, in fact, different phenomena. . . . Hostile attitudes do not necessarily result in conflict, nor need we expect that objective discrepancies in power, status, income, and the like will necessarily lead to the outbreak of conflict, although they can be conceived as potential sources of conflict.\**

In sum, it is entirely possible for us to be in conflict with each other and yet like each other, just as it is possible for us to dislike each other and not be in conflict. By extension, conflict need not be detrimental to the parties involved—or to anyone else. In a sense, conflict is simply another face of competition.

Notes Joe Paterno, football coach at 1982 national champion Penn State (and 1982 NCAA Coach of the Year): "I tell my players, 'Love your opponent, because he's the person who gives you a reason to excel. If he were a pushover, there wouldn't be any point to playing the game.'"

Paterno adds:

> *There's nothing greater than to be in the locker room before a big football game, where you see a bunch of people who aren't concerned about what's in it for themselves but people who actually, physically, want to hang on to each other. I've been in locker rooms where our players embraced before a game with tears in their eyes. We've said a prayer before a game, with men on their knees, holding hands—these men who are so strong, so aggressive, so ambitious, so determined to be recognized. To see them lose themselves at that moment, it's almost an act of love. And then to go out and perform superbly—to me, these are the joys you get out of a sport like football.*

Viewed in this light, conflict is not an impediment to the efficient functioning and successful operation of an organization; it is—or can be—a spur toward excellence and achievement. No matter the type of organization—church, school, hospital, small business, large corporation—conflict can be valuable.

*\*International Encyclopedia of the Social Sciences,* Vol. 3, p. 233.

Indeed, no matter the type of organization, conflict, properly managed, is essential to growth. To suppress conflict can be even more costly to the organization than rampant, uncontrolled conflict. Take away conflict, and you also take away the incentive to develop, to excel. The ideal situation is one in which there is a *healthy* level of *controlled* and *contained* conflict.

In the chapters ahead, I'll discuss how this can be brought about. First, however, let's look at the reasons why conflict is inevitable within organizations.

# ══4══WHY CONFLICT IS INEVITABLE WITHIN ORGANIZATIONS

Inherent in the structure of every organization are unavoidable sources of conflict. Indeed, it may be definitional that "to organize" is to introduce sources of conflict.

Let's go to the Random House dictionary definition: "to form as or into a whole consisting of interdependent or coordinated parts." The parts may indeed be interdependent (and coordinated), but chances are that each of them sees itself as more important than any of the others.

Think about your own organization. If it is industrial, it probably has units given over to three basic functions: production, sales, and finance. If it is not industrial, it probably has comparable units. For example, in a governmental agency (such as the FBI or

the Department of Health, Education, and Welfare), the people responsible for obtaining funding are the equivalent of a commerical
organization's treasurer, who—in effect—solicits money from
stockholders or lenders to finance the organization's operations;
likewise, in a school district, the teachers are the equivalent of an
industrial organization's production people, delivering the goods
or services that are the organization's raison d'etre.

Naturally, each unit, department, or division within an organization will develop goals, values, objectives, and procedures appropriate to its mission. If I am a teacher, I will want whatever I think
is necessary for me to do my very best work: a comfortable and
well-lighted classroom, a certain number of pupils, certain text-
books or other teaching materials. If I am a sales manager, I will
want whatever I think is necessary for me and my subordinates to
do our best work: products of high quality, attractive packaging,
advertising and promotional support, quick delivery, quick and
relatively lenient credit approvals, and so on.

All of these desiderata, however, are likely to conflict with the
desiderata of other departments within the organization. If you are
the president of the school board in the district in which I am
teaching, you have to answer to taxpayers who may be unwilling
to pay for the personnel, facilities, and materials that I regard as
necessary. Likewise, if you are the credit manager of the company
in which I am the sales manager, your responsibility to minimize
losses conflicts with my responsibility to maximize sales.

Most of us can, in situations of this kind, appreciate the other
person's problems and point of view. But the fact remains that
each of us has a mission, and the other person represents a barrier
to our accomplishment of that mission.

Not surprisingly, we usually assign higher priority to our own
mission than to the other person's. In the process, we may lose
sight of the organization's overall goals, values, objectives, procedures, and reasons for being. In any event, conflict is inevitable as
our quest for what we feel we need clashes with colleagues' quests
for what they feel they need.

Each of us, it seems, tends to identify with the smallest work
unit within an organization. If I am a reporter in the business sec-

tion of the local newspaper, I may feel loyalty to a number of enti-
ties: the profession of journalism itself, the newspaper for which I
work, the division of the newspaper that deals with "breaking"
news (as opposed to features), and the subdivision that deals with
business news. However, my primary loyalty probably will be to
the subdivision, that is, the business section. Thus if my newspaper is the object of a merger offer by a chain that is known to emphasize feature material at the expense of business news, I probably will oppose the merger—even though I may believe that the
merger will serve the best interests of the newspaper itself.

Each of us also, it seems, tends to apply the standards of his or
her own work unit to the other work units within the organization.
Reporters in the business section may be proudest of the speed and
accuracy with which they report the news; reporters within the
food section or arts section may take greater pride in their ability
to write entertainingly. If a development at the newspaper seems
likely to encourage speed and accuracy at the expense of entertain-
ing writing, we in the business section are likely to favor it while
those in the food section and arts section are likely to oppose it.

In sum, subgroups within an organization tend to think of themselves as primary, and the members of each subgroup tend to apply
their own standards to the other subgroups—with the result that
conflict is inescapable.

Another illustration of this point comes from a study my company conducted for a leading manufacturer of plastics. We asked
managers in three departments—production, sales, and
research—how they felt about the formal structure of the organization, about the goals and objectives of each department, and
about how important they perceived relationships among employees to be.

Managers of production departments preferred rigid formal
structure. They wanted to know who reported to whom, when, and
under what circumstances. They placed low priority on
interpersonal relationships. They emphasized goals that related
mainly to the integrity of the product and to the efficiency of the
manufacturing process. They did not care whether or not employees liked each other.

Sales managers, on the other hand, preferred only a moderate degree of formal structure. They wanted to know to whom to send reports, but they preferred to submit reports without deadlines and they wanted as much flexibility as possible regarding the details of the reports. They placed a very high priority on interpersonal relationships. They wanted a cohesive team of salespeople who had excellent rapport with each other as well as with customers. They emphasized goals that related to the problems of customers, the activities of competitors, and other marketplace-related factors.

Finally, managers of research departments preferred minimal formal structure. They liked nothing better than to be left alone. They placed low priority on interpersonal relationships. They emphasized goals that related to long-term improvements of the manufacturing process or of the quality of the product.

Please note that each department had developed goals, standards, and objectives appropriate for itself. Not surprisingly, conflict arose when these departments began to evaluate *each other* in terms of these same goals, standards, and objectives.

Sales managers said, "Those clowns in production spend all their time trying to get the product down to .001 millimeter of perfection. They don't understand that if we don't get it to customers on time, this company won't be around for very long."

Production managers said, "Those guys in sales have no ethics. They'll sell *anything*. They don't understand that if we don't provide our customers with quality products, this company won't be around for very long."

Both sales and production managers were in close agreement about the people in research: "They are so out of touch with what keeps this company going, it's ridiculous. They sit around smoking their pipes and doodling on their drawing boards, and they couldn't care less what happens to the rest of us."

Meanwhile, the research people held an equally dim view of the people in sales and production.

A good case might be made that the potential amount of conflict within an organization is directly proportional to the number of levels in the organization, the number of distinct job titles or specialties within each level, and the number of distinct steps required to complete the product or service that the organization provides.

Does this mean that as organizations grow larger there will be more conflict? Yes—inevitably!—for "to organize" is to divide and subdivide, and the greater the number of divisions and subdivisions, the greater is the potential for conflict.

Meanwhile, in certain situations, conflict inheres in the job description. Police officers, for example, cannot do their job without being in conflict with law breakers. Lawyers trying a given case are, of necessity, in conflict with each other. In many companies, an internal auditor or controller is required to seek out examples of wasteful spending; if no examples are found, the jobholder is perceived as not doing his or her job.

In other occupations, while conflict is not exactly definitional, it usually goes with the territory. For example, we can safely assume that a governmental safety-and-health (OSHA) inspector and a plant manager will usually be in conflict. In theory, they may both want the same thing—a safe and healthy environment in the workplace. However, from the plant manager's point of view, the inspector might be seen as a petty autocrat whose goal is to find violations requiring costly changes or modifications. Meanwhile, the inspector may see most plant managers as corporate lackeys who want to save money for their companies, no matter what the risks to employees.

Another illustration:

☐ On a college campus, the security department has as its primary mission the protection of college property, while the faculty has as its primary mission the teaching of students. The roles are not mutually incompatible, but sometimes they may entail conflict.

☐ The faculty, for example, may want the students to have 24-hour access to certain expensive equipment. The security department may wish to restrict access to certain hours when the equipment can be guarded properly.

☐ The security department, to be sure, does not seek to *deprive* students of the equipment, just as the faculty does not desire that the equipment be placed *at risk*. All the same, if the security department is to perform its mission optimally, it probably will attempt to limit use of the equipment to a narrower time frame than the faculty deems desirable.

Let's now consider some other common sources of conflict within organizations.

# COMPETITION FOR LIMITED RESOURCES

No matter what the organization and no matter how abundant its resources, those resources are finite. Thus mathematically speaking, anything that you claim as your own is something I cannot claim as my own.

Granted, the more there is to go around, the less likely you and I are to fight over it. No one covets sand in a desert. In most situations, however, there is not quite enough of *any* resource to go around. Thus those of us who seek it are playing a zero-sum game in which you cannot win except at my expense and I cannot win except at yours.

When we speak of resources within organizations, most of us probably think immediately of money. Well, no question about it, money is a resource, and no matter how much of it there may be, the quantity is finite. However, there are a great many other resources over which people may compete, and some of these are far more important—in certain contexts—than money.

To wit:

## Responsibility

Some of us may shirk responsibility, but a great many of us—probably most of us—want more of it than we have. A few of us want as much as we can possibly get. We may want it mainly because of certain prerequisites that accompany it. The president of the United States commands Air Force One; you and I don't. But most of us, I think, want responsibility mainly because of the chal-

that it offers—the challenge to test the limits of our abilities, our dedication, our imagination.

Whatever the reasons for wanting it, we may be sure that other people within our organizations want it also. And whatever the organization, we are playing a zero-sum game, for neither of us can increase his or her area of responsibility except by diminishing someone else's.

## Personnel

In a sense, the number of people we have reporting to us is merely a reflection of our responsibility, but in another sense—larger and more important to a great many of us—these people are what makes it possible for us to do our job as well as we can. Thus in most organizations there is intense competition over personnel, and given that there are only so many people to go around, conflict is inevitable.

## Space

Like personnel, space is both a reflection of responsibility and a contributor to improved performance. Yes, I want the large corner office because it has the most attractive view and because my clients will be impressed; however, I also want it because the light is better, because there is enough room for me to work without feeling cramped, and because I will not be disturbed by traffic that passes other offices on the way from the reception desk. (And, of course, the large corner office is also a badge of power and prestige; the little guys do not get the big offices.)

## Tools and Equipment

The better ours are, the better we are able to do our jobs. And as is the case with personnel and space, the supply is finite.

The tools and equipment need not be limited to those under our exclusive control. In most companies, computer time—an extremely valuable resource—is shared by a variety of people. And there is never enough computer time: every minute that you claim is a minute that I cannot have.

## Access to Superiors

If you are the chairperson and Marge is the president, I, as executive vice president, would prefer to report directly to you—not only because a certain amount of prestige attaches to such a relationship but also because you, as the ultimate decision-maker, can facilitate my achieving my work-related goals.

Meanwhile, you could not do your job as chairperson if you made yourself available to the dozens or hundreds or thousands or even (in certain organizations) millions of people who would like your attention. So you must establish reporting channels to limit the number of people who have access to you. Obviously, those who seek access are in conflict with each other, and we who report to Marge will feel bettered by those who report to you—just as those who report to junior officers will feel bettered by those who report to Marge.

Let's look now at a textbook example of a conflict over limited resources:

☐   A manufacturing company for which I was a consultant decided during the last recession to reduce the size of its training department. The only employees who would not be transferred were the director and her assistant. Meanwhile, the activities of the department would be restricted to orienting new employees. Inasmuch as very few people were being hired, there would not be much orienting to do.

☐   Not surprisingly, the director of the department and her assistant felt threatened. They could not help but wonder how useful they were to the company and how long they would remain on the payroll if they were not doing anything.

☐   In fact, the president of the company had no intention of firing them; he saw the situation as temporary and intended to restore a full workload as soon as business improved. He tried to convince the director of this, but she was not persuaded. Accordingly, she began trying to make herself more valuable by expanding her activities into the customer service area. However, this company already had a customer relations department, and its activities also had been cut back. Thus the people in each department were in conflict with each other over the amount of responsibility each would be permitted to claim.

☐   The president understood the conflict for what it was: competition over a resource (responsibility) that the parties felt was limited. He decided that the best way to deal with the situation was to increase the apparent amount of the resource. Thus he created projects for each department—a special assignment for the training department in minority recruitment and a special assignment in the customer relations department relating to responses to an advertising campaign. The people in both departments felt busy once again and no longer had a reason to be in conflict.

There are, I think, several very good lessons here.

First, and probably most obvious, is that it sometimes may be prudent to practice minor deceptions in the interest of resolving conflicts. Had the president told both departments the unvarnished truth (that is, that their competition was pointless and potentially damaging to the company), they probably would have kept right on competing.

If they did not, they might nonetheless respond viscerally to the reduced workload and be dissatisfied with their jobs because they felt unproductive, unneeded, and coddled. Or they might, after a time, grow comfortable with their minimal workload and feel exploited when circumstances changed and the workload returned to normal.

In either event, seeing them idle could be demoralizing to fellow employees whose workload had not been reduced. By playing the psychologist and theorizing about their *real* (as opposed to apparent) needs, the president concluded that it was best to give them more work.

The second—and far more important—lesson to be drawn from this situation is that the *appearance* of a desideratum may sometimes be substituted for the desideratum itself. The president diagnosed (correctly, I believe) the conflict as competition over the resource of responsibility, but he did not actually give the parties more responsibility; he merely gave them more *work,* which they equated with responsibility.

The fact is that in a great many conflicts an apparent desideratum can be substituted for a real one. Also, one real desideratum can be substituted for another.

An illustration of the latter premise:

☐   Space, responsibility, and access to superiors are all limited resources. Let us say that a situation arises in which you, as president of a company, must take away space from one department and give it to another. If you simply announce what you intend to do and explain why it is being done, you probably will not satisfy the people in the department from which the space was taken.

☐   However, if you give that department additional responsibilities and/or more desirable reporting channels, the loss of space can be seen as a *trade-off* for these other desiderata. You will have, in effect, balanced the scale—not in an illusory way, as with assigning unnecessary work, but in the very real way of giving people something they want in return for something you have taken away. Of course, if you can give them more of the new thing than you have taken away of the old, you'll be doing very well indeed.

The final and most important lesson to be drawn from this situation is that the parties to a conflict do not always—or even usually—have a clear idea of what the conflict is about. They may believe they are doing battle over space when what they really want is more responsibility. The main reason that they are battling over space is that they regard space as a *symbol* of responsibility.

Far, far too often we humans fight over symbols without stopping to think about what the symbols symbolize. During the last four years of the Vietnam War, you may recall, the main reason put forth by the United States for not withdrawing from Vietnam was not that there was any practical reason for continuing to fight but rather that such a withdrawal would entail "losing face."

In sum, the source of a great many conflicts within organizations is competition over some resource that the parties feel is limited but that in reality can be expanded or augmented by some other resource. Critical in the resolution of such conflicts is timing, for experience shows that conflict increases as the parties perceive that resources are shrinking.

The following model* illustrates the point:

XXXXX

XXX

X

XXX

XXXXX

Regard the Xs as units of a given resource. We start with five of them, then have only three, then have only one. Then the situation improves and we return to three, then to the original five.

In fact, we would be likely to have conflict even if the original number of units of this resource (five) never declined, for most of us expect to progress rather than merely to maintain the status quo. However, when the number of units declines, the likelihood of conflict increases exponentially.

Therefore in the model above the stage of conflict begins somewhere between the top row of five Xs and the next row of three Xs—in other words, at the point where parties begin to perceive that the units are decreasing. The conflict intensifies as the units continue to decrease. Then, as the units begin increasing, the conflict eases.

In other words:

XXXXX

      Conflict begins.

XXX

      Conflict is at its most intense.

X

      Conflict begins to ease.

XXX

      Conflict is resolved.

XXXXX

*I first presented this model in my book *The Process of Interpersonal Communication* (San Francisco: Canfield Press, 1976) pp. 167–168.

In still other words, the conflict intensifies at a faster rate than the units of the resource decline, and the conflict reaches its peak even before the units have reached their lowest level—this because the competitors perceive a (to borrow from the language of the stock market) bottoming-out. Then, on the upswing, the conflict eases as the *promise* of more units materializes—and the conflict is resolved even before the original number of units has been restored.

The pattern should encourage managers who make no attempt whatever to manage conflict, for the pattern suggests that when conflict is a result of competition for a declining resource, the conflict will end even before the original quantity of the resource is restored. However, I suggest that the conflict would *never arise* if managers knew how to offer substitutes—or, if you will, *relevant alternatives*—to the diminishing resource.

Let's look at it again schematically:

XXXXX
          Conflict begins.
XXX    XXXXXXXX    Relevant alternatives are introduced.
          Conflict ends.
X    XXXXXXX

XXX    XXXXX

XXXXX       XXX

None of the above is to say that you will resolve all your subordinates' conflicts by providing substitutes for shrinking resources. There is no question that many resources are finite—money perhaps the most ardently desired among them—and many people will not accept substitutes. Indeed, if you appear to be offering a merely cosmetic substitute for a desired resource, chances are that your people will regard you as insulting their intelligence and will be even more resentful than if you had made no attempt to offer a substitute.

The fact remains, however, that some resources are indeed susceptible to replacement by relevant alternatives. Much conflict will be eliminated by managers who learn to look *beyond* the apparent desiderata of the parties in conflict and identify the *real* desiderata or relevant alternatives.

## CLASHES OF VALUES

The world offers virtually limitless examples of personal or political conflicts that grow out of clashes of values. You think that your teenagers should be home at a certain hour, and they believe that they should have the freedom to set their own hours. A teacher of English in high school wants certain books in the library, and the PTA objects to their use of sexual language. Russia claims the right to station troops in a given nation, and NATO argues that Russia does not have that right.

It may at first seem that clashes over values would be far less common in the workplace, where most activities remain far outside the ambit of ideology. In fact, value-related conflicts are extremely common in the workplace—both among individual employees and among departments or other divisions of an organization.

One of the most common sources of value-related conflict is a difference in philosophy about the purpose of the organization or the purpose of being part of it. Far, far too many corporate managers feel that employees have no interest in overall corporate objectives and that the principal motive for working in the organization is to earn a living. In fact, a great many employees—probably a majority—have strong moral feelings about the sort of work that they do, and a very high percentage could probably make more money doing something else.

The moral feelings of employees about their corporations' objectives and activities were demonstrated dramatically recently when the president of a large hotel chain resigned after his board of directors voted to acquire a gambling casino. During the Vietnam War, many thousands of people left or refused to accept jobs in war-related industries. Many people today refuse on ethical grounds to work for manufacturers of munitions, firearms, alcoholic beverages, or tobacco products, or for companies perceived to be spoilers of the environment or exploiters of the hapless. However, a much more commonly encountered source of value-related conflict has to do with philosophies of what the *primary* mission of an organization should be.

In some hospitals, for example, professional administrators think of themselves as being in a "service industry" and make their decisions accordingly. To these people, efficiency, return on investment, and similar desiderata are paramount. Other employees of the hospital—nurses, for example—may view their work as a calling to help the sick and injured, no matter what the cost. (It is significant that nurses as a class get paid far less than hospital administrators, who have no greater investment in training or experience.)

Among attending physicians at a given hospital, there almost certainly are some who subordinate economic considerations to a sense of doing good, and there almost certainly are others who are far more interested in doing *well* than in doing good. It is relevant to compare the earnings of physicians in different specialties. Though training and experience may be identical, pediatricians and psychiatrists on average earn less than a quarter the income of the typical surgeon or anesthesiologist. Indeed, in 1983, it was not uncommon for anesthesiologists to have an annual income of $400,000 to $500,000, billing one third of the fees of the surgeons whom they assisted, while individual surgeons with narrow specialties could take home $750,000, $1 million, or even more.

Add to these groups the hospital employees who look on their work as just another job. These may include some physicians, nurses, and administrators, but they probably consist mainly of maintenance, clerical and other employees whose functions would be much the same whether they worked at a hospital or in an organization entirely unrelated to medical care.

A conflict arises: A patient complains to a nurse about maintenance employees who perform certain noisy chores late at night. The nurse might feel that it is terribly wrong for the maintenance people to disturb the patients. The maintenance people might argue that they should not have to alter their work schedule simply because one fussy patient is bothered.

Certain physicians might side with the nurse and argue that the patient's comfort is paramount. Others might feel that the patient is a charity case and should not complain. Still others might expect the hospital's administrators to devise an equitable solution to the problem—for example, by moving a more tolerant patient to this room or assigning the maintenance people another place to work.

If hospital administrators fail to take into account the *values* of the parties to the conflict, they are likely to conclude that all except one of the parties are "wrong" and that whoever is "right" should prevail. However, for our purposes, as students of the phenomenon of conflict, *none* of the parties should be regarded as wrong.

I'll say it again:

**None of the parties (whatever the conflict) should be regarded as wrong.**

There is, I suggest, no place whatever in the study of how to manage conflict for consideration of who is "right" and who is "wrong." The manager's role is not like that of the umpire in baseball, who rules a player safe or out, or the jurist, who decrees a defendant guilty or not guilty. The manager's role is to resolve the conflict in such a way that the best interests of the organization—and, one hopes, the best interests also of the individual parties to the conflict—are served.

Accepting this point of view may be difficult for many of us. We have, after all—most of us, anyway—been raised with the idea that right should prevail over wrong. Many of our institutions, including the entire judicial system and most religions, have as their raison d'etre the task of distinguishing between right and wrong.

However, I suggest that in situations of conflict over values, "right" and "wrong" are irrelevant. Typically, each party regards his or her values as right and the other party's as wrong.

In other words, values make perfect sense to the people who hold them. If we did not find them logical, we would not subscribe to them. And if they differ from the next person's values, we are unlikely to conclude that we are wrong and the other person right.

Indeed, we are much more likely to conclude that the other person is wrong and we are right.

Conflict arises when we project our own values on the other person. The nurse, for example, argues that the maintenance employees *should* be more considerate of the patient. The maintenance employees respond that they have work to do; it is not *their* problem that the patient is disturbed.

If the hospital's administrators think only in terms of right or wrong and attempt to *adjudicate* rather than seek a solution that will keep everyone happy, they are likely to alienate every party to the conflict except one (the one whose point of view prevails). However, if the administrators look *beyond* "right" and "wrong," they may—indeed, they should be able to—come up with a solution that satisfies everyone.

In the chapters ahead I'll discuss how such solutions might be developed. First, however, let's look briefly at some other situations in which clashes over values lead to conflicts within organizations.

In many schools and colleges, today's administrators are yesterday's teachers. Many of them believe that teachers' rewards should be based wholly on performance. Meanwhile, many new teachers believe that performance cannot be measured objectively and that, in any case, salaries should be based on the number of hours worked rather than on any measure of performance or longevity.

Obviously, the vested interests of the two groups may—and almost always will—color the group's perceptions of what is right or wrong. The point here is that *each* group believes that it is right. The solution to the conflict lies not in *adjudication* but in bringing about *accommodation*.

Another example:

☐   In profit-making (or purportedly profit-making) organizations, it is virtually axiomatic that customers must be satisfied if they are to continue doing business with the organization. However, different employees at different levels within the organization may have different philosophies about how far the organization should go to satisfy customers.

Should a difficult customer be placated at all costs? If not, where should the line be drawn? How much attention should the customer get from senior executives of the company?

Most companies will at least pay lip service to the nostrum that the customer is always right. However, while senior executives may make speeches or issue memos to this effect, lower-echelon employees—the ones who actually have contact with most difficult customers—may regard the customer more as a nuisance who interrupts the day's work than as the person whose satisfaction is the purpose of the day's work.

The *values* of the lower-echelon employees often will give customers a totally different impression of the company than the senior executives intend—as you well know if you have been treated rudely by a gas station attendant or made to wait overly long in a line at a supermarket.

We can, I think, safely assume that no senior executive wants his or her chain of food stores thought of as one that treats customers rudely, makes them wait too long, or otherwise serves them poorly. Yet customers receive indifferent or even downright hostile service in many supermarkets. Somewhere between the check-out counter and the executive suite is a manager—or several of them—who did not investigate with sufficient vigor the attitudes and behavior of lower-echelon employees.

The values of senior executives, as reflected in their companies' ways of dealing with customers, can tell us a great deal (for better or worse) about the executives' policies. The following story reveals how these philosophies can affect a company over the long term.

☐   A friend of mine who makes his living writing novels in 1960 bought a used 1958 Mercury. A year or so later, the automobile's steering mechanism failed, and my friend was almost killed while driving on a turnpike.

☐   This same friend, having survived the automotive incident, became a customer of IBM during the mid-1960s, buying one of that corporation's first Mag-Card Selectric typewriters. Fifteen years later, after spending many thousands of dollars on IBM equipment, he tried to finance the purchase of an IBM word processor. Not only was his credit application rejected, but also the person to whom he complained about the rejection treated him in a manner that he regarded as imperious and otherwise impertinent.

☐ In yet another incident, my friend, as a customer of California's Crocker Bank, became dissatisfied with the service at one of Crocker's branches, where lines were extremely long and where his secretary was not permitted to cash checks on his behalf. When he complained to the branch manager, he was told, in effect, to take his business elsewhere.

☐ In all three situations, my friend wrote a letter of complaint to the chief executive of the relevant company.

☐ His complaint to John Place, Chairman of Crocker, was answered by a consumer relations underling who said, in effect, that the complaint was unwarranted. Angry, my friend closed his account at Crocker.

☐ His letter to Henry Ford III was answered by another consumer relations underling who said that Ford would not take responsibility for used cars except when those cars were sold through authorized Ford/Lincoln/Mercury dealers. Angry, he never again bought a Ford product—and, over the next two decades, he embarrassed Ford whenever he got the opportunity. In half a dozen novels or screenplays, he wrote scenes in which an automobile broke down or otherwise malfunctioned in a critical situation; in each of these scenes, the automobile was a Lincoln, a Mercury, or a Ford.

☐ His letter to Frank T. Cary, chairman of IBM, was answered—three days after he posted it—by a phone call from IBM's regional manager, who requested (in the most ingratiating manner) an appointment at my friend's office. My friend scheduled the appointment, and the IBM regional manager explained what the problems were with regard to my friend's credit. My friend provided additional documentation about his financial status, and the credit was approved. In the years since, he has bought more than $100,000 worth of IBM equipment.

None of the above is to say that my friend was "right" with IBM and "wrong" with Crocker or Ford. Actually, in all three conflicts, the case might be made that my friend expected more from the company that he had any "right" to expect.

However, rightness and wrongness are irrelevant for the purposes of this discussion. The point is, IBM resolved the conflict by satisfying my friend—and making him a continuing customer. Crocker and Ford, whether rightly or wrongly antagonized him, lost his business, and may in the future continue to suffer the slings and arrows of his outrage—perhaps long after the executives who antagonized him have retired.

Here is one final example regarding conflicts related to clashes of values:

☐   Some years ago, I was retained by one of the nation's 100 largest companies to investigate a rapid build-up in conflicts between employees. The company, a nonunion firm that was more than a century old, naturally had not been immune to conflicts in the past; however, very few of these conflicts—far fewer in the typical corporation of this size—reached such a level of intensity that middle or senior managers had to intervene.

☐   Then, seemingly all of a sudden, things changed. Quarrels between lower-echelon employees began breaking out with great frequency over the most trivial matters—for example, one's place in the cafeteria line. Personnel turnover rose dramatically, and a much larger percentage of departing employees quit than were fired. The number of complaints to managers did not rise appreciably, but the number of complaints to federal and state regulatory agencies did.

☐   One incident proved to be the proverbial straw that broke the camel's back and persuaded senior managers to seek help.

☐   A man who had been with the company for six months drove a shuttle bus between buildings at a large manufacturing facility. His shift ended at 3 P.M. According to the company's procedures manual, he could sign out early if he reached the terminal between 2:45 and 3; however, if he reached the terminal before 2:45, he was required to make another round of the buildings, which might mean returning to the terminal a few minutes after 3.

☐   On the day of the incident, he reached the terminal at 2:44

and attempted to sign out. The dispatcher informed him that he would have to make another round. He protested to no avail and finally, around 2:55, left for the final round. Then, at exactly 3, with the shuttle bus full, he stopped between buildings, turned off the motor, and started walking toward the parking lot.

☐   A midlevel executive who had been on the bus followed the driver and tried to persuade him to complete the trip to the terminal. The driver refused, and the executive attempted to restrain him physically. The driver pushed the executive, the executive pushed back, and soon a fist fight had erupted.

☐   "Can you imagine," said the senior vice president who retained me to investigate, "*that* kind of behavior in a company like *this?*"

☐   He added that senior managers had done everything they could to keep lower-echelon employees happy. The company's pay scale was significantly higher than those of comparable firms, and the employees had a benefits package that union leaders often used as an example when bargaining with other companies.

☐   "If all of this had happened within a few weeks or even a few months," the senior vice president continued, "I'd be tempted to conclude that a union was sabotaging us as a preliminary to a recruitment effort. But it has been going on for several years, and that's just too long for a sabotage scenario."

☐   What made the situation even more bewildering to the senior vice president was that the company had for so long prided itself on its esprit de corps. Unlike so many firms, which recruited senior managers from other companies, this organization boasted that all of its divisional presidents and senior vice presidents had worked their way through the ranks. This was a company that believed in loyalty and rewarded loyalty, a company that cared for its employees and made every effort to show that it cared.

☐   That this perception might not be shared by new employees apparently did not occur to the senior vice president who retained me—but that is exactly what developed in interviews that my staff and I conducted as the first phase of our investigation.

☐   We asked midlevel and senior managers, "Do you believe you will be rewarded for your work?" Without exception, they answered in the affirmative. When we asked the same question to new employees, they literally laughed at us—as if they could not imagine that we were serious. They believed that promotions and other rewards were unrelated to performance. They made such statements as, "It all boils down to who gets 'in' with whom."

☐ For midlevel and senior managers, the company was the equivalent of a family. They had, with few exceptions, spent their entire careers here. They *cared for* the company and for each other, and they *felt* cared for *by* the company and *by* each other. They could not imagine that any reasonable person who shared the company's embrace would have a different point of view.

☐ Meanwhile, lower-echelon employees—especially those who had been hired within the past few years—looked on their work as an undesirable but necessary means of support. The things that were important to them took place off the job. They did not feel cared for by their employer, nor did they care about the company. If anything, they wished the company harm: Several of our interviewees boasted of not using the company's products, and several others predicted with pleasure that it would not be long before the company went "down the tubes."

☐ Midlevel and senior managers had an inkling about these attitudes, but they did not see them as a ramification of conflicting values. The managers' feeling was that the rebellious employees were part of a "spoiled" generation that expected more emoluments than it deserved. One executive told me, "I'm afraid they're hopeless. We're just going to have to keep paying more and more for less and less until the whole thing falls apart."

☐ Lower-echelon employees, meanwhile, looked at the midlevel and senior executives and said, "Is that any way to live? They spend 12 hours a day at the office, and then they take their work home with them. They're overweight and have ulcers and probably will die 20 years before they should. I don't want to be like that."

☐ The problem, as I analyzed it, had historical roots. The company underwent a 20-year period of very brisk growth that ended about 10 years before the current period of discord. Most midlevel and senior executives had been employees during or even before the fast-growth period. Consequently, they were promoted faster than their counterparts in other companies. They also were better paid, and they shared a greater number of benefits and other rewards. For them, the secret of a happy career was to commit oneself to the company and trust the company to take care of everything else.

☐ The newer employees, meanwhile, had signed on during a slow-growth period. They saw few opportunities for advancement: The "old guys" had everything bottlenecked. True, the company offered excellent salaries and benefits, but the newer employees saw these as bribes—something that the company had to do in order to keep fully staffed and prevent unionization. For them, The Company was a malign clique of avaricious old men who deserved the worst they could get.

☐ The solution to the problem, as I envisioned it, was to work slowly but steadily at giving the newer employees a meaningful stake in the success of the company and, in the process, giving them reason to *change their values.* This might mean deviating from the long-established system of rewarding seniority more than initiative or other desiderata. It also might mean decentralizing decision-making so that people in the lower echelons had greater control over the particulars of their work.

☐ On my recommendation, one of the first things the company eliminated was the finely detailed procedures of the shuttle bus schedule. Instead of signing out based on whether they reached the terminal at 2:44, or 2:45, or 2:46, the drivers were left to resolve among themselves how to pass the reins from shift to shift.

☐ As more recently arrived employees were given greater control over the circumstances under which they worked, they developed a sense of being *part of* the company—and their attitudes *and values* became much more closely aligned with those of senior and midlevel managers.

In sum, values make perfect sense to the people who hold them. Conflict arises when we project our own values on the other person. Do not assume that you will be able to motivate others by the same values that motivate you. In a great many situations you will not. The trick is to learn the other person's values and then determine a way to give that person what he or she wants or to offer a desirable alternative.

# POORLY DEFINED RESPONSIBILITIES

Imagine, for the purpose of illustration, that you and I decide to start a business. We agree that you will take responsibility for producing the product and I will take responsibility for marketing it.

That seems sufficiently straightforward, does it not? Hardly any room for ambiguity there, eh?

Of course there's room for ambiguity.

Let's say that people who buy our product want to see it demonstrated before they make a commitment. In my opinion, demonstrating the product falls within your responsibility as producer; in your opinion, I, as marketer, should have the responsibility.

We are in conflict *not* because either of us is seeking to take advantage of the other, *not* because we entered our agreement in bad faith, *not* because we are cantankerous or quarrelsome, but simply because we failed to provide for a contingency that was not anticipated when we came to our original agreement.

Let's further say that we have agreed to divide evenly the profits of the business. After a year, we have net earnings of $X million, and I seek to take my half. You object, arguing that most of the money should be kept within the corporation to fund growth.

Neither of us seeks something that is contrary to the letter or spirit of our original agreement, but what each of us seeks is incompatible with what the other seeks.

Someone might argue that the agreement that you and I struck was insufficiently detailed—thus our conflicts have arisen as a result of our lack of thoroughness. However, no matter how thorough and detailed an agreement may be, there always is room for differences of interpretation. Were this not so, there would be no need for a judicial system; legislators would merely legislate, and the executive branch of government would simply enforce the (totally unambiguous) laws.

Organizations have, especially in recent years, attempted to leave as few as possible of their members' obligations open to interpretation. Thus we have elaborate and extremely lengthy constitutions, by-laws, corporate charters, and similar documents. Moreover, instead of merely permitting managers to hire and fire at will, as many organizations did a few decades ago, we now have union contracts, job descriptions, arbitration proceedings, and similar vehicles for defining or clarifying our responsibilities to each other.

Unfortunately, useful as these vehicles may be, there always seems to be an element that eludes definition. Significantly, the undefined element frequently emerges as a major source of conflict between parties who have never wanted anything but harmonious relations.

A case in point:

☐   You hire me as your secretary. We discuss such matters as how I should deal with telephone callers, how I should screen your mail, and how much time I should take for lunch. Also, you tell me that my responsibilities will include making coffee every morning.

☐   I dislike the idea of making your coffee. I regard the task as properly within the province of a maid or waiter, not a secretary. However, this is a small office, and there are no other employees to do the job, so I agree to do it.

☐   A year passes. Each morning I have made your coffee, and you have often complimented me on how tasty it is. In fact, on more than a few occasions, you've invited friends from the office down the hall to have a cup with you. I have uncomplainingly—but with mounting displeasure—continued to make the coffee . . . and to serve it to you (and your friends) . . . and to wash the cups and saucers and spoons . . . and to make sure you do not run out of cream or sugar.

☐   Comes now a morning when I am feeling particularly put-upon. My workload has been increasing, my salary has not. You have said that you intend to hire a part-time employee to relieve me of my more trivial tasks, but you have not done so. My patience is wearing thin.

☐   When you arrive at the office—characteristically late—you are accompanied by several colleagues. I serve coffee to all of you, but after your colleagues have left, I tell you that this is the last time I will do so. You remind me that when you hired me you stated emphatically that this was part of the job. I reply that I agreed only to *make* coffee, not to serve it and to wash the cups. Moreover, I agreed to make coffee only *for you,* not for an unlimited number of visitors.

☐ From your point of view, my attitude is unreasonable. As you see things, the task described as "making coffee" entails serving it, washing cups, reordering when current supplies are depleted, and everything else that is necessary to ensure that you will have a satisfactory cup of coffee on your desk whenever you want it. Moreover, in your view, the requirement that I serve coffee to you extends automatically to serve your guests, washing their cups, etcetera.

☐ However, from my point of view, you are demanding far more than I agreed to provide. If I wanted to be a waiter, I would have applied for a job in a restaurant, not an office. If I don't draw the line somewhere, there's no telling what you'll expect me to do next—wash windows, maybe, or scrub floors.

☐ You and I probably would agree that lines must be drawn *somewhere* as to what "making coffee" actually entails. Obviously I could not have expected when I accepted the assignment that my only task would be to pour coffee-grounds into a percolator that you already had filled with water and to notify you when the coffee has been brewed. Obviously you expected that I would—at the very least—fill the percolator with water and turn on the hotplate.

☐ Presumably you also expected me to reorder coffee and other supplies as they ran out. Also, assuming that there is no one else in the office who has the assignment, you presumably (and rightly) expected me to empty whatever coffee remained in the percolator at day's end, wash the percolator, dry it, and bring it back from wherever I washed and dried it to wherever it had been before I did the washing and drying.

☐ It is hard to imagine that any reasonable person would dispute that these tasks were part of "making" the coffee. (Likewise, if you had given me an addressed envelope and told me to mail it, I should have understood that you did not merely expect me to place it in our building's mail chute; I should have understood that you assumed I would first stamp and seal the envelope.)

☐ However, there is room for disagreement about how much you might have a right to expect beyond this. Obviously you could not reasonably expect me to serve coffee daily to thousands of people and to wash all their cups, saucers, and silverware. If thousands are out of the question, what number is reasonable? Two? Five? Ten?

☐ Would I be reasonable in demanding that you not offer guests coffee unless you yourself intend to serve it—and wash the cups, saucers, and silverware? Should I expect you to use disposable cups instead of china if your guests number more than two? Should I argue that you should use disposable cups for your own coffee if you do not wish to wash your own china cup?

In theory, job descriptions are supposed to anticipate and provide for any contingencies that may arise. In fact, no job description can address every possible contingency. Most of us understand this and attempt to be flexible. However, there are limits to the flexibility of just about everyone. When those limits are reached—and sometimes even when they are merely approached—conflict is inevitable.

Just as undefined elements in a job description can lead to conflict betwen co-workers, ambiguous or insufficiently thought-out policies can lead to conflict between an organization's divisions. A case in point:

☐ During a period when enrollments in universities were on the decline, the administrators of a university in the Northeast attempted to enlist the faculty in a recruitment effort. When mere exhortation failed to produce the desired results, the administrators established a faculty-to-student ratio for each department. In effect, faculty members were put on notice that if their departments did not attract certain numbers of students, teaching jobs would be lost.

☐ The faculty, as would most people in such a situation, promptly went to work. The biology department recruited from the chemistry department. The English department recruited from the psychology department. The math department recruited from the physics department.

☐  What the administrators had hoped, of course, was that the faculty would recruit *new* students—that is, high school seniors, transfer students from other universities, or young adults who at present were not attending college. No administrator intended to encourage a zero-sum game in which individual departments competed for the students who were already enrolled in the university. However, the policy failed to anticipate that this might happen and failed to establish preventive mechanisms.

☐  Just as nature abhors a vacuum, members of organizations abhor ambiguities—and rush in to fill them with their own understandings.

## CHANGE

Most of us became acquainted fairly early in life with the paradoxical maxim that there is nothing so constant as change. And most of us—even those who fancy themselves the most flexible—have some difficulty dealing with change.

This is, I suggest, eminently reasonable. Variety may be the spice of life, but most of us have devoted a great deal of effort to arranging the circumstances in which we currently live. The better we like those circumstances, the more apt we are to resist change.

Within organizations, the prospect of change is ever present. Indeed, changes of one sort or another are always taking place. People quit, get fired, retire, or die. Departments or entire companies merge, reorganize, get acquired, or get spun off. We change from a manual system to a computer system or from one computer system to another.

Managers usually are very careful in planning the mechanics of change, but few are nearly as careful in planning how the change will affect the people who are involved.

For an extremely elementary case in point, let's return to the recent illustration in which you and I, as boss and secretary, were in conflict about my responsibility to prepare and serve coffee to your guests. Let's say that I suddenly objected to having anything whatever to do with serving coffee in the office.

In other words, one day I approached you and said something to the following effect: "Yes, I know that when I started working here I agreed that making coffee would be part of my responsibilities. Yes, I know, you're the boss and I'm the secretary and there's no one else to make the coffee if I refuse to do it. Yes, I know your time is more valuable than mine—at least insofar as our wage scales are concerned—and the company will lose more money if you must make your own coffee than if I make it for you. But frankly, Scarlet, I don't give a hang: I am so repelled by the job of serving your coffee that I will do just about anything to avoid it. So fire me, if you wish, or do whatever else you choose, but henceforth I will never make coffee for you again."

Assuming that you found me a valued employee, and assuming also that you are convinced that I meant what I said, you might very well make some other arrangement for your coffee. Either you would buy take-out coffee somewhere or you would brew your own or you would assign the task to someone else or you would stop drinking coffee. Whatever you did, you probably would be less satisfied with the situation than with my making coffee for you— and this change in our relationship might very well be a source of irritation (and conflict, even if never expressed) for quite some time.

Now let's turn the situation around. Let's say that I do not object to serving coffee to you and your guests. In fact, let's say that I prefer that to filing—a task that thus far has been the responsibility of a junior clerk in our department. Now, however, our budget has been reduced, and the clerk is being transferred to another department, and you considerately have decided that it would be unfair to ask me to absorb the additional responsibilites without reducing some of my existing responsibilities. So you tell me that henceforth I am going to do the filing and you are going to buy your coffee at the neighborhood newstand.

While I may be grateful for your considerateness, the fact remains that the new situation is less desirable to me than the old. Thus the change is a source of conflict: Even though I do not blame you for what has happened, I now like my job less than I used to, and I have a grievance that I did not have before.

Increase the number of people affected by a given change and you almost invariably will increase the organization's conflict quotient. Consider, for example, the changes that come about when two companies merge. There can be only one chief executive; whoever it is that surrenders a chief-executiveship must either leave or adjust to reporting to someone else. Many managers who heretofore reported to the chief executive will be required to report to an intermediary. Some jobs will be eliminated, others will be combined.

People who used to be very close to the top of the seniority list will, of a sudden, be not nearly as close. People who considered themselves very close to a major promotion now may find that there are twice as many competitors. People who used to work the day shift may suddenly find themselves—to their great dissatisfaction—forced to work nights.

None of this is to say that change and its attending conflicts are not manageable. However, managers who do not plan adequately for change—and its attending conflicts—will almost certainly be the poorer for their lack of planning.

## NORMAL HUMAN DRIVES FOR SUCCESS, RECOGNITION, POWER, AND OTHER DESIDERATA

Every few months, it seems, newspapers report another instance of some scientist who falsified data in order to support certain conclusions. Some of us—especially those with an idealistic regard for science—may find this difficult to understand.

Ideally, of course, the fundamental task of scientists is to determine The Truth. Astronomers should not look to the skies hoping to confirm someone's preconception of what is out there but rather to determine what actually *is* out there. Likewise, physicians should not test a series of drugs hoping that Drug A is more effective than Drug B; they should experiment with an open mind, hoping only to learn how effective—if at all—each drug is.

Scientists speak of the null hypothesis—that is, the prospect that none in a series of experimental attempts will succeed. Ideally, an experiment that proves the null hypothesis—that is, an experiment in which all attempts fail—is no less valuable than an experiment in which one of the attempts succeeds, for each experiment reveals Truth.

The purpose of an experiment is not to win (that is, to discover the miracle cure for a disease or the answer to an ostensibly insoluble problem) but rather to *test* a specific approach under a specific set of circumstances. Eliminating an unsuccessful approach is, in the long run, as important as discovering a successful approach. The knowledge derived from the "unsuccessful" experiment contributes to an understanding of the problem—and to its ultimate solution. Indeed, such knowledge often contributes also to the solution of problems far more important than those that the researcher was addressing.

For example, in 1882, German physicist Robert Koch identified a microorganism—the tuberculum baccillus—responsible for that century's most dreaded disease, tuberculosis. At the time, microscopists used—as they do today—a variety of dyes to color cells and thus better observe them.

Dr. Koch's junior colleague, Paul Ehrlich, noted that certain dyes stained bacteria without staining other cells. He reasoned that strong concentrations of the dyes might serve as a "magic bullet," killing the bacteria without damaging other cells.

Dr. Ehrlich eventually discovered Trypan red, a dye that would cure African sleeping sickness. However, it was inefficient: Most patients could not tolerate doses strong enough to eradicate their bodies' stores of the responsible trypanosome bacteria.

Dr. Ehrlich tested 605 compounds without success. His 606th compound, also ineffective against African sleeping sickness, cured syphillis, and his work, which won him the Nobel Prize, set the stage for the discovery of the wonder drugs of the twentieth century—sulfanilamides and, later, penicillin and other antibiotics.

Was Dr. Ehrlich's 605th test less valuable to humanity than his 606th? Was his 505th less valuable, or his 432nd, or his 115th, or his 10th? From the scientist's point of view, each of the tests was equally valuable, in that each of them demonstrated a Truth.

All this having been said, the fact remains that no scientist ever was awarded the Nobel Prize for proving the null hypothesis. No psychologist became famous for *not* establishing a link between schizophrenia and diet or heredity. No chemist achieved world renown for discovering that a given nickel alloy was *weaker* than tempered steel.

And that takes us back to those scientists who falsify data. While we may condemn their doing so, we should not be astonished that they did. They were operating within the context of our society's system of rewards and punishments. They, like most of the rest of us, were responding—albeit unethically (in your opinion and mine)—to normal human drives for success, recognition, power, and other desiderata.

These desiderata are not "limited resources" within the context of our earlier definition. In theory, the capacity of the world to bestow recognition on us may be finite, and there may be a smaller quantity of success, power, and other desiderata than all of us, in the aggregate, may desire. In practice, however, the vast majority of us can attain a satisfactory amount of all of these desiderata without robbing the next fellow.

All the same, our appetites for success, power, recognition, and the like may place us in conflict with people who are similarly driven. We observe their achievements, and they observe ours, and each of us feels in some way diminished—even though both of us may have gained.

A case in point:

☐    You and I work for the same television network. You are in charge of comedy series, and I am in charge of sports. Over a given period of time, the number of television sets tuned to your programs may increase at a rapider rate than the number of television sets tuned to mine. I may regard your success as a threat—even though my programs do not compete with yours, and even though my programs are drawing better viewer response than sports programs on other networks, and even though I may have received as many encomia from our bosses as you have.

Of course, if drives for success and power entail competition for resources that *are* limited (or are *perceived* as limited), the likelihood of conflict is commensurately greater. Throw change into the bargain, and the likelihood is greater still. To wit:

☐   One of my clients, a distributor of office equipment, discontinued a line of desktop calculators, replacing it with a line of desktop personal computers. Of a sudden, the people who used to sell the calculators were no longer called "sales representatives;" they were known as "data consultants."

☐   Their duties were essentially the same, as were their earnings, but their new title drew envy from other employees who continued to be called "sales representatives." The new title was seen as a badge of success and recognition, and the drives for success and recognition of the people who did not receive the new title were frustrated.

☐   Thus far—in theory, anyway—no limited resource was involved, for bestowers of titles may bestow them pretty much as they see fit. The president of this company, whose idea it was to change the title from "sales representatives" to "data consultant," could have, if he chose, dubbed everyone on the payroll "data consultant."

☐   In practice, however, he would not do this—for he deliberately was using the title selectively as a motivational tool. Thus what was, strictly speaking, an unlimited resource was *perceived* by employees as a limited resource, and for their purpose it became one. (Not insignificantly, it was their perception of a title as a resource that made it a resource in the first place; had none of them attached importance to a title, the title would be valueless.)

☐   Meanwhile, the change of titles stimulated intense conflict in the company's training department, even though members of this department did not aspire to the new title. One division of the department trained sales personnel; another trained managers. The division that trained managers regarded the change of titles as more than merely cosmetic. This division viewed the change as a symbol that the new line of desktop computers represented a priority project. The division therefore wanted the responsibility for training the new "data consultants," who under their old titles would have been trained by the other division. This was competition not for a nominal resource but for a real one: The responsibility brought with it an increase in budget, an increase in personnel, and an increase in authority—all important desiderata.

☐    Please note that none of this conflict came about by accident. The president of the company orchestrated the changes intending to accomplish exactly what he did. He *wanted* conflict of the sort he got because he wanted the competition that it stimulated. He realized that there are productive as well as destructive uses of conflict, and he very skillfully arranged and managed this conflict to maximize its productive uses and minimize its unproductive uses.

In later chapters I'll deal in greater detail with the productive and destructive uses of conflict. The point here is that there are within organizations certain inescapable sources of conflict— sources that inhere in the process of organizing. The next chapter will offer an exercise in which you can practice your skills at identifying sources of conflict.

# 5 ONE IS NOT ENOUGH

## OR IDENTIFYING
## THE SOURCES OF CONFLICT

---

Herewith, a dramatization:

☐ Jeff is vice president of employee relations, a position he has held for seven of his 17 years with The Company. He enjoys good relations with other executives and is generally thought of as a good manager. He will, however, freely admit to one blind spot: He does not believe that women can function effectively as executives.

Susan is director of management training. She reports to Jeff. However, she was not appointed by Jeff; she was appointed directly by The Company's president, who did not consult Jeff about the appointment. Before her appointment, Susan had been a secretary in another department. The position to which she was appointed had been vacant for about a year, during which time the duties of the director were shared by Jeff and several of his subordinates.

☐ The dialogue that follows occurs in Jeff's office. It may strike you as somewhat overblown and unrealistic, but please go along with me. The conflict between Jeff and Susan is based on a conflict episode recorded by my former colleague, Allan Frank, of the Brockport campus of the State University of New York. The dialogue compresses a number of exchanges that occurred between Jeff and Susan over a period of several weeks.

JEFF: Hi, Susie, how are you doing today?

SUSAN: As if you'd really care to know.

JEFF: What's that supposed to mean?

SUSAN: Don't act naive, Jeff. If you had your way, I'd never be an executive except in name only—and probably not even in name.

JEFF: I don't understand what you're talking about. You *are* an executive.

SUSAN: No one would ever know by the way you treat me—or any other woman, for that matter.

JEFF: Susan, don't confuse sexism with an awareness of your inexperience. I've given you all the responsibility I think you can handle. Stop being so impatient.

SUSAN: I can't believe this. Are you saying that the president didn't know what he was doing when he appointed me?

JEFF: I'm saying that I don't think you have the experience or the background to take on more responsibilities than I've given you.

SUSAN: I was hired by this company with a B.S. in business administration and fifteen credits toward an M.B.A. I spent almost a year here being nothing more than a clerk. If you don't give me the responsibility, how do you expect me to get the experience?

JEFF: You're being too impatient. Things like this take time. When you're my age you'll—

SUSAN:   If you had your way, I'd be a secretary now, and I'd be a secretary when I was your age, too. What you're really saying is that *no* woman deserves managerial responsibility. Well, if that's your attitude, let me put you on notice: I was appointed to an executive position, and I demand to be allowed to assume my rightful duties *now*. If not, I'm going to initiate a sex discrimination suit against The Company and against you personally.

JEFF:    That's ridiculous.

SUSAN:   If you're saying that you don't intend to change anything, I'll have a federal investigator here as soon as I can get one.

JEFF:    I won't be threatened, Susan. I am relieving you of all your duties, effective immediately. You will hear from The Company's attorney.*

Yes, I will grant you that neither Jeff nor Susan deserves an award for diplomacy.

You might say that Susan provoked the confrontation with her very first comment—"As if you'd really care to know." Obviously, this is not the way one speaks to one's boss—or to anyone else, if one is skilled at relating to people.

You might also say that Jeff has to be the managerial dunderhead of all time to respond, "What's that supposed to mean?" Whatever the problem may be, if Jeff wants to ameliorate rather than exacerbate it, he should avoid sarcasm and belligerence; instead, he should directly—and sincerely—ask why Susan feels as she does.

However, the question now before us is not how the parties' reactions to each other are fanning the flames of conflict; the question is, what are the *sources* of conflict.

Before reading further, please make a list of what you perceive as the sources of this conflict. List as many sources as you can,

---

*Reprinted with permission from Allan D. Frank, *Communicating on the Job* (Glenview, Illinois: Scott, Foresman, 1982).

even if some of them seem relatively minor. You may reread the dramatization any number of times.

Have you completed your list? Very well, let's proceed.

## JEFF'S VALUES ABOUT WOMEN IN MANAGEMENT

Most of us, I think, will identify Jeff's values as a major source of this conflict. While he does not come right out and tell Susan that he does not believe women are capable of functioning as managers, he has on other occasions admitted freely that this is his attitude (see the second paragraph of this chapter) and, in any event, he does not challenge her perception when she accuses him of holding this attitude.

Obviously, if he does not believe that women can function as managers, he will always be in conflict with any woman manager with whom he must deal, whether as a subordinate, a superior, or a peer.

## THE SOCIETAL CHANGE WHEREUNDER WOMEN HAVE BEGUN TO ENTER MANAGERIAL POSITIONS IN SIGNIFICANT NUMBERS

While male managers still outnumber female managers by a very wide margin, the fact remains that there are more female managers in the workforce today than at any time in the past. This change cannot fail to be a source of conflict, for change itself is a source of conflict.

None of the above is to say that women should not claim an even larger role in management. Conflict does not arise only when there is a change for the worse; a change for the better can also be a source of conflict.

In the Jeff–Susan controversy, Jeff clearly was not prepared for the change whereunder women began entering the managerial ranks in significant numbers, and he certainly is resisting it. The change itself is one major source of the present conflict, and Jeff's resistance to the change is another major source.

## SUSAN'S BELLIGERENT MANNER

There is no question that Susan is short on charm and tact. Even if Jeff had no predispositions whatever against female managers, he might well object to her simply because of her abrasiveness. He doubtless would object also to any male manager who was similarly abrasive.

This is not to say that Susan is not justified in feeling that she is the victim of sexual discrimination. However, the question here is not one of right versus wrong. As we noted a chapter ago, values always make perfect sense to the people who hold them.

## JEFF'S PATRONIZING MANNER

Although Jeff may express himself less belligerently than Susan does, he gives no indication that he understands or cares about her frustrations. If she were not hostile to begin with, his manner might very well inspire hostility.

## SUSAN'S THREAT TO JEFF'S POWER AND AUTHORITY

Personalities aside, there is no question that Jeff feels threatened. He did not promote Susan; the president did. Presumably he cannot fire her without the president's approval.

She reports to Jeff, but he clearly does not enjoy autonomy in dealing with her. He can hardly fail to feel that his power and authority are being threatened.

## JEFF'S FAILURE TO DEFINE SUSAN'S RESPONSIBILITIES

This conflict could not possibly have come about if, when Susan began working for Jeff, he gave her a clear and comprehensive description of what her duties would be and how quickly she might expect to claim additional responsibilities.

She might at the time have felt that she was not being given enough responsibility. If she could not persuade Jeff that she should have more, the two of them obviously would be in conflict. However, the conflict would be much smaller in dimension than the present conflict.

The above list of sources of conflict is not exhaustive. If we worked at it, we probably could come up with quite a few additional entries. However, even these few entries are more than most readers probably would develop on their first analysis of the dramatization.

This leads to a proposition that may be the most important one in this entire book:

**There never is** *only one source of conflict.*

I'll say it again: There never is *only one* source of conflict. There may be one source to which both parties attach more importance than any other, and that source may or may not be the precipitating factor when the conflict flares up. However, inevitably, inescapably, and invariably there will always be at least one *secondary* source.

It may be an underlying attitude (or several of them). It may be a limited resource (whether identified or unidentified). It may be a change (anticipated or unanticipated, for better or for worse). It may be a clash of values, a quest for power or success or recognition or some similar desideratum, or a failure by one or more of the parties to define responsibilities.

Whatever the case, there will *always* be at least two sources of conflict. This is extremely important because, as will be demonstrated in subsequent chapters, one of the most effective techniques in conflict management is to identify *all* the sources of a particular conflict and to persuade the parties to compromise on some in order to obtain concessions on others.

I'll pursue this proposition at greater length some pages hence. First, however, let's return to Jeff and Susan.

An important consideration in their conflict is the role of the president. Is he a neutral bystander, or is he a party to the conflict? What is his interest, if any, beyond ensuring that the conflict will not impede the department's successful operation?

It would be a mistake to say that Jeff and Susan are the only parties to the conflict. The president, when he appointed Susan without consulting Jeff, became a party. He was—whether he realized it or not—setting the stage for conflict. He may not have been the person who lit the fuse, but he certainly inserted the fuse into the dynamite. He is perceived by both Jeff and Susan as a *partisan* if not a party, and that makes him—ex officio—a party.

The above is not merely an exercise in semantics. In attempting to manage a conflict, it is useful to identify *everyone* who is a party. Failure to do so often exacerbates the conflict.

For example, if the president, for whatever reason, had sought to act as an arbitrator or mediator in this situation (a "third-party neutral," as the jargon has it), his efforts would be undermined by the fact that both Jeff and Susan perceive him as being involved.

If he summoned Jeff and Susan to his office to discuss the situation, what might Jeff think? "Hey, what's this guy up to? First he appoints Susan without consulting me, and now he's asking me to answer for the way I supervise her. Do I have authority over my own department or not?"

Meanwhile, what might Susan think? "Well, Jeff has finally gone too far. Now he's going to get his." Or: "Why am I being called in? Am I going to be reprimanded for insisting on the authority I need to do my job? Was this whole thing just a charade to get me into a fight with Jeff so that these guys could cite my intransigence as evidence of executive inability?"

Whatever the thoughts of Jeff and Susan, the point is that no one who is in any way perceived to be a party to a conflict can act as a third-party neutral.

I'll say it again:

**No one who is in any way perceived to be a party to a conflict can act as a third-party neutral.**

This is especially important because parties who see themselves as third-party neutrals and take great pride in their objectivity often make matters worse by attempting to intercede as arbitrators or mediators. *They* believe that they are neutral, objective, unbiased, and interested only in truth, goodness, fairness, and justice. However, the parties to the conflict perceive them as hypocrites.

Apropos the relationship of the president of The Company to the conflict between Jeff and Susan: If he is not neutral, is he a bumbler? *Why* didn't he consult Jeff before appointing Susan? If Jeff's attitudes about women were so well known within The Company, could a competent president have been unaware of them? Being aware of them, should not our president have taken steps to ensure that this conflict would not arise?

When I present this dramatization at seminars on conflict management, participants—especially those in middle-management or lower corporate echelons—almost invariably agree that the president handled the situation poorly. The president's poor judgment, in the view of these seminar participants, was the main reason the conflict came about.

As one of the participants put it, "If I were the chairman of the board of The Company, I'd fire the president, and I'd tell him that on his way out he should take Jeff and Susan with him."

Well, okay, if we take what we've seen at face value, the president may indeed seem incompetent. But consider this: Might the president have deliberately provoked this conflict?

You're astonished? You can't imagine that he would do such a thing?

Well, think about it for a moment—and please do not be afraid to indulge your most deeply suppressed Machiavellian impulses.

Might the president have provoked the conflict because he was looking for an excuse to get rid of Jeff? If that were his intention, he could hardly have done a better job. Can you imagine a labor relations investigator finding fault with a president who fired (or requested the early retirement of) an executive who worked so assiduously at frustrating the letter and spirit of the many laws that purport to ensure equal opportunity in employment?

Or might the president have provoked the conflict because he was looking for an excuse to get rid of Susan? That also could have worked. No one could accuse him of gender-related discrimination after he had promoted her to director of management training. If she proved—whether by her belligerence, her incompetence, or whatever else—unequipped to handle the job, the president could always take refuge in the fact that he had given her a chance.

The less cynical among us might resist such explanations, but let us not be naive. Those who understood conflict and its productive and destructive uses may in certain circumstances find irresistible—and perfectly permissible ethically—the temptation to manipulate a situation by stimulating conflict. If we close our eyes to the fact that such things are done, we limit unnecessarily our ability to understand—and manage—conflict.

So much for the president and his role. Let's return to our consideration of the sources of this conflict.

Perhaps you have on your list, "Failure to communicate," or something to that effect. You will notice that no similar explanation appears on my list.

"Failure to communicate" has in recent years become an extremely popular explanation for a wide variety of maladies. I suggest, however, that conflict is not possible *without* communication.

The communication need not be verbal. In other words, we may, by our actions, provide others with what political scientists call "indications" of our positions. For example, if the United States objects to certain newly announced policies of a given Mediterranean country, it might, without saying anything to or about the leaders of the Mediterranean country, demonstrate its opposition by staging naval and air maneuvers off the shore of that country. (For more on this proposition, consult my book, *Conflict Resolution Through Communication*, published by Harper & Row in 1973).

In any event, Jeff and Susan definitely *are* communicating. They may not be communicating *effectively*—that is, they may not be getting across to each other the points that they *want* to get across—but they are unquestionably exchanging messages about how they feel toward each other and how they feel about the conflict that they are experiencing.

Herein lies an extremely important lesson for anyone who seeks to become skillful at managing conflict. The problem is not to get the parties *to communicate*; the problem is to get them communicating *effectively* about issues where there are *opportunities for agreement*.

Imagine, for example, that we could get Jeff and Susan to list some goals that they both shared. One goal might be a reduction of the hostility between them. (Presumably they do not *enjoy* being constantly at each other's throat.) Another might be resolution of their conflict without involving anyone outside the department or outside The Company. (It will not look good for either of them if the controversy must be brought before a federal agency or a court.) Yet another might be a salary increase or additional vacation time or some other benefit that was not related directly to their relationship with each other.

Whatever their goals, Jeff and Susan cannot fail to have some in common. Can they be persuaded to regard each other *not* as adversaries in a zero-sum game but rather as potential allies in an enterprise from which both can emerge victorious? If so, they almost certainly will find ways to resolve their differences.

In sum, the main task of those of us who want to manage conflict productively is *not* to encourage the parties to communicate—they already *are* (and *have been*) communicating—but rather to teach them *how* to communicate in a way that will help them resolve their differences.

An analogy:

☐   Have you ever attempted to dance with someone who does not know how to dance? If you have, you know that the two of you did not dance together very well—no matter how good a dancer you yourself might be.

☐   It serves no purpose, of course, to accuse your partner of being a lousy dancer. That will not help him or her dance better, and it will not make the two of you a better-dancing couple.

☐ The solution lies in *teaching* your partner to dance. Once you have done so, you will get more pleasure from dancing with that person, and the two of you will get more pleasure from dancing as a couple.

☐ Consider now a situation in which *two* people who do not know how to dance are trying to dance together. Eventually, of course, they might through trial and error become superb dancers—just as, eventually, a chimpanzee who sat at a piano might randomly strike in perfect sequence and rhythm and volume all the notes of Beethoven's *Emperor Overture*.

☐ "Eventually," unfortunately, is a very long time. Thus if two nondancers wish to learn to dance, they will better their chances by enlisting the help of someone who knows how. Likewise, if two people who are in conflict do not know how to communicate effectively, they need help.

If you're a manager who seeks to resolve conflicts among subordinates, your primary mission is to teach them how to communicate effectively—that is, how to "fight." Likewise, if you're in conflict with someone who does not know how to fight, your primary task is to teach that person what *productive* fighting entails.

I'll address the specifics of all this in future chapters. Meanwhile, let's return to Jeff and Susan for an update of their conflict:

☐ Susan did complain to the federal government, and she was given a hearing before the Human Rights Commission, which ruled in her favor. According to the ruling, she had experienced "sex discrimination" and must be "made whole." In other words, The Company had to remove "all impediments" to her performing the job to which she had been appointed.

☐ Did Susan "win"? Legally speaking, she certainly did. Practically speaking, she did not.

☐ Can you imagine what life is now like for Susan at work? Is her conflict with Jeff resolved? Of course not. Jeff almost certainly is now doing—on the surface, anyway—everything that he should to fulfill the ruling of the Human Rights Commission. However, where no one can see him, Jeff probably is doing everything possible to ensure that Susan will fail.

☐ The conflict has gone underground. No one will ever be able to fault Jeff for his visible behavior toward Susan, but the likelihood is that he will do whatever he can to sabotage her performance.

☐ Does that mean that *he* has won? No, it does not. He, after all, is in charge of the department in which she manages a division. Problems in her division—encouraged and exacerbated by him—will hamper the operation of his department and will reflect poorly on his managerial abilities.

☐ Susan, having "won" before the Human Rights Commission, has lost the more important battle of establishing herself as an executive within The Company. Jeff, too, has lost. And the president has lost—even if his only purpose was to set an example discouraging other women from seeking to exercise their rights against discrimination in the workplace.

☐ Whatever the president's purpose, The Company has lost—for inordinate amounts of time and other resources were wasted on a conflict that did not contribute one whit to productivity. What might initially have been seen as a minor and easily manageable conflict was permitted to escalate into a major and extremely damaging one.

That often happens.

# 6 ON THE ESCALATOR

## OR HOW SMALL CONFLICTS QUICKLY BECOME LARGE ONES

I was angry with my friend;
I told my wrath, my wrath did end.
I was angry with my foe:
I told it not, my wrath did grow.
And I water'd it in fears,
Night and morning with my tears;
And I sunned it with smiles,
And with soft deceitful wiles.
And it grew both day and night,
Till it bore an apple bright;
And my foe beheld it shine,
And he knew that it was mine,
And into my garden stole
When the night had veil'd the pole:
In the morning glad I see
My foe outstretch'd beneath the tree.
WILLIAM BLAKE

Virtually every major conflict started as a minor one. This is true on a personal scale, as in divorce, or on a global scale, as in war. The escalation from minor to major is a result of things the parties do—often unwittingly, invariably unsuccessfully—while attempting to deal with the conflict.

Let's look again at the conflict in Chapter 5 between Jeff and Susan, this time with an eye toward determining the points at which escalation took place.

The stage was set for conflict before Jeff and Susan's first day as manager-subordinate, but this does not mean that conflict was inescapable. Either Jeff or Susan could have taken steps to avoid the conflict—or, at the very least, to establish ground rules for productive "fighting."

For example, Jeff, on being informed of Susan's appointment, might have tried to talk the president into assigning her elsewhere. Failing this, Jeff might have decided that everyone's best interests would be served if he made a determined effort to have harmonious relations with her.

His thinking may have proceeded along these lines:

"Well, I don't want her working for me, but that's beyond my control. If I let my emotions also go out of control, I may wind up ruining the department and wrecking my career. Obviously I shouldn't let my dissatisfaction with this one situation poison the rest of my professional life.

"I've long believed that women cannot be effective managers, but I may be wrong. This will be an excellent opportunity to put that belief to a test. If I treat her as I would any male executive, and if she performs well, my belief will have been proven wrong, but I'll be the richer for it. It's far better to find out that you have been wrong and to change your ways than to live in error and suffer its effects for the rest of your life.

"On the other hand, if I am right that women cannot be effective managers, Susan soon enough will make some serious mistakes. These may hamper the performance of her division and, by extension, my department. However, if I supervise her as closely as I would any other new manager, I should be able to minimize the damage she can do. Meanwhile, every mistake that she makes strengthens my argument that she is not equipped for the job. If she really botches things up, and if I carefully document her mistakes, I can go to the president and lay the record on his desk and insist that she be transferred."

Having reasoned thus, Jeff might have made it a point to discuss the problem with Susan on her very first day working for him. He might have invited her into his office—or, better yet, taken her to lunch—and said something like this:

"Susan, you've probably heard that I'm an old-fashioned guy who hasn't quite adjusted to the idea of women as executives. Well, that may be true, even though I'd like to think I'm open minded about these things. It's no secret that I wanted your new job to go to a man, and the president appointed you against my wishes. This puts a burden on me, and it also puts one on you.

"We can be at each other's throat for as long as we work together, and we can both suffer the accompanying unpleasantness and emotional strain. Both of us would work less effectively because of it. On the other hand, we can decide right now to cooperate at trying to overcome our differences. If we see ourselves as allies against a common problem, we will have a much better chance of getting along and working effectively together.

"I've resolved that I'm going to try to overcome whatever biases I have about working with women managers. In all my dealings with you, I intend to treat you no differently from any man who held the job. If you ever—under any circumstances—feel that I am treating you differently, I want you to tell me. I may not agree with you, but at least we can talk things out, and each of us will know where the other stands."

Susan, for her part, apparently started her new job with a chip on her shoulder. Her thinking may have proceeded thus:

"Well, I got my promotion—a lot later than I should have—and look at what they gave me. Everybody knows that Jeff is a Neanderthal. How could any woman be expected to work effectively for a boss like him? What was the president trying to do, sabotage my career?

"Well, I'm not going to let these male chauvinists do a number on me. I'm going to insist on every advantage that they would give to a man. I'm going to demand as much responsibility, and I want it as fast as a man would get it, and I am not going to accept anything less. The days of sexism in the workplace are over. There are federal laws mandating equality of opportunity, and if these people discriminate against me, they are going to have to answer for it."

If she began the job with this attitude, she could hardly fail to antagonize Jeff and probably a great many of her co-workers—not all of them men. Few of us, after all, enjoy working with people who are hostile, bitter, belligerent, and inflexible.

I am *not* saying, mind you, that such an attitude would be wrong. As I have argued in earlier chapters, values make perfect sense to the people who hold them. If we wish to manage conflict productively, our task is not to pronounce judgment on whose values are right or wrong but rather to try to channel the parties' behavior toward productive ends.

Let's now, therefore, without trying to change the basic attitudes expressed above, envision a way in which Susan might approach the new job with better chances for success:

"Well, I got my promotion—a lot later than I should have—and look at what they gave me. Everybody knows that Jeff is a Neanderthal. How could any woman be expected to work effectively for a boss like him? What was the president trying to do, sabotage my career?

"Well, if that's what's in the works, I am not going to play into these guys' hands by personifying all their stereotypes. If they want an excuse to criticize my performance, they are going to have to look very hard to find one.

"I am going to do everything I can in this job to give them reason to change their thinking about women. I'm going to go all out on every assignment. If I don't do it better than everybody else did, it won't be for lack of trying.

"I'm also going to try to win over Jeff personally. I can't let myself forget that his antifemale biases are a result of his ignorance or weakness. He didn't simply wake up one morning and say, "I think I'll be a real fool and start discriminating against women." His biases took a long time to develop, and he probably is becoming hardened in them as he feels threatened by the increasing number of female successes that are taking place all around him.

"The very worst way to deal with that kind of man is to be belligerent and combative. The best approach is to eliminate his reasons for feeling threatened. If Jeff can be made to see me as an asset—as someone whose excellent performance will reflect on his excellence as a manager—then he will have every reason to support me rather than oppose me.

"Of course, if Jeff and the president are really out to get me, it may take a lot more than good work to overcome their opposition. But I'm not alone in this fight. There are federal laws mandating equality of opportunity, and if these people discriminate against me, they are going to have to answer for it.

"However, if they make it necessary for me to go to the government, I'm not going to go poorly equipped. I'm not going to give them a chance to criticize me for being uncooperative or unreasonable. In fact, I'm not going to give them a single negative to hold against me. I'm going to build a record as a model executive. Let them try to fight against *that!*"

Having reasoned thus, Susan might approach Jeff on her first day as his subordinate and say something along these lines:

"I know you didn't choose me for this job, and if I were in your place I probably wouldn't feel good about having a subordinate who was appointed by someone else. Well, I want you to know this situation makes me even more eager than I normally would be to do a first-rate job for you. I want you to be really happy with my work. I'm going to do everything I can to make you say, 'Maybe I didn't chose her, but I'm sure glad I got her.'"

If Susan felt that by taking the initiative she might seem even more threatening to Jeff, she might say nothing unless he introduced the subject, in which case she could express these sentiments in response to whatever he said. In any event, had *either* Jeff *or* Susan taken one of the approaches suggested above, the likelihood is that their relationship would have begun fairly harmoniously. *Either* person could have reduced significantly the prospects that their differences would lead to a rapidly escalating battle in which one party could win only if the other lost.

Indeed, even if Jeff and the president *had* conspired to sabotage Susan's performance as a way of arming themselves to justify firing her, they might—had she operated as suggested above— have changed their minds after seeing that she was far more of an asset than either of them had realized she could be. If she could not win them over, she would nonetheless have prepared herself to do battle with them in a way that served her purposes much better than the scenario in Chapter 5.

Let's assume, for the purpose of illustration, that Susan followed the suggested approach and Jeff did not. Let's further assume that she refrained from approaching him on the first day for fear that he might deem her overly aggressive. Where might conflict first arise, and what should be done about it?

Jeff, it appears from the case study presented earlier, had chosen the tactic of baiting her by not giving her responsibility. In other words, his strategy was to deprive her of an important limited resource, then sit back and wait for her to get frustrated and behave rashly.

She could have thwarted that strategy. Once she saw what he was doing, she could have approached him and asked for more responsibility. If he replied—as he did in the original dialogue—that he felt she did not have the experience or the background, she could have said something along these lines:

"I can understand why you would feel that way, especially since I did mainly clerical work before I got appointed to this job. But I was hired by this company with a B.S. in business administration and fifteen credits toward an M.B.A. I didn't accept the job with the expectation of being a clerk, and I don't think the president appointed me as director of management training because he expected you to do my work for me. If you're dissatisfied with my performance, tell me where it's deficient. If you're not dissatisfied, then start giving me more responsibility."

If Jeff responded with only vague generalizations, as in the dramatization in Chapter 5 ("You're being too impatient. Things like this take time. When you're my age you'll . . ."), Susan could demand that he be more specific. How much time did he believe it would take before he increased her responsibilities? What more, if anything, did he expect as she performed the work she was now assigned? What sort of timetable did he have for eventually turning over to her the full responsibility and authority for running her own department?

In effect, such an approach would force him to establish criteria and assign himself deadlines. If she met the criteria, he could not reasonably refuse to meet the deadlines. He might not like being put on the spot this way—much less having her take the initiative in putting him on the spot—but he would have little choice in reacting to the *reasonableness* of her position. If he continued to resist her, he would be risking problems with the president and with the government if at some future time she complained and supported that complaint with a carefully documented history of Jeff's foot-dragging.

In sum, by approaching the matter in this way, she could present Jeff with an avoidance-avoidance conflict in which increasing her responsibility was a far less undesirable alternative to defending why he did *not* increase her responsibility. Moreover, she would accomplish this without demonstrating hostility or belligerence, or otherwise giving Jeff something to use against her.

Perhaps the most useful aspect of this approach is that it gives Jeff the opportunity to save face. She is not telling him, "Give me more responsibility or else . . . !" She is not—with equal or worse effect—supporting his biases by invoking the name of the president in a way that would reinforce Jeff's probable stereotype of female executives: shrewish, bitchy, unfair, and ready at a moment's notice to play squealer (a stereotype Susan did reinforce in the dialogue in Chapter 5). Instead, she is letting him appear to remain in full control of the situation by hearing her out, giving her the chance to prove herself, and rewarding her according to her efforts and results.

Let's now consider some other ways in which Jeff might respond to her request for an itemization of her inadequacies.

If instead of being vague he gave her a laundry list of complaints, she could make a judgment about whether these were bonafide and substantive or whether he was nit-picking. If she decided that his grievances were justified, she could work at eliminating them, then renew her request for more responsibility. If she decided he was nit-picking, she could request that he and she meet again in two weeks to discuss whether she had improved.

His awareness of her determination to gain his approval could help overcome his disapproval—if only by putting him on notice that she was not going to sit idly by while he attempted to suffocate her with indifference.

If Susan felt that the time was opportune to be even more forceful, she might challenge Jeff's judgment about her inadequacies and suggest that he and she seek the president's intercession in their controversy. This last course of action, while extreme, might be warranted if she concluded that she had exhausted all other approaches to resolving the conflict.

However, should Susan invoke the name of the president, she should not do so in the snide, innuendo-laden manner that she employed in the dramatization in Chapter 5. ("Are you saying that the president didn't know what he was doing when he appointed me?") Rather, she should straightforwardly—and in the most unemotional language possible—tell Jeff exactly what the situation is: She believes that she has exhausted all other approaches to resolving the conflict, and if he cannot see his way to exploring new avenues of cooperation with her, she will have no choice but to accuse him of bad faith and ask the president to arbitrate.

All of these approaches would serve Susan better, in my opinion, than the approach she took—which consisted mainly of expressing hostility through innuendo and sarcasm. All except the last approach (seeking the president's intercession) invited a cooperative response by Jeff. Even the last, however, left room for cooperation and compromise. None of the approaches encouraged escalation of the conflict.

The conflict escalated when Jeff and Susan, instead of seeking conciliation, began attempting to punish each other. He apparently fired the first round by withholding responsibility and by not telling her he was doing so and why. She responded in kind, assuming his decisions were a personal attack (or a broadside against the whole of working-womanhood). She did not explore any legitimate reasons he may have had for not giving her more responsibility.

On the day of the dramatized confrontation, neither party made any attempt to investigate the other's point of view or to convince the other of anything. Instead, they simply exchanged insults.

The escalator picked up speed when Susan threatened to involve the federal authorities. Jeff at that point might have bought time—and, in the process, contributed to the resolution of their conflict—by acknowledging that she might indeed have legitimate grounds for complaint. He could have invited her to spell out her grievances and, if only as a token, made certain concessions.

Instead, he ignored the *substance* of her complaint and fixed on a *symbol*—"I won't be threatened, Susan"—as if the *manner* in which she sought redress of her grievance were more important than the grievance itself.

In effect, he left her with little choice but to carry out her threat. Then, once the government got involved, the stakes were higher and the incentives of each party to "win" rose commensurately. Now neither could back down without admitting to being "wrong."

The escalator continued to climb when the Human Rights Commission ruled in Susan's favor. Jeff now had nothing to gain by working harmoniously with her. She had defeated him, and he wanted to get even. To reverse this defeat became a holy cause, a mission of overwhelming importance. Jeff thirsted for *victory*—even if that victory were pyrrhic. He would settle for nothing short of unconditional surrender. Thus did what could have been a bite-sized, easily containable conflict escalate into all-out war.

Four conditions normally must exist before a small conflict can become a large one. I'll first list and characterize all four, then offer illustrations of each.

1. *Mirror Image.* Each party regards the other's position as exactly opposite—and wholly inimical to—his or her own; accordingly, both parties are blind to opportunities for accommodation or compromise.

2. *Differing Interpretations of the Same Facts or Behaviors.* The parties, in effect, see only what they want to see; they favor whatever interpretation they regard as most compatible with their predetermined ends.

3. *Double Standard.*   The parties judge their own acts by a different standard from their adversaries' acts; "one man's meat" is *not* necessarily "another man's poison."

4. *Polarized Single-Issue Positions.*   The parties focus on one issue and perceive each other as representing the opposite extremes on that issue; thus, they see the conflict as having only one source, and they regard their task as forcing their adversaries to surrender unconditionally.

Let's look at some examples of these phenomena, both in the Jeff–Susan contretemps and in other conflicts.

## MIRROR IMAGE

Jeff and Susan apparently cannot conceive of an interest that they have in common. Neither of them seems to recognize—or, in any event, to attach importance to—their mutual interest in enhancing their own careers by contributing together to the betterment of The Company. Neither seems aware that both will benefit if they overcome their differences and learn to work in harmony.

Instead, each sees himself or herself as the other's victim and bête noire. Jeff, from his point of view, would not have this problem if Susan were not such an uppity, aggressive, impatient, win-at-any-cost harridan. Susan, from her point of view, would not have this problem if Jeff were not such a hard-headed, old-fashioned, ignorant, totally-unwilling-to-listen-to-reason, male chauvinist pig.

It apparently does not dawn on Jeff that his attitudes might be part of the reason that Susan is behaving as she does. Meanwhile, she apparently does not realize that her behavior is reinforcing his attitudes. *Neither* party seeks to *understand* the other's point of view.

A parallel might be drawn to the attitudes of the nations that fought in World War II.

From the standpoint of most Americans, the Axis "powers," as we so often referred to them, were the embodiment of everything evil. Hitler was a lunatic and a sadist, Mussolini a strutting buffoon, Tojo a malevolent automaton, and Hirohito a religious fanatic. (Not insignificantly, almost half a century after that war, only Hirohito—who outlived the others by several decades—appears to be thought of somewhat less malignly.)

My point is not that the Axis cause was just or the means for pursuing it moral. My point is that our stereotypes discourage consideration of the merits of any position but our own. We were the Good Guys. They were the Bad Guys. Everything else is irrelevant.

Few of us ever think of inquiring about how the citizens—approximately a quarter billion of them—of the Axis nations *viewed themselves*. Did they think of themselves as the Bad Guys? If not, how did they justify their failure (or refusal) to oppose the actions of their leaders? Were they all a pack of sniveling rats who did not have the courage to stand up for what they believed was right? Or did they—some of them, anyway—believe that we were as bad as we believed them to be?

I have chosen World War II as an example because relatively few people are alive today who have ambiguous feelings about it. There is much less agreement about the Korean "conflict" (as American officialdom inevitably described it at the time, seeking to avoid the word *war*) or the Vietnam experience (substitute *war, adventure, involvement, fiasco,* or any other word you like).

Significantly, the feelings of partisans on either side of these fundamentally unsuccessful exercises in conflict management are virtually identical. Whether you favored or opposed involvement in Korea or Vietnam, chances are you believe you were right *and the other side wrong*.

In just about every instance of escalated conflict, each party believes himself or herself to be the innocent victim who represents Truth, Justice, and Honor and who is being attacked maliciously by an evil enemy. Each claims to want only a just and fair resolution, while the other wants something else—ergo, by the process of elimination, a resolution that is both unjust and unfair.

In sum, each party in the typical escalated conflict looks into the mirror and sees exactly the opposite of his or her own point of view—no matter how many mitigating circumstances there may be and no matter how many mutually compatible goals the parties may share.

## DIFFERING INTERPRETATIONS OF THE SAME FACTS OR BEHAVIORS

Ask parties to an escalated conflict what the conflict is about, and you almost certainly will get dramatically different answers. For example, in the race-related conflicts that were so prominent in the United States during the 1960s, many people spoke of civil rights versus states' rights. If you did not have a scorecard and did not know the players, you might not have any idea that racial discrimination was an issue.

Few of the states' rights people came out openly and said they believed blacks should be subjugated. Rather, affecting the posture of constitutional scholars, they argued that, whatever the gritty details of the current controversy, the overriding consideration should be a clause in a two-centuries-old document that sought to establish jurisdictional harmony between state and federal governments.

Likewise, many who were interested specifically in the elimination of discrimination against blacks spoke in the most general terms about "equality of opportunity," as if racial barriers were only one of a broad spectrum of issues. Indeed, to speak of racial barriers in this context is somewhat euphemistic, for only one race was involved. Asian Americans and native Americans were not being ordered to the back of the bus.

Let's return now to the much more modest scale of conflicts within the workplace—and, more specifically, to our conflict between Jeff and Susan. If you were to ask them what their conflict is about, you almost certainly would get dramatically different answers.

Jeff might discuss the conflict in terms of challenges to authority and attempts at disrupting the usual (and, therefore, "right") order of things. He quite likely would see Susan as an iconoclast, an agitator, and someone who wants something for nothing.

Being older than she, he might also interpret her ambitions as an attack on older people by younger people. And he probably would find it very hard to accept that she simply sought the opportunity to compete equally with men for the same desiderata that he already possesses.

He more likely would believe that she was attempting a short cut, seeking to use affirmative action or other political weapons to avoid "paying her dues." He might also entertain the suspicion that she would not have been promoted had she not been sexually intimate with The Company's president. (It is significant that one of the most widely publicized personnel controversies of the early 1980s arose when a 29-year-old woman was promoted to vice president of a Fortune 500 company. The woman was known as a social acquaintance of the chief executive. Even the stodgiest newspapers and magazines did not avoid thinly veiled innuendos that the relationship was also sexual. Had the youthful vice president been male, would even a fraction as many people have taken notice that she and the chief executive knew each other socially, let alone speculate that the relationship might be sexual?)

So much for how Jeff might view the conflict. How would Susan view it? She probably would think in terms of women's rights and equality of opportunity. She might, in fact, see herself as champion of a New Order and Jeff as a reactionary fighting a rear-guard action against the wave of the future.

She probably would think of him as inflexible, selfish, and intolerant—while never for a moment imagining that these same adjectives might be applied to her. Being younger than he, she might also interpret his resistance more broadly as a defense against encroachments on the "establishment" by outsiders. If he were a member of an ethnic and/or religious group more closely associated with "old wealth" than her ethnic and religious peers, she might see ethnic or religious discrimination in his behavior.

In escalated conflict, each party seems to be keenly sensitive to an adversary's ignoble acts or motives. Each in turn seems completely blind to the possibility that his or her own acts or motives may be other than Pure, Good, and True.

In a study within a large federal agency, executives were asked to recall and describe episodes of conflict. They characterized their adversaries as having "demanded," "insisted," "threatened," "warned," "ordered," "refused," "disagreed," and "said it couldn't be done." They described themselves as having "requested," "suggested," "advised," "cautioned," "recommended," "explained," "urged," "had misgivings," "expressed reservations," and "sought assurance."

In sum, the executives described their adversaries as having acted competitively (if not also imperiously, hostilely, and contrary to the better interests of everyone involved). They described themselves as having acted cooperatively (if not also helpfully, graciously, charitably, and otherwise in consonance with the Boy Scout oath).

Readers of George Orwell are unlikely to find any of this astonishing. It is not without reason that what used to be called the War Department is now called the Department of Defense. It is not without reason that banks, insurance companies, and prospective employers, *require* us to *apply* for loans, policies, and jobs, whereas institutions that are less intent on intimidating us invite us to "Reach out and touch someone" or "Go for the gusto" or—classic of classics—"Fly the friendly skies."

Likewise, it is not by accident that insurance companies *require* us to file a *claim,* accompanied by *proof of loss,* and then turn the whole thing over to an *adjustor* (the implication being that what we asked for will be "adjusted" downward), and plaintiffs file a *complaint,* normally including a *demand* for relief and sometimes also including a *demand* for trial by jury. Nor is it without reason that traditionally styled courthouses resemble ancient Greek temples and cannot be entered unless one climbs a long flight of stairs, or that judges sit on elevated platforms and wear clothing symbolic of royalty and are addressed as "your honor" and expect everyone to rise when they enter the room.

In the Orwellian language favored by parties to escalated conflicts:

I offer help; whereas you meddle.
I am flexible; you have no backbone.
I have the strength of my convictions; you are stubborn.
I have wide-ranging interests and the ability to move from one to

another quickly, whereas you lack the ability to concentrate.

I am moral; you are a moralist (and perhaps also a prig and a prude).

I am an idealist; you are an ideologue.

I am a realist; you are unprincipled.

I am pragmatic; you would sell your best friend down the river.

I am a romantic; you are a dreamer.

I am forceful; you are aggressive.

I am quick to take action; you are brash.

I am sensitive; you are merely easily hurt.

I am direct; you are tactless.

I am introspective; you are an egomaniac and you waste too much time thinking about things that aren't important.

# DOUBLE STANDARD

This may at first seem to be simply an extension of the above category (Differing Interpretations of the Same Facts or Behaviors), but there are significant—if subtle—differences.

The principal difference has to do with the establishment of ground rules. Parties in escalated conflicts almost invariably believe that they are entitled to liberties to which their opponents are not.

Acts of terrorism are perhaps the ultimate expression of the double standard. Few if any terrorists would argue that it is morally desirable to kill innocent people. Yet terrorists do it all the time; it is their stock-in-trade. Their justification: this is the only way they can apply leverage against their opponents, who are inestimably more powerful than they.

Meanwhile, the governments that the terrorists oppose often practice their own equivalents of the terrorists' acts—summary execution, false imprisonment, torture of prisoners, confiscation of property. Strictly speaking, what they are doing is legal—for the government itself is the source of the law. Yet most human beings would regard the government's acts as immoral.

How does the government justify these acts? It claims that they are necessary if law and order are to be preserved. "This is the way these people have to be treated," the argument goes. "If we don't do it, they'll overrun the country and then you'll see a bloodbath the likes of which you never imagined."

There are other examples of the double standard in the world of corporate espionage.

Every so often someone is arrested for stealing corporate documents or other secret materials. The booty might be circuit diagrams for computers, sales records, design specifications for a new automobile, lists of individual customers' transactions, or any of a myriad other items that competitors could put to profitable use.

Legally, of course, there is no justification for such a theft. Yet the likelihood is that the executives who ordered the theft—or who bought goods stolen by a freelancer—consider themselves moral. They probably justify their behavior thus:

"Yeah, under ordinary circumstances it's wrong to steal. I certainly wouldn't take *money*—especially from someone who needs it. But what the heck, this isn't a simple matter of stealing. That company has been dominant in this industry for years. It's got more money than any 10 of the rest of us combined. It's got half the U.S. Senate and two-thirds of the House of Representatives in their pocket. For goshsakes, its house counsel is a former attorney general! If you want to compete against those guys, you can't do it by the Marquis of Queensberry rules."

Yet another example of the double standard is found in a well-known story involving a celebrated lawyer who was defending a man accused of wife-poisoning. Just before delivering his summation to the jury, the lawyer drank a quart of buttermilk to line his stomach. Then, as the brief summation came to a close, he guzzled down the remains of a bottle of poison that the prosecutor had contended the defendant had employed to commit the murder. As soon as the jury retired to deliberate, the defense attorney rushed to a waiting ambulance, in which he was taken to a hospital to have his stomach pumped.

Is it ethical to deceive a jury? Most lawyers probably would answer in the negative—especially if they are speaking on the record. Yet many lawyers have been known to encourage witnesses to lie—or at the very least, to conceal certain germane truths.

What is the justification? "The situation is stacked in favor of the other side."

If a prosecutor encourages police officers or other witnesses to testify untruthfully against a defendant, the rationale is that the defendant is guilty—of many other crimes as well as this one. "This is the only way we can be sure we'll put the rat behind bars, where he belongs."

If the defense attorney suborns perjury, it is because The System is against his client. "The police and the prosecutor have violated the poor kid's rights, and this is the only way to get him off."

Ask anyone who is involved in an escalated conflict to explain behavior that most people would regard as unethical, and you probably will be told that the behavior was *necessary* under the circumstances. If the other guy does it, it's a dirty trick. If I do it, I'm only being pragmatic and playing the game the way it has to be played.

The other guy is malicious; I'm smart!

In the conflict between Jeff and Susan, we have evidence that both parties believe they are entitled to liberties that the other party should not take.

Susan, for example, apparently has no qualms about speaking sarcastically to Jeff, accusing him of ulterior motives, and issuing an ultimatum. Of course, none of these acts is illegal, and most people would regard none of them as immoral, so they certainly do not fall within the same category as a lawyer's suborning perjury or tricking a jury by swallowing poison while an ambulance waits. All the same, the likelihood is that Susan would regard one of *her* subordinates as behaving improperly if that subordinate acted toward her in the same way that Susan acted toward Jeff.

Jeff, for his part, also seems to subscribe to a double standard. He presumably would feel agggrieved if one of his bosses, whether male or female, spoke patronizingly to him or cut off a discussion by saying, "I won't be threatened. I am relieving you of all your duties, effective immediately." But he apparently sees no fault in speaking this way to Susan.

Possibly the best recent historical examples of the double standard come from American presidential politics. Is it not significant that more than one candidate who presented himself as a champion of law and order ultimately gave evidence that he considered himself and his aides above the law?

If you are inclined to regard this as a partisan statement, you may be guilty of applying your own double standard. Think back, please, not only on Watergate but also on the clandestine tape-recording by Franklin D. Roosevelt and John F. Kennedy of conversations that occurred in their offices.

Please recall also Lyndon B. Johnson's use of the questionable Gulf of Tonkin incident to obtain a congressional resolution that he subsequently employed as his justification to escalate combat in Vietnam. Recall also Gerald R. Ford's pardon of Richard M. Nixon not only for all crimes of which Nixon had been accused but also for "any crimes that he *may* have committed."

Would any of these presidents, as a high school orator in the Voice of Democracy contest, have condoned such presidential behavior? I think not.

## POLARIZED SINGLE-ISSUE POSITIONS

In escalated conflicts, parties tend to focus on a single issue and perceive each other as representing the opposite extremes of that issue.

A classic example occurred at a high school in the Northeast during the early 1950s and triggered what apparently was America's first strike by students. The principal of the high school had incurred the animosity of a substantial segment of the student body and virtually all of the faculty. She was a political appointee who had no experience as a teacher and was named principal immediately after serving as secretary to the local political boss. A small but extremely vocal group of students was attempting to persuade other students to stage a strike. However, while the students had many grievances against the principal, the would-be strike leaders could not arouse sufficient ire to trigger a walk-out.

Then, in a controversy that had nothing whatever to do with the students' grievances, the principal suspended the vice principal on charges of insubordination. The vice principal was a fairly popular member of the faculty but by no means a champion of the causes of the rebellious students. However, the would-be strike leaders found in his suspension the catalyst they needed to mobilize the rest of the student body.

On the Monday morning after the suspension, only a handful of students appeared for classes; the remainder were parading outside the school, carrying banners and placards that had been constructed hastily over the weekend. "No Jim, No School," the signs proclaimed, "Jim" being the name of the vice principal, although none of the students had dared refer to him by his first name before the strike.

For several days, the principal, the superintendent, and the school board made no attempt to address the students' grievances. Their only response was a statement to the effect that: (a) the strike was illegal; (b) the principal had full authority to suspend any subordinate and was not accountable to the students for such action; (c) each day that the students remained on strike would have to be "made up" during summer vacation in order to meet the state's attendance requirements; and (d) students who returned to class immediately would not be punished, but those who delayed would be expelled and required to repeat the entire school year.

Only a handful of students returned. Meanwhile, the strike had become a cause celebre in newspapers throughout the Northeast. A number of parents took up the students' cause, demanding not only that the vice principal be reinstated but also that the principal resign. The students prepared a list of grievances against the principal. A local lawyer volunteered to negotiate on behalf of the students.

Recognizing the broad base of opposition to the principal, the superintendent prevailed upon the mayor to call a town meeting. The superintendent also persuaded the suspended vice principal to urge the students to return to school pending resolution of their grievances. The vice principal complied, but the students remained on strike.

The town meeting was held. The students' grievances were heard. The superintendent promised to address them after the students returned to school. Members of the school board assured the students—and their parents and other interested citizens, who by this time outnumbered the students—that justice would be done. The superintendent added that, earlier threats to the contrary notwithstanding, striking students who returned to class immediately would not be expelled. The students' self-appointed lawyer told the students that he thought they were getting a very good deal.

The students' reply? "No Jim, No School."

The students' lawyer continued to negotiate with the superintendent and the school board. Quite a few of the students' demands were met. Indeed, the lawyer told the students he thought they were getting a much better deal than they had any right to expect. He added that if they did not accept the offer, he feared they would have backed the superintendent and board into a corner where there would have been no choice but to break off negotiations, declare the students truant, and call in the police.

The students' reply: "No Jim, No School."

They obviously had lost sight of the fact that the vice principal's suspension was only a *symbol* of what they found objectionable. They also seemed to have forgotten their original grievances. By making the vice-principal's suspension their single issue, they were, in effect, throwing away everything they originally had sought.

The administrators, meanwhile, were committed to the opposite extreme on the issue of the vice principal's suspension. They were determined not to be perceived as having backed down. They would, in effect, have given away virtually anything so long as they did not have to force the principal to reinstate the vice principal—an act which would be tantamount to unconditional surrender.

Negotiations were suspended. The administrators continued to threaten expulsion and involvement of the police. The students continued to chant, "No Jim, No School." And then—

And then someone on the side of the administrators came up with a solution that was elegant in the extreme and wholly cosmetic.

The principal announced the reinstatement of the vice principal. Careful to point out that she was not acceding to students' demands, she said that she had intended originally that the suspension would last for only 10 days; the 10 days now had elapsed, and therefore the vice principal could return to work. She added that students who did not return to class within 24 hours would be arrested for truancy.

The students were left without a cause. They had staked their strike on a single issue, and the issue had been—in one stroke—taken away from them. In dismissing earlier attempts to resolve their other grievances, they had acknowledged—in effect—that these grievances were minor. They therefore had lost all justification to continue their strike. If they disobeyed the principal's ultimatum to return to class, they would be seen as mere troublemakers. The students returned to class without a single concession by the principal or the school's administrators.

The outcome of this strike is not surprising to those of us who specialize in conflict management. Single-issue conflict permits only two outcomes: One party wins or both parties lose. There is no room for ambiguity, no room for compromise. Either you are right or I am right, but we cannot both be right. To compromise is to give in, to surrender, to lose face.

Isn't it ironic, then, that so many people attempt to resolve conflicts by encouraging the parties to focus on a single issue?

Would-be mediators ask, "What's your disagreement *really* about? What is *the* issue here?" By doing so, they encourage the parties to harden their positions on a single issue. In the process, escalation of the conflict is encouraged.

In my opinion, the parties should be urged to recognize that the conflict has *more* than one source. Mediators should strive to make the conflict seem *rich* with multiple, overlapping, inextricably intertwined issues. The greater the number of issues that the parties can identify, the more room there is to structure an outcome in which both parties can perceive themselves as winners.

Issues need not even be germane. Indeed, some of the most effective negotiators are those who can persuade parties to accept concessions on nongermane issues in exchange for concessions on germane issues.


☐    For example, in 1982, when French president Francois Mitterand attempted to open diplomatic relations with North Korea, officials in South Korea threatened to oppose that country's purchase from French companies of certain transportation and electricity-generation equipment costing billions of dollars.

Mitterand countered by promising to persuade at least one Soviet-bloc nation to open diplomatic relations with South Korea once France sent an ambassador to North Korea. In reply, South Korea demanded that the Soviet-bloc nation be either Russia or China rather than one of the so-called satellites.

We can envision the sort of haggling that might have gone on as the negotiators exchanged offers.

FRANCE:         Look, we can't get you Russia or China, but how about Hungary and Yugoslavia?

SOUTH KOREA:    Who needs 'em? They are Western puppets any-way. Now if you could get us Poland and Albania. . . .

FRANCE:         Well, Albania is out of the question—we have no influence there. Poland, maybe. . . .

SOUTH KOREA:    For Poland alone, the most we'll do is withdraw our opposition to French involvement in the pro-ject for a high-speed train on the Seoul-Pusan railway. If you also want to get involved in building the proposed Pusan subway, you've got to give us more than just Poland. How much influence do you have with the Czechs?

Obviously, the participation by French companies in South Korean construction projects was not germane to any ideological differences France and South Korea might have had regarding France's proposed diplomatic relations with North Korea, nor was French president Mitterand's offer to recruit Soviet-bloc recognizance relevant to the construction projects. However, by expanding single-issue conflicts into a multiple-issue conflict, France and South Korea found opportunities to compromise and make peace.

In single-issue conflict, the parties see themselves as having no choice but to force an adversary to surrender unconditionally. However, if the parties can be persuaded to see the conflict as multidimensional, they often will be able to agree on acceptable trade-offs and compromises.

Looking again at the strike at the high school, we can see that the students had many opportunities to better their situation by accepting the offers of the superintendent and the school board. They lost everything by sticking to the single issue of the vice principal's reinstatement.

It is ironic—and doubly noteworthy—that this issue was, in reality, only a symbol. The students did not *care* about the vice principal. They had seized on his suspension as a vehicle for protest, and then they confused the *vehicle* with what was supposed to be the *cargo*. Their symbol *supplanted* what it was supposed to symbolize.

Symbolism did not play quite so large a role in the conflict between Jeff and Susan at The Company, but they, too, permitted a single issue to dominate.

Each of them presumably had a myriad of interests in the conflict. For example, Susan probably did not object merely to being deprived of responsibility; she also wanted the many other desiderata that usually accompany responsibility: more interesting and challenging work, the concomitant feeling of accomplishment, recognition within the company, higher pay, and a better benefits package. Jeff likewise probably did not object merely to having a female manager as his subordinate. He presumably objected also to not having had a say about her appointment, and he probably was concerned with such tangential matters as what this appointment signified with respect to his standing within the company. He also may have been concerned that she could not do the job and that her mistakes would reflect negatively on his managerial abilities. Indeed, this may have been his biggest concern.

If either Jeff or Susan had seen the other's situation in perspective, either could have (in the manner of the French and South Korean negotiators) offered help in achieving what the other was seeking. Failing that, either could have traded one desideratum for another.

For example, Jeff, not wanting Susan within his bailiwick, might have sung her praises to a colleague in another department or in another company who might have hired her away from him.

She might thus have achieved all her desiderata—none of them at Jeff's expense.

Susan, for her part, instead of waiting for him to give her more to do, might have assumed some tasks on her own—perhaps working on them after-hours—and presented the completed work to him as a fait accompli. Or she might have presented him with proposals that he could recognize as contributory to his overall mission. If nothing that she did won him over, she might have approached him and said candidly, "Look, if you want to get rid of me, I'll make it easy for you. Write me a nice letter of recommendation and introduce me to some people in other departments or companies."

Instead of recognizing such possibilities, Jeff and Susan took polar positions on a single issue. She probably saw the issue as women's rights versus sexism, whereas he probably saw it as managerial autonomy versus interference. Whatever their perception of the issue, they both dug in for a last stand on it—and both lost.

Let us now look at another example of negotiators who have shown themselves adept at identifying a broad range of relevant issues in an ostensibly single-issue conflict. Not surprisingly, the richest source of examples is the world of professional diplomacy.

☐ The United States since World War II has maintained military bases in Greece. About 3,700 Americans are stationed at the bases, which employ 2,500 Greeks and contribute an estimated $70 million annually to the Greek economy. The bases are authorized by an executive agreement between the nations. An executive agreement, one step down the ladder from a treaty, does not require ratification by the U.S. Senate, but it does require approval by Greece's parliament.

☐ In 1981, Andreas Papandreou, as Socialist candidate for prime minister, promised to remove all foreign military bases from Greece. His pledge obviously was directed at the United States, for no other nation had comparable installations in Greece. Therefore the logical assumption was that when he won the election the American bases would soon be shuttered—right? More precisely, when the five-year executive agreement regarding the bases expired on December 31, 1983, it would not be renewed—correct?

□    Well, not exactly. In October of 1982, 15 months before the agreement was to expire, the United States and Greece began negotiating its renewal. You and I—or Jeff and Susan—might conclude, based on the announced position of Papandreou, that there was nothing to negotiate. We would be wrong. Reginald Bartholomew, chief negotiator for the United States, and Greek deputy foreign minister Ioannis Kapsis "unpacked" the single-issue conflict by introducing a number of side issues.

□    For example, under the U.S. security assistance program, Greece had been receiving $280 million a year. This program had not been linked to the military bases, but a link quickly was found. The Reagan administration requested of Congress an increase to $500 million in security assistance funds for 1984—but contingent on successful conclusion of the negotiations. Thus negotiator Bartholomew was able to both dangle a carrot and brandish a stick.

□    Another side issue: While the agreement expiring on December 31, 1983 did not establish deadlines or spell out procedures for troop withdrawals, Bartholomew proposed that a renewal of the agreement contain a provision whereunder troops would be withdrawn within 17 months of the agreement's expiration. This was an American carrot without a stick, and a rather cosmetic carrot at that, but it provided Papandreou with a useful vehicle for propaganda. More on this point a few paragraphs hence.

□    The negotiations continued for nine months and, to all outward appearances, were both intense and acrimonious. Wrote one journalist: "The sometimes-bitter negotiations [were] punctuated by outbursts of anti-American rhetoric" from Papandreou. However, in July of 1983 the governments of the United States and Greece jointly announced that the agreement had been extended for another five years. The announcement described the two nations as "close friends and allies."

□    Did Papandreou go back on his campaign promise? Well, not exactly. In a statement issued in Athens independent of the binational announcement, he pointed out that the new agreement guaranteed the removal of all U.S. forces from Greece within 17 months of the expiration date of December 31, 1988. He characterized this provision as "an historic recovery of Greek national sovereignty."

☐  (In Washington, meanwhile, State Department sources told reporters that the agreement was substantively identical to the one it replaced. These sources added that the new agreement called for renegotiation or extension of base rights after five years, just as the old agreement did. The sources characterized the 17-month "guarantee" as a grace period during which either government could decide to extend or renegotiate the pact.)

☐  Also, Papandreou was quick to disabuse his constituents of the notion that the United States might have bought the agreement by almost doubling Greece's security assistance payments. He pointed out that the United States had years earlier established a ratio of 10 to 7 in military aid to Turkey and Greece—that is, Greece would receive $7 in aid for every $10 received by Turkey. The request for Turkey in 1984 being $755 million, the request for Greece ($500 million) was in line.

☐  Moreover, while the aid request was not part of the executive agreement regarding the military bases, Papandreou announced that negotiator Bartholomew had agreed to it in an exchange of private letters with Greek negotiator Kapsis. (Bartholomew would not comment, but State Department officials told American reporters that there was no such side agreement and that Bartholomew did not have the authority to enter into such a side agreement.)

☐  Whatever the truth about any of this, the point is that the American and Greek negotiators, rather than getting polarized on a single issue ("get rid of the bases" or "leave them in place"), found ways to introduce additional issues and to trade concessions on one for concessions on another. In the process, everyone was able to save face.

Conflicts escalate when parties polarize on single issues, apply a double standard regarding each other's behavior, interpret the same facts or behaviors differently, and see each other's positions as mirrorlike opposites. Conflicts deescalate—and get resolved—when parties recognize mutual interests and multiple issues, then trade concessions on some issues for concessions on others.

A few chapters hence I'll explore the techniques of conflict resolution in considerably greater detail. First, however, let's look at some of the destructive and productive uses of conflict.

# ≡≡≡7≡DESTRUCTIVE AND PRODUCTIVE USES OF CONFLICT

$S$ome of the destructive consequences of conflict may be apparent to even the most casual observer. They include:

*1.* Stress and its concomitant physical and psychological toll on human beings

*2.* Misallocation of personal and/or organizational resources as parties devote time, thought, and material to doing battle instead of doing business

*3.* Diminished across-the-board performance as parties let the conflict sap them of energy, determination, and dedication

Each of these consequences may have consequences of its own, and not all of these are so readily apparent. A sometimes unrecognized consequence of conflict-related stress is the unwarranted extension of hostility to people who are not really involved in the conflict.

For example, you and I have a conflict at work. That evening, I meet a friend for dinner and get into a pointless quarrel about some plans we have made. You, meanwhile, go home and speak abusively to your spouse, who in turn mistreats your child, who in turn kicks the family's dog.

These domino-effect subordinate conflicts can eventually take on a life of their own and become another source of continuing stress that exacerbates the original conflict.

For example, your spouse, weary of having you come home in a bad mood because of your workplace conflicts with me, may demand that you change jobs if you cannot better handle the pressures of this one. Your child, yet another step removed from the original conflict, may become troublesome at school. And the poor dog, still another step removed, may get you into a lawsuit by biting your neighbor.

Some organizations, aware of the damage that is possible in domino-effect conflicts, provide gymnasia or other sports facilities for employees, hoping that conflict-related hostilities can be worked off physically rather than get directed against innocent parties.

Conflict-related misallocation of resources can be seen in the unsigned poison pen letters sent to regulatory agencies by disgruntled employees or in the malicious anonymous "memos" posted overnight on companies' bulletin boards. Misallocation can also be seen in extended and animated discussions at the water cooler: Employees begin investing the organization's time—and, by extension, the organization's money—in the conflict.

And then there is the "work-to-rule" game, which aggrieved employees ofttimes play: "I'm going to do only what they pay me to do—nothing else. *I'll* show *them*."

Of course, no job description can be truly complete (refer to Chapter 4), and therefore all sorts of things get neglected that ordinarily were done as a matter of course: "Alright, the job description says I have to make coffee, but it doesn't say I have to pour it, or wash the cups afterward, or fill the coffeepot with water beforehand, or keep track of how much sugar or cream we have. . . ." In effect, the job description has become a weapon in the conflict.

In yet another destructive second-stage consequence of conflict, workers use their job-related perquisites to damage their opponents. For example, a credit department might find reason to reject every new account brought in by the sales force.

The people in the credit department can be very sanctimonious about their behavior: "We're only trying to protect the company. If the sales people would find some good accounts, we'd be delighted to extend them credit." In fact, the credit people may simply be attempting to retaliate for a real or imagined offense by the sales people.

A special—and ofttimes difficult to identify—destructive consequence of conflict is sabotage. I use the word advisedly, recognizing that for many people it invokes images of spies planting explosives in munitions plants. Well, yes, that *is* sabotage, but there are quite a few subtler forms: for example, work slowdowns, waste, or personal appropriation of company resources.

Sabotage occurs most frequently in situations where one party has a great deal of power and another party has little or none. The powerless party sees sabotage as one of the only ways to "get back" at the powerful party.

For example, we are not apt to see much sabotage when the parties to a conflict are two senior executives fighting over who will take command of a new project or two secretaries competing over a boss' time or use of certain equipment. In peer or near-peer relationships, sabotage is unnecessary; the combatants have far more efficient weapons.

But we are apt to see a great deal of sabotage when the main office issues an edict that is deemed exceptionally onerous by the rank-and-file in the branches—especially if there is no channel through which these employees can air their grievances.

The techniques of sabotage usually are legal. They aim at inflicting a loss on the people in power, or disrupting the work of those people, or otherwise embarrassing the people or the company as a whole.

For example, a lower-echelon employee might leave on the hot water tap in a rest room, causing the waste of a great deal of fuel and perhaps also flooding the room and surrounding areas. Or the employee might dispatch hundreds of letters with the postage meter set at $3.70 instead of $.37.

What can a manager do when faced by employees' acts of this sort? If it were possible to determine which employee had left the hot water tap on or had failed to reset the postage meter, should the company demand that the employee pay for the damage? Should the employee be fired? Should some other penalty be exacted?

Actually, just about any attempt to punish the employee will prove counterproductive. Punishment is apt to arouse sympathy among other employees and incur their animosity toward the company and/or the manager. The attitude is likely to be something to this effect: "It was only an accident. What kind of company are we working for when you can't even have an accident without getting punished? This is worse than the army. The company has money coming out its ears, and here we are barely making a living, and they treat us this way."

Indeed, if you have an employee whom you want to fire under circumstances of this kind, you probably would be better off postponing the firing until some time when it would not seem to be punishment. Other workers are likely to perceive punishment as unfair even if a given employee repeatedly made costly "mistakes." Most workers will not see these "mistakes" as sabotage.

How can we be sure they *are* sabotage? We can't—short of catching someone in *flagrante delicto,* holding the proverbial smoking gun. I suggest, however, that people who *care* do not let costly "accidents" happen. Even people of extremely low intelligence, if they care, do not let these things happen.

*Care*lessness is just that—an absence of care for the party whose resources are damaged or placed at risk. In the workplace, not caring is an expression of hostility, a statement to the effect that "the company doesn't care about me, so why should I care about the company?"

☐    An excellent example of sabotage that might appear to be something else occurred in a division of a fast-food chain. The company, which was very careful about quantifying everything that took place at its outlets, observed a slow but steady increase in food costs versus revenues. Given that purchasing and distribution were centralized, the only explanation was that food was being wasted. That is, more food was being used per dollar of revenue in this division than in others, and therefore employees either were stealing the food, giving it away (whether to customers in larger portions or to friends without charge), throwing it away, or handling it improperly and letting it spoil.

Less sophisticated managers than the senior executives of this company might have concluded that the problem was merely one of pilferage or of inadequate indoctrination of employees on size of portions or food-handling and storage. Such managers might attempt to address the problem by posting signs about waste and portion control, by publishing brochures on the obligations of employees, or by threatening the managers of the individual outlets. Yet another unsophisticated approach might be to hire a private investigator to catch errant employees in the act, then punish them as an example to the others.

All such approaches, however, would attack the symptoms rather than the underlying disease—and would, in the vast majority of cases, only make things worse. Chances are that posters or brochures would be the butt of jokes. Employees probably would decorate them with graffiti. Threatened managers might regard a threat as the proverbial last straw and quit a job that was not all that desirable to begin with. Subordinates in the outlets, mostly high school students working part-time, might quit if one of their peers was punished or might engage in costlier forms of sabotage—for example, leaving a freezer unplugged or burning out a microwave oven.

Recognizing the possibilities of such consequences, and concluding that the problem really was sabotage—an attack by the powerless against the powerful—the managers of the fast-food chain sent an employee relations consultant to the division that was having the problem. The consultant scheduled weekly "gripe sessions" for employees. He also developed an incentive program whereunder the managers of the outlets and their subordinates could win fly-away vacations.

The consultant never said one word to the managers or their employees about waste, pilferage, or rising costs. Yet, over the course of several months, the problem was eliminated. Indeed, the division soon began to show a lower ratio of costs to revenues than the average within the company.

In sum, the consultant recognized that waste, pilferage, et cetera, were sabotage and that these acts of sabotage were symptoms of employees' malaise. Rather than addressing the symptoms, he addressed the disease, and, when the employees' grievances had been eliminated, the problem also was eliminated.

It is easy for managers to fail to recognize sabotage. When there is pilferage, waste, inordinate absenteeism, damage to the company's property, or similar misallocation of resources, the tendency of many managers is to generalize about workers' irresponsibility, indifference, low motivation, or lack of respect. However, in a great many—if not most—of these instances, the workers are performing sabotage, whether calculatedly or unthinkingly, and the redress of workers' grievances leads to the elimination of the problem.

☐   In a case in which I was involved personally, managers at a manufacturing plant were dissatisfied with the productivity in one of their factories. They sent in efficiency experts (engineers who specialize in the processes of manufacture) to analyze the problem and recommend solutions.

These experts concluded that the temperature in the factory was too high and that workers therefore were lethargic. The experts recommended that the temperature be lowered over a period of three weeks (so that workers would not notice an abrupt change) from 72 to 65 degrees Fahrenheit.

Their recommendation was followed, and management got no feedback—positive or negative—from the workers. There were scattered complaints to supervisors, but when the supervisors replied that nothing could be done, there was no follow-up. There were no complaints to the union, no petitions to senior managers, no off-duty meetings of disgruntled employees.

What did happen was that absenteeism increased, damage to equipment increased, and productivity decreased. Management was dumbfounded, wholly unable to understand why the carefully thought out solution of the experts had backfired.

That's when I was called in. I evaluated the situation and concluded that the lowering of the temperature had been counterproductive. I recommended that management, without announcement, increase the temperature to its former level and concurrently initiate certain incentive programs based on increases in productivity.

Productivity promptly returned to its original level and then rose slightly above it. It was one of the easiest fees I ever earned.

I stress, the workers in this factory need not have made a deliberate decision to sabotage the company. They may simply have become more disgruntled about jobs with which they were more than passingly disgruntled in the first place. Accordingly, they may have begun taking off more time and paying less attention to the maintenance of their equipment. Whatever the case, their decreased productivity can be seen as a direct consequence of management's ill-advised attempt to lower the temperature in the factory.

In some situations, there is no question that sabotage is carefully planned. A master of certain sabotage techniques—all perfectly legal—was Saul Alinsky, a labor and community organizer of the 1960s and 1970s who frequently worked with minority groups.

☐   As the story goes, in Rochester, New York, Alinsky had the task of persuading community leaders that certain grievances of minority groups should be redressed. When conventional methods failed, he opted for a more dramatic approach.

Among the many civic institutions of which Rochester is justifiably proud is the Eastman Symphony, named after the founder of Rochester's largest employer, the Eastman Kodak corporation. Alinsky bought a great many tickets for a performance by the symphony and announced that he would give the tickets to members of the minority group with which he was working. This, in itself, was obviously not an act with which the city fathers could take issue; indeed, it was one they had no choice but to encourage.

Alinsky then announced that, on the evening of the performance, the ticket holders would be his guests at a buffet dinner. This, too, was a legal act with which no one could quarrel. Certainly, on the face of developments so far, no one could accuse Alinsky of having anything but the highest motives.

Come the buffet dinner and Alinsky served . . . beans! There were other foods, but all in rather short supply. Imagine casserole upon casserole of beans: lima beans, kidney beans, fava beans, lupine beans, northern beans, pork 'n' beans, baked beans, boiled beans, stewed beans, pureed beans.

The concert was, to put things mildly, a less-than-total success. Alinsky, without doing anything illegal, achieved his aim of demonstrating his ability to disrupt community life. If Rochester's leaders had responded punitively (assuming that they could find a justification for punishment), Alinsky and his allies would have won sympathy.

In the negotiations a few days after the concert, Alinsky obtained a great many of the concessions that he had been seeking. His adversaries had little choice but to recognize that his power to disrupt community life was greater than their power to keep him and his allies at bay.

The point here—it cannot be overemphasized—is that sabotage is not *the* conflict; it is merely a consequence of the conflict and a symptom of the conflict. And, lest you be inclined to think that sabotage is a rather uncommon phenomenon, let me call your attention to a few statistics.

In a study conducted by the University of Minnesota for the U.S. Department of Justice in 1983, one third of all retail, manufacturing, and hospital workers were found to have stolen from their employers. More than two thirds engaged in "counterproductive behavior," such as excessively long lunches and/or breaks, sloppy workmanship, abuse of sick leave or other perquisites, and/or working while under the influence of alcohol or drugs. According to the study, pilferage by employees costs American businesses as much as $10 billion annually.

The researchers concluded that "a feeling of being exploited" was far more often the motive for theft by employees than economic pressures on the worker or other factors. This was especially true among workers aged 16 to 25: "Not only was their level of dissatisfaction higher, but we also observed that these employees were not much deterred by the typical sanctions of dismissal for employee-theft violations."

Noting that employers frequently offer the best fringe benefits and other perquisites to employees with the most seniority, the researchers observed: "As a technique for reducing theft and deviance in the workplace, this policy may be precisely the worst thing that the organization could do."

Finding it "most perplexing and unexpected" that employers do not pay more attention to the problem, the researchers concluded: "Draconian security-hardware, such as cameras, one-way glass, mirrors, and the like may be a deterrent to shoplifters, but when directed at employees they tend to convey a message of distrust. Our research suggests that social controls, not physical controls, are in the long run the best deterrents to theft and deviance in the organization."

"Social controls," of course, is merely jargon for creating an ambience in which people behave in a desired way because they *want* to behave that way.

So much for the destructive consequences of conflict. The fact is that conflict can have productive uses also. Indeed, conflict can yield profit far disproportionate to the conflict's potential for damage, and some organizations foster certain levels of conflict for the express purpose of stimulating maximum performance.

For example, when the late Werner von Braun was in charge of the United States' Marshall Space Flight Center (then headquarters of this nation's space program), any employee who noticed a defect in a piece of equipment was immediately put in command of a task force to correct that defect. A mere private first class or G-3 (one of the lowest-ranking civilians in governmental employ) could be made the boss of company- or even field-grade officers.

The competition to find defects was, in some ways, demoralizing to senior members of the organization. However, it also resulted in significantly higher quality control. (Let us not forget that von

Braun and his team put men in space without a single serious accident, let alone a fatality.)

Another example of the productive uses of conflict can be found in professional football, where coaches routinely refrain from announcing the new season's starting team until the last possible moment, thus encouraging competition for each position. To be sure, the competing players are in conflict with each other—each player's goal can be achieved only at the expense of the other player. However, the conflict is viewed as productive in that it stimulates players to higher degrees of excellence than they might achieve if they did not have to compete.

"Love your opponent," Penn State football coach Joe Paterno exhorts his players. "He's the guy that's forcing you to be as good as you can be."

Those of us who look on conflict as malum in se, or intrinsically evil, may resist the idea that conflict can have productive uses. However, it is undeniable that some of society's most beneficial changes are an outgrowth of conflict.

Had there been no Revolutionary War, there would be no United States. Had there been no confrontation at Runnymede in June of 1215, there would be no Magna Charta. Of course, it's better still to achieve the benefits of conflict *without* going to war—and that's part of what this book is about.

Conflict persuades—or should persuade—people to recognize their problems and take steps to solve them. People are more willing to build dams after a flood. They are more willing to use fertilizer after a crop failure. They become more attentive to matters of health after a siege of illness. (If there is anyone more zealous than a reformed smoker, it is a reformed drunk.)

Of course, villains are as capable as heroes of seeing this, and the logical next step for those of villainous bent is to create conflicts that can be used to persuade people to follow a desired course of action. Probably the best example in recent times of this sort of manipulation of public opinion was the Reichstag fire in Germany during the 1930s, wherein Hitler and his cohorts set ablaze the building in which their nation's parliament met, then blamed the fire on vandals and used the spurious threat of vandalism to justify repressive measures that Hitler had been planning from the start.

Those of us who are on the side of Goodness and Light can only recognize that this is a potential weapon in the armamentarium of our unscrupulous adversaries and be ready to counter its deployment whenever we can. Meanwhile, the fact that conflict can be exploited by the malevolent should not prevent us from recognizing that conflict can be used productively—and creatively—by the benevolent (that is, you and me).

Some organizations, wholly benevolently, establish a "control unit" to encourage productive conflict. In other words, these organizations appoint a person or group to serve as a watchdog against other members of the organization.

The controller or comptroller plays this role in corporations. The General Accounting Office does in the U.S. government, and the Inspector General does in the Armed Forces. An ombudsman does in other institutions—for example, many newspapers use the ombudsman to judge complaints by outsiders against writing that appeared in the newspaper.

One purpose—in most organizations, the *main* purpose—of these control units is to nip problems in the bud. If you discover a conflict early, before anyone has had an opportunity to escalate it, chances are that you can set matters straight relatively easily. (The ombudsman at a newspaper can order a retraction that may placate someone who might otherwise have sued for libel. Once the suit got started—perhaps with the aid of a lawyer who was working for a percentage of the plaintiff's reward—the newspaper might be totally unable to placate the plaintiff and would have no choice but to defend a hopeless cause and eventually pay a formidable judgment.)

However, another purpose of control units—a purpose at least as salubrious—is to keep people on their toes. When they know that someone is watching, there is less likelihood that they'll take a chance doing something that they should not.

Sociologist Irving L. Janis explores the dangers of *not* using control units in his book, *Victims of Groupthink** in which he cites numerous examples in government and industry of great evils that were perpetrated simply because no one within an organization

---

*Irving L. Janis, *Victims of Groupthink: A Psychological Study of Foreign-Policy Decisions and Fiascoes* (Boston: Houghton, Mifflin, 1972).

had the daring to speak out against a plan that appeared to enjoy the support of everyone else. The pages of today's newspaper almost certainly will provide evidence of still other such evils that came about because no one dared to stand up and object.

It is well known, for example, that the drug Thalidomide, which maimed countless babies, was marketed despite the fact that the manufacturer had evidence that the drug was dangerous. No one within the pharmaceutical company was willing to speak out against what became by default, if not by actual agreement, the majority position.

Likewise, the Ford Motor Company, knowing that its Pinto was equipped with a gas tank that was especially susceptible to damage and explosion in rear-end collisions, decided not to recall the automobile, reasoning that a recall would cost far more than the company was likely to lose in lawsuits by people who were maimed or killed in the relatively small number of explosions that could be foreseen as statistically likely to take place. No one within Ford was willing to stand up against the Pinto, to demand that the car be recalled, and to take the matter to the public—whether through the newspapers or the Congress or some other institution—when management callously decided that the company's beloved "bottom line" would suffer relatively little impact from a few charred corpses.

During the Eisenhower presidency, when "groupthink" was the order of the day, there was an unstated but universally accepted mandate to keep a lid on any situation that might conceivably lead to conflict—especially publicly visible conflict. Conversely, in the Kennedy White House, conflict was encouraged. Indeed, there was a built-in control unit in the person of the president's brother and attorney general, Robert, who regularly made it a point to play devil's advocate when controversial ideas were on the agenda.

Many veterans of the Kennedy White House have told of sessions in which consensus appeared to have been reached in a meeting with the president, whereupon the president would leave the room and his brother would attack the idea on which everyone had agreed. In the absence of the president, members of the Cabinet and other officials felt freer to speak their minds—especially when they believed that the president's brother might be on their side!

Of course, the concept of a control unit does not originate with the Kennedy family. Alfred Sloan, who built General Motors from a foundering collection of failing garages into one of the world's industrial giants, was known to challenge vigorously any idea that subordinates seemed to accept without question. Sloan would demand, "Hasn't anyone been able to come up with any reasons why we *shouldn't* do this?"

Actually, long before Sloan, the ancient Persians reportedly had their own approach to such a control unit. The ancient Greek historian, Herodotus, writes of them:

> *They are accustomed to deliberate on matters of the highest moment when warm with wine; but whatever they in this situation may determine is again proposed to them on the morrow, in their cooler moments, by the person in whose house they had before assembled. If at this time also it meets their approbation, it is executed; otherwise it is rejected. Whatsoever also they discuss when sober is always a second time examined after they have been drinking.*

The idea found its way into other cultures. Thus we find the Roman, Valerius Maximus, writing in the first century A.D. of an "appeal from Philip drunk to Philip sober." And some seventeen hundred years later, Lawrence Sterne, in *Tristam Shanty,* wrote:

> *The ancient Goths of Germany . . . had all of them a wise custom of debating every thing of importance to their state, twice; that is, once drunk and once sober; drunk—that their councils might not want vigour; and sober—that they might not want discretion.*

In my own work, I've had many occasions to create control units of one sort or another to combat groupthink within organizations and to foster creative levels of tension. One of the easiest ways to make this approach work is by creating an ad hoc unit that conducts a weekly session during which any member's actions of the previous week can be challenged without fear of reprisal.

☐    I created such a review session when consulting at a hospital in northern California that had been experiencing an extraordinary amount of uncontrolled conflict, characterized by gossip, backbiting, and negativism. The hospital's executives and I met each Friday morning. The only rules of the meeting were that (1) discussion was limited to matters that had transpired during the previous week; (2) everyone was free to criticize everyone else; and (3) no one could be punished in any way for anything said in the meeting.

The sessions accomplished several objectives:

We contained conflict among the executives to that single one hour period. The executives no longer felt the need to challenge each other during their ordinary workday or to attempt end-runs around each other to enlist the support of a peer or a supervisor. Everyone knew that he would have the Friday morning equivalent of a day in court and that the conflicts that were discussed on Friday would be resolved in a reasoned and unemotional atmosphere. (Of course, the conflicts would not always be resolved to everyone's satisfaction; but everyone would have an opportunity to persuade everyone else of what he believed was the best approach, and all opinions would be taken into account before a final decision was made.)

Merely by scheduling the session and administering it fairly, we persuaded the executives that their opinions were important and eagerly sought. They no longer had reason to believe—as many of them had before—that "no one around here cares."

I ensured, by serving as moderator of the sessions, that no one would pull rank or get away with rhetorical tricks. In a sense, I served as a judge—not in that I had the authority (or the desire) to impose my will on others, but in that I was able to control the flow of the conversation and ensure that everyone observed the rules. (Having an outside party to direct traffic at meetings of this sort is invaluable. The party's lack of a vested interest—thus his impartiality—is his best credential. If there is any doubt about the person's impartiality when the sessions begin, a good moderator can quickly dispel that doubt by conducting the sessions in a way that leaves no doubt.)

We accented the positive and sought to develop useful programs. Our emphasis was more on finding solutions than on determining how the problems had come about or who was to blame. Thus the people attending the session had a *good feeling* about them; they knew that action would be taken on what was discussed, and they felt that their time was well spent.

The sessions served as an "invisible police officer" of each participant's work all week long. Everyone knew, understood, and appreciated that his actions could—and would—be challenged, whereas in the past many actions might have been ignored by peers and might have gone unnoticed by supervisors. Thus everyone was kept on his toes.

Let me emphasize that the manner in which such a review session is conducted is of paramount importance. The participants must be persuaded that they are working together to solve problems in which they share an interest. They cannot think of the meetings as mere gripe sessions, as opportunities to express hostility or solicit sympathy. The focus *must* be on *cooperatively making things better.*

Irving Janis, in *Victims of Groupthink,* offers nine precepts that are invaluable to anyone who seeks to limit the destructive uses of conflict and maximize the productive uses. Here are the precepts, along with my advice thereon:

1. *Establish an Atmosphere in Which People Will Feel Free to Raise Appropriate Objections.* In fact, make people believe that it is part of their job to raise objections. If they don't feel free to say what they think is wrong, you'll lose an invaluable opportunity to spot problems before they become critical. You'll also encourage an attitude of not caring about individual performance "because nothing I do around here matters anyway."

2. *When Soliciting Opinions, Do Not Define the Results That You Expect.* In fact, do not even give a hint about what you expect *or* desire. The last thing in the world that you want is to have your people telling you what they think you want to hear. What you really want is to convince them that it's safe—nay, even profitable—to tell you what you *don't* want to hear.

3. *Set up Parallel, Independent Policy-Making Groups.* Take advantage of the encouragement to excellence that comes when groups compete. Also take advantage of the independent thinking that occurs when two groups approach a problem without knowledge of what the other group is doing.

4. *If Personnel Is Limited, Periodically Divide the Policy-Making Group into Two or More Subgroups.* In other words, go as far as resources allow in your attempt to achieve the objectives of Precept 3.

5. *Have Representatives of Each Group Act in Liasion with Other Groups.* It's more efficient to funnel information through a representative than to have each member of each group hear from each member of each other group. The whole point of subdividing is to eliminate the sort of free-for-all that occurs when too many people are addressing the same problem at the same time. (If you don't appreciate the problems inherent in that sort of free-for-all, try asking a group of 50 or 60 people for suggestions about where to have lunch. Actually, if there are more than four or five members in the group, you'll usually fare much better by proposing several alternatives and letting the members vote. Otherwise, the discussion/debate could continue well past dinnertime.)

6. *Invite Experts Who Are Not Members of the Group to Challenge the Views of the Core Members.* Remember my role in the review sessions at the hospital? Someone who is independent is more likely to feel free to speak her mind. An outsider also is likely to raise important questions that insiders never consider because they take so many things for granted. And people in the group are apt to weigh an outsider's opinions objectively, whereas opinions by a member of the group usually will be viewed in the context of what the others in the group feel toward the expresser of the opinions.

7. *Encourage Someone to Play Devil's Advocate.* There is, of course, a point of diminishing returns in devil's advocacy; if someone challenges *everything* that is said, many people quickly get the idea that it's too much of a hassle to say *anything*. But judicious devil's advocacy can be extremely productive, encouraging the

meek and shy to express contrary opinions where they ordinarily would not and also encouraging the proposers of ideas to examine those ideas critically.

8. *Try to Think Like Your Competition.* There's no better way to understand your problems than to examine your own behavior from the perspective of someone who is trying to outdo you by taking advantage of your weaknesses.

9. *Before Ratifying any Decisions, Hold a Second Meeting to Rethink the Issue and Explore Any Residual Doubts.* Remember Herodotus' ancient Persians who debated each issue twice—once while drunk, once while sober.

# 8≣AN EXERCISE IN DEALING WITH CONFLICT

And now, let's look at the way you and some of your friends deal with conflict. We'll do so in an exercise that is—for good reason—very popular in business schools. You'll need at least six participants, plus one person to supervise the play, but any even number of additional people may participate at the same time. In fact, the more players you have (short of the point of unmanageability, which in most situations will occur circa 100–200 players), the more instructive the exercise can be.

Okay, if you have six or eight players, divide them into two groups. Obviously enough, you will have either three or four players per group. If you have 10 players, divide them into two groups of three players and one group of four players.

If you have 12 players or more, you're ready to add another dimension to the game. Before dividing the players into groups, organize the players into pairs. Once this has been accomplished, divide the pairs into groups, then structure the groups as you would have in the earlier example when there were no pairs—that is, groups comprising three or four pairs apiece, up to any number of groups.

Okay, the groups (whether comprising individuals or pairs) have been designated, and now it is time to discuss the rules of play.

Our exercise will be divided into five rounds. In each round, each player or pair of players will choose one of two letters: an X or a Y. The scoring will be determined by the pattern of choices within a given group.

Before I tell you how to keep score, let me say that my instructions may seem somewhat vague. This is intended. I'll explain why at the end of the exercise. But please promise me that you'll perform the exercise at least once before you look at my explanation of the reason for the vagueness. If you knew the reason before you performed the exercise, you would not get the full benefit of the exercise.

Okay, that having been said, here is the method of scoring when there are three players or pairs:

| | |
|---|---|
| If all 3 choose X . . . | all 3 lose $100 apiece |
| If there are 2 Xs and 1 Y . . . | the Xs win $100 each and the Y loses $300 |
| If there are 1 X and 2Ys . . . | the X wins $300 and the Ys lose $100 each |
| If all 3 choose Y . . . | all 3 win $100 apiece |

And here is the method of scoring when there are four pairs:

| | |
|---|---|
| If all 4 choose X . . . | all 4 lose $100 apiece |
| If there are 3 Xs and 1 Y . . . | the Xs win $100 each and the Y loses $300 |
| If there are 2 Xs and 2 Ys . . . | the Xs win $200 each and the Ys lose $200 each |
| If there are 1 X and 3 Ys . . . | the X wins $300 and the Ys lose $100 each |
| If all four choose Y . . . | all 4 win $100 each |

In the instructions that follow, I will pretend that the exercise involves six or 12 people—two groups, each comprising three individuals or pairs. If you perform the exercise with a different configuration of players, simply adapt my instructions to your circumstances. Each player should have a copy of the scorecard on the bottom of this page.

Very well, let's begin!

## Round One

You must decide between an X and a Y. If you are playing without a partner, simply make your decision and enter the letter in the "Choose" square on the line designated "Round 1." If you are playing with a partner, the two of you must make the decision together. Neither of you may discuss your decision with any other player. If you and your partner cannot agree on which letter to use,

| Round | Rule | SCORECARD | | | |
|---|---|---|---|---|---|
| | | Choose | Group's Pattern | Payoff | Balance |
| 1 | Partners only | X Y | __ X __ Y | | _____ |
| 2 | Discussion within group | X Y | __ X __ Y | | _____ |
| 3 | Twice the $ | X Y | __ X __ Y | | _____ |
| 4 | Twice the $ (secret ballot) | X Y | __ X __ Y | | _____ |
| 5 | To be announced | X Y | __ X __ Y | | _____ |

your team forfeits this round and loses the maximum amount—$300.

Very well, the letters of everyone in the game have been entered on the scorecard. Now compare the results with other members of your group (but not with anyone from an opposing group). Did you get three Xs? Three Ys? Two of one and one of another?

Enter the group's pattern on the scorecard in the column marked, appropriately enough, "Group's Pattern." For example, one X and two Ys. Or three Xs.

Next, calculate your own payoff. For example, if every member or pair in your group chose a Y, your own payoff would be $100—as would be the payoff of every other member or pair in your group. Meanwhile, if you chose an X and the two other members or pairs chose a Y, your payoff would be $300—and each of the other members or pairs would lose $100.

Please note: your responsibility is to keep track of only your own score, not the scores of other members or pairs in the group. Therefore, in the payoff block of Round One, you should enter only the amount of *your own* payoff—$100, $300, −$100, or whatever.

Finally, calculate your running total. In this case, since we are in Round One, the running total will be the same as the round's payoff.

Allright, on to—

## Round Two

Again you must decide between an X and a Y. This time, however, you (with or without a partner) may consult with other members of your group. Make your decision, and enter the result on your scorecard. If you cannot decide which letter to use, you forfeit the round. If any member of your group forfeits the round, the other players within the group may enter a letter on behalf of the forfeiter.

Okay, the letters have been chosen, the group's pattern has been recorded on the scorecard, and each member or pair has tabulated and recorded a payoff and a running balance. Now on to—

## Round Three

Once again, you (with or without a partner) must decide between an X and a Y, and once again you may consult with other members of your group. Please note, however, that the "Rule" block of the scorecard now calls for *twice* the dollars as in rounds one and two.

Make your decision, and enter the results on your scorecard. If you cannot decide which letter to use, you forfeit the round. If any member of your group forfeits the round, the other players within the group may enter a letter on behalf of the forfeiter.

Okay, the letters have been chosen, the group's pattern has been recorded on the scorecard, and each member or pair has tabulated and recorded a payoff and a running balance. Now on to—

## Round Four

As in previous rounds, you (with or without a partner) must choose a letter, and, as in round three, you are playing for double the amount of money as in rounds one and two. However, in this round, you (with or without a partner) must choose your letter *without* conferring with other members of your group.

Make your decision, and enter the result on your scorecard. If you cannot decide which letter to use, you forfeit the round. If any member of your group forfeits the round, the other players within the group may enter a letter on behalf of the forfeiter.

Okay, the letters have been chosen, the group's pattern has been recorded on the scorecard, and each member or pair has tabulated and recorded a payoff and a running balance. Now on to—

## Round Five

Once again, as in previous rounds, you (with or without a partner) must choose a letter. You may, if you wish, consult with other members of your group. The special feature of this round is that you will be playing for *10 times* the money of rounds one and two.

That's right, your wins or losses on this round can range from $1,000 to $3,000 rather than from only $100 to $300. And, as you can readily see, what you do on this round can dramatically change the fortunes of any player or pair in your group. (The reason I was secretive about the amount of this payoff until now is that if you knew earlier what I had in mind, you obviously might have played quite differently.)

Okay, make your decision and enter the result on your scorecard. If you cannot decide which letter to use, you forfeit the round. If any member of your group forfeits the round, the other players may enter a letter on his or her behalf.

And now the game is over.

Tally your running total, then compare scores with other players—those in your own group and those in other groups also. Before reading any further, discuss the scores with your fellow players—again, those in other groups as well as those in your own.

Has the exercise taught you anything about your own style of game playing? Has it taught you anything about the styles of other players?

If you were given a chance to replay the game, what might you have done differently? What, if anything, should other players have done differently?

I suggest that you close the book at this point and think more about what you have done in the exercise and what your decisions may reveal about your own style of play and the styles of your friends. Please do not resume reading until you've satisfied yourself that you've given this matter sufficient thought.

Okay, welcome back. Now I'll give you my ideas about the exercise.

You may recall my saying earlier that my instructions were intentionally vague. The most important point about which I was vague was the *goal* of the exercise. I didn't tell you whether your goal was to get the highest possible score for yourself (with or without a partner) or to cooperate with your group in getting the highest team score against other groups.

For example, if you and the other players in your group chose from the start to cooperate with each other, you would have selected nothing but Ys in every round. This would have meant that each player (or pair) would have a running total of $100 in the first round, $200 in the second, $400 in the third, $600 in the fourth, and $1,600 in the fifth. The three-unit group, meanwhile, would end the game with a total of $4,800—the highest that is mathematically possible.

However, if you (with or without a partner) chose not to cooperate, you could have achieved a much higher individual score than $1,600. For example, if you (with or without a partner) chose an X in the first round while the other two players in your group chose a Y, you'd have a payoff of $300, and the others would lose $100 each. If the same thing happened in the second round, you'd have a running total of $600, and the others would have a running total of −$200 each.

If you repeated this performance in the third round, you'd have added $600 to your score, and the others in your group would have lost another $200 each, meaning a running total of $1,200 for you and −$400 for each of them. Yet another repeat performance in the fourth round would have boosted your running total to $1,800 and would have left each of them with a running total of −$600.

Finally, in the fifth round, when everyone was playing for 10 times the money of the first and second rounds, your choice of an X against your counterparts' choices of a Y could have added $3,000 to your score, producing a running total of $4,800. The others, meanwhile, would have tallied losses of $1,000 apiece, giving each a running total of −$1,600.

Well, there's no question about it, if you took this tack you would have single-handedly (or pair-handedly) run up a score equal to that of an entire group that chose nothing but Ys (and, in the process, obtained the highest possible group score). However, your high score would have come at the expense of your teammates; the net score for your group would be your own $4,800 minus the $1,600 of each other individual or pair, or a net of only $1,600.

Who won the game?

You tell me. Or, to put it another way, nobody won—or everybody won.

The point is, I never did define what constitutes *winning*. The purpose of the exercise was not to produce a "winner" but to give you insights into how you—and your friends—played the game.

If you think about this for awhile, you probably will agree with me that there are two distinct *styles* of play—*cooperative* and *competitive.*

The quintessentially cooperative players have faith in each other from the start. They look at the system of scoring and recognize that the group will benefit most if each player selects a Y in each round. It never occurs to these players that someone else in the group may choose an X to the other players' Ys and thereby upset the group's applecart—or, if it does occur to them, they trust the others not to do it. (It is not without reason that I referred to this group of players—from the start—as a "group" rather than a "team." The latter word connotes cooperative effort, and I did not want to risk influencing you in that direction.)

Competitive players, meanwhile, are innately cynical and seek any advantage they can get. They not only try to out guess their group mates; they may even, during rounds when discussion is permitted, lie about what letter they intend to choose. In fact, I have administered this exercise in certain situations where I have seen a player repeatedly persuade his peers that he planned a cooperative vote, then turn around and double-cross them on round after round. How did he get away with it? I don't know. I can only say that his powers of persuasion were perfectly matched to their gullibility.

Which style is better or worse?

You tell me.

I say that neither style is *intrinsically* better or worse. It's all a matter of circumstances—principal among which is the *definition of a goal.* If the goal is for the group to achieve the highest possible score, the cooperative style obviously is the best. If the goal is for a single player or team to achieve the highest possible score, the competitive style is the best.

*You* set the goal, and *you* decide which style is best.

Interestingly—at least to me—I have staged this exercise throughout the world and have found distinct national patterns.

No nation produced more consistently cooperative groups than Japan. In fact, in the course of conducting management seminars in that country, we eventually stopped using this exercise because everyone regarded it a waste of time. *Everyone* played cooperatively. (Presumably the Japanese philosophy of business and management holds out as the ultimate desideratum the group-identification of members of every unit—the members subordinate individual goals to the desire for the group's success against other groups, trusting that their own personal success will be a result of the group's success.)

Meanwhile, in the United States—and Italy, France, and Germany—I found a decided tendency toward competitive play. The ideal in these nations apparently was: Each Player for Himself. They have been more than a few cooperative groups but a far greater number of competitive groups.

What's the lesson in all this for the person who wants to develop skills at managing conflict productively?

There are several lessons:

1. Don't assume that everyone else shares your goals. (I hope you remember that I've said this before.)

2. Whether or not others share your goals, whether you win or lose depends on how *they* play as well as how *you* play.

3. Whether you win or lose, you can learn a lot by watching the other players. In fact, the biggest value of the exercise is that it gives you insights into how you and others play in the biggest game of all, Life.

Now that you've been through the exercise once, you'll never again be able to play it with the freshness that you did the first time. However, this does not mean that you cannot profitably play it again. I suggest that you do it several times with different groups of friends and colleagues. In these replays you may not learn a great deal more about yourself, but you should learn quite a bit about your colleagues and friends!

# ≡≡≡9≡GETTING PAST "YES"

## OR THE THEORETICALLY PERFECT RESOLUTION OF ANY CONFLICT

$W$hat is the best possible resolution of a conflict?

1. You win everything.
2. Your opponent wins everything.
3. Neither of the above.

Resist it though you may, the answer is: 3. Neither of the above.

Yes, I know, most of us have been taught that we should strive for victory. The more extreme of us buy the philosophy articulated by the late football coach, Vince Lombardi: "Winning isn't everything, it's the *only* thing." By this standard, the only acceptable resolution of any conflict is unconditional surrender by one's opponent.

Actually, this is usually an undesirable resolution—and often the worst possible resolution—not only for the surrendering party but also for the victor.

Why? Because the surrendering party almost certainly will feel aggrieved and either avoid future dealings or seek to "get even" for the loss. Thus the ostensibly satisfactory resolution of the present conflict will either kill the relationship or set the stage for future (unnecessary) conflicts.

Let us, for a moment, consider the relationship.

It is possible to have a conflict that is not part of an ongoing relationship. For example, a stranger's car sideswipes yours, and each of you believes that the other is at fault. But most conflicts involve people who have dealt with each other in the past and intend to deal with each other in the future. To wit:

> Your spouse wants a beige lampshade for the living room, and you want a peach lampshade.
>
> You have been late making payments on your charge account at a department store, and the store has reduced your credit limit.
>
> After you enrolled your child in a private school, the school billed you for "tuition insurance." The policy guarantees that the full year's tuition, which you paid in advance, will be refunded by the insurance company if for one reason or another your child does not finish the year. The cost of the insurance is rather small—$55.90—but you object on principle to *having* to pay for it, especially because no one told you beforehand that the insurance was a requirement of the school.

In all three of these situations, it would be possible to end the conflict simply by ending the relationship: Enroll your child in another school, stop shopping at this particular department store, and divorce your spouse.

The fact is, however, that you do not *want* to end the relationship. You love your spouse and want to stay married. You like shopping at this department store, even though you dislike the way its credit department has responded to your late payments. And, disgruntled though you are about the school's demand that you purchase "tuition insurance," you sincerely believe that there is no better school for your child.

The question, therefore, is *not* how to bend your adversary to your will but rather how to devise a solution that will satisfy both you *and* your adversary—and, in the process, permit your relationship to continue at pretty much the same level of amiability as before the conflict arose.

At the risk of seeming to oversimplify, I shall explore this proposition in a bit more detail. Let's start with the situation in which your spouse wants a beige lampshade for the living room and you want a peach lampshade. Think for a moment about all the possible ways in which this conflict might be resolved. In fact, before reading any further, list on a sheet of paper at least five ways that the conflict could be resolved—not necessarily in a manner that will preserve your relationship. If you have trouble thinking of five approaches that seem reasonable, list some that seem unreasonable. In any event, do not continue reading until you have listed five ways to resolve the conflict.

Have you listed them? Okay, your next assignment is to list five more. Impossible, you say? Well, try anyway. Be as creative as you can. It is more important that you develop a substantial number of approaches than it is that you develop *practical* approaches. Please do not continue reading until you have listed five more approaches.

Allright, you've now listed a total of 10 possible resolutions to the conflict. I will list 22—some practical, some absurd, and some that don't fall neatly into either category. Let's see how many of mine match yours.

1. *Kill Your Spouse.* (That certainly would resolve the conflict, though it would also—to say the least—end your relationship.)

2. *Surrender.* In other words, let your spouse choose the lampshade. (You might not be happy about it, but you will indeed have resolved the conflict.)

3. *Pretend to Surrender—Variation 1.* Let your spouse choose the lampshade. Then, when it is installed, deface it. That will teach your spouse not to mess with you when you've made up your mind about something. (If your spouse has the temerity to replace the shade that you defaced, deface the replacement, also. Keep doing this until your spouse gives up and lets you have your choice of lampshade.)

4. *Pretend to Surrender—Variation 2.* Let your spouse choose the lampshade. Then, when it is installed, complain incessantly about it. Make your spouse feel really awful about having prevailed in this conflict. You will thereby mitigate your displeasure about living with the new lampshade, diminish your spouse's pleasure, and help weaken your spouse's resistance to your will in future conflicts.

5. *Bully Your Spouse—Variation 1.* Threaten that if you don't get your way you will punish your spouse in some manner—perhaps by defacing the new lampshade once it has been installed, perhaps by refusing to entertain guests in the room that contains the lamp. (If you credibly threaten something that is sufficiently unsettling to your spouse—suicide, murder of your spouse's best friend, etc., etc.—your spouse almost certainly will conclude that the color of the new lampshade is not worth the threatened consequence.)

6. *Bully Your Spouse—Variation 2.* Start spending weekends at the home of a friend. Tell your spouse that you won't end the practice unless you get your way on the lampshade.

7. *Take Unilateral Action.* Buy the lampshade that you want and install it without even discussing the matter with your spouse. This probably will lead to a quarrel, but after the quarrel the lampshade will still be there—and will still be the color that you favor (unless your spouse employs "Pretend to Surrender—Variation 1," in which event you will have to fall back on one of the other tactics.)

Okay, those are seven possibilities. Any one of them could resolve the conflict, although none of them is likely to be a *satisfac-*

*tory* resolution to the conflict. (Indeed, if any of the above approaches *does* resolve the conflict to either party's satisfaction, I suggest that the *real* conflict goes far beyond any disagreement over what color that new lampshade should be.)

Please note one element that all seven approaches have in common. In all of them, one party's will prevails. There is no attempt at negotiation, no attempt at finding a mutually acceptable alternative to the parties' initial desires. One party wins, one party loses—period.

Now let us consider some approaches in which the parties work cooperatively at finding a solution rather than fighting each other for supremacy:

8. *Take Turns at Playing Dictator.* In other words, you and your spouse agree that neither of you can be completely happy in this situation, and therefore, to preserve your domestic tranquility, one of you will accede to the other's wishes, in exchange for which the other party will accede in the next conflict.

9. *Attempt to Develop a Mutually Satisfactory Third Choice—Variation 1.* Rule out both the peach shade and the beige shade, and try to find a color that pleases both of you.

10. *Attempt to Develop a Mutually Satisfactory Third Choice—Variation 2.* Rule out both the peach shade and the beige shade. If you cannot then find a color that pleases both of you, devise some system for assigning numerical scores to the other lampshades that you may be considering. For example, rate each shade on a scale of 1 to 10. When all have been rated, you and your spouse can compare your scores and select the shade that received the highest total.

11. *Test Both the Peach Shade and the Beige Shade Before Making a Final Decision.* In other words, prevail (if you can) upon the seller to let you try each shade for one week. Perhaps seeing the shades in your living room will persuade one or both of you that the other spouse's choice is not all that bad. Perhaps the test will end with both of you favoring the same shade. If not, one of you may agree that the other's choice is acceptable. If not, you can explore other approaches to a resolution of the conflict.

12. *Agree to Put a Price on the Right to Make a Choice.* For example, agree that whoever chooses the shade must pay for it. If you both still want to prevail under these circumstances, hold an auction: The higher bidder must pay for the shade, and whatever is left after the shade has been purchased becomes the property of the other spouse.

13. *Enlist the Services of a Mediator.* In other words, select someone whose taste both of you respect, and authorize that person to make the final decision about which shade will grace your living room—whether the peach shade, the beige shade, or yet another color that the mediator deems preferable.

Please note that these six approaches (numbers 8 through 13) are at least as likely to resolve the conflict as the first seven approaches. The crucial difference is that this second group of approaches will bring about—or help bring about—a solution that both parties are *far more likely to regard as acceptable.* The relationship of the parties will not be damaged by the way in which the conflict was addressed; indeed, the relationship might even be strengthened because of the good feelings the spouses felt toward each other while working cooperatively toward their mutual goal.

And now let's explore still other approaches to the problem.

Whenever I find myself feeling unimaginative and at a loss for creative approaches to problems, I pose the problem to children and ask them to turn loose their imaginations. The following suggested approaches to the lampshade problem are courtesy of three young ladies who are daughters of friends of mine: Laura Schechter, age eight; Giuliana Gillette, age seven; and Caroline Gillette, age four.

14. Buy a shade that contains both peach and beige, thereby satisfying both spouses.

15. Move a lampshade that both spouses like to the living room from another room.

16. Don't buy a lamp at all; use candles instead.

17. Buy two lamps—one with a peach shade, one with a beige shade.

18. Buy a lamp without a shade.

19.   Have a contest—for example, drawing numbers from a hat or finishing a crossword puzzle—and let the winner select the color of the shade.

20.   Flip a coin, and let the winner decide.

21.   Invite some friends to vote on which lamp looks best in the living room and abide by their decision.

22.   Make a deal that whoever does certain undesirable things can make the decision about which shade to buy—for example, taking out the garbage or doing the dishes for a year, watching the children every Saturday, and so on.

I leave it to you to decide whether the children's approaches are better than my own or your own. My main point is that the conflict should not be permitted to destroy—or even to mar—the relationship. The relationship is much more important than the conflict.

Because this will be true in the vast majority of conflicts in which you find yourself, I'll say it again, this time in capital letters:

## THE RELATIONSHIP IS MUCH MORE IMPORTANT THAN THE CONFLICT.

If I seem to be overstating the obvious, think about some conflicts in which you've been involved wherein the relationship was permitted to suffer because one party or another sought to *win* rather than to *resolve* the conflict. I'll wager that you can think of more than one. In fact, if you're over 25 years of age, I'll wager that you can think of more than a dozen. Far too many of us, when we are involved in a conflict, think mainly—or only—of the "win," when our best interests would be served if we thought instead of the *relationship* with the person with whom we are experiencing the conflict.

Few spouses would, if they were confronted point blank with the question, argue that their marriage was less important than the choice of a lampshade. Yet many of us—in our marriages, our relationships with our children, our business dealings, and other activities—let ourselves become committed irrevocably to positions that destroy relationships because we feel that we must take a stand on a particular issue. We throw the baby out with the bathwater, as it were, but we demand, along with Roman Emperor Heliogabalus, *fiat voluntas meas et pereat mundus,* loosely translated as, "Let my will prevail, even if it means that the world must perish."

The question of how to preserve relationships while pursuing the resolution of conflicts is addressed by Roger Fisher and William Ury—professors at Harvard University who are, respectively, director and associate director of the Harvard Negotiation Project—in their best-selling book, *Getting to Yes: Negotiating Agreement without Giving In.**

I applaud much of what Fisher and Ury say, but I suggest that their subtitle—*Negotiating Agreement without Giving In*—is not merely oxymoronic but an utter impossibility. You can't *negotiate* agreement without giving in. If you *never* give in, you're not negotiating, you're merely forcing the other folks to bend to your will.

Fisher and Ury begin with a nigh-irresistible premise:

> *Any method of negotiation may be fairly judged by three criteria: It should produce a wise agreement if agreement is possible. It should be efficient. And it should improve or at least not damage the relationship between the parties. (A wise agreement can be defined as one which meets the legitimate interests of each side to the extent possible, resolves conflicting interests fairly, is durable, and takes community interests into account.)†*

The authors also argue persuasively in favor of separating the disputants from the dispute:

> *Figuratively if not literally, the participants [in the conflict] should come to see themselves as working side by side, attacking the problem, not each other. . . .*
>
> *When negotiators bargain over positions, they tend to lock themselves into those positions. The more you clarify your position and defend it*

*From *Getting to Yes: Negotiating Agreement without Giving In.* Copyright © 1981 by Roger Fisher and William Ury. Reprinted by permission of Houghton, Mifflin Company. Penquin edition published in 1983.

Permission to use these excerpts does not imply approval of Mr. Jandt's comments on them. The authors of *Getting to Yes* feel that Mr. Jandt's characterizations of their arguments are often at odds with the plain meaning of the quoted passages and the book as a whole.
†Ibid., p. 4.

*against attack, the more committed you become to it. . . . As more at-
tention is paid to positions, less attention is devoted to meeting the
underlying concerns of the parties. Agreement becomes less likely.
Any agreement reached may reflect a mechanical splitting of the difference between final positions rather than a solution carefully
crafted to meet the legitimate interests of the parties. The result is frequently an agreement less satisfactory to each side than it could have
been.\**

### And:

*It is easy to forget sometimes that a negotiation is not a debate. Nor is
it a trial. You are not trying to persuade some third party. The person
you are trying to persuade is seated at the table with you. If a negotiation is to be compared to a legal proceeding, the situation resembles
that of two judges trying to reach agreement on how to decide a case.
Try putting yourself in that role, treating your opposite number as a
fellow judge with whom you are attempting to work out a joint
opinion. . . .*

*As a negotiator, you will almost always want to look for solutions that
will leave the other side satisfied as well. . . . The relationship between the sides, often taken for granted and overlooked, frequently
outweighs in importance the outcome of any particular issue. . . . In
almost every case,* your satisfaction depends to a degree on making
the other side sufficiently content with an agreement to want to live
up to it *[emphasis added].†*

All of which, I suggest, is eminently reasonable and very well
expressed. However, where Fisher and Ury get into trouble, in my
opinion, is where they suggest that disputes may be resolved by
establishing *objective criteria* which can be applied to the settlement of the points in controversy. They write:

*However well you understand the interests of the other side, however
ingeniously you invent ways of reconciling interests, however highly
you value an ongoing relationship, you will almost always face the
harsh reality of interests that conflict. . . . Typically, negotiators try to
resolve such conflicts by positional bargaining—in other words, by
talking about what they are willing and unwilling to accept. . . .
Whether the situation becomes a contest over who can be the most*

---

*Ibid., pp. 11; 5.
†Ibid., pp. 36; 75.

*stubborn or a contest over who can be the most generous . . ., this*
*negotiating process focuses on what each side is willing to agree to.*
*No negotiation is likely to be efficient or amicable if you pit your will*
*against theirs, and either you have to back down or they do. And*
*whether you are choosing a place to eat, organizing a business, or*
*negotiating custody of a child, you are unlikely to reach a wise agree-*
*ment as judged by any objective standard if you take no such*
*standard into account. If trying to settle differences of interest on the*
*basis of will has such high costs, the solution is to negotiate on some*
*basis independent of the will of either side—that is, on the basis of*
*objective criteria.\**

I agree that positional bargaining—about which I will write in
considerable length some chapters hence—is a bad idea. However,
I feel that the idea that there are *objective criteria* on which disputants will agree assumes either that one of the disputants is naive
or that the other is Svengali-like in his or her ability to persuade.

As I argued at considerable length—and, I hope,
persuasively—in Chapters 5 and 6, there is no objectivity in
conflicts. The problem usually is not that you are "right" and I am
"wrong," or vice-versa, but rather that each of us *thinks himself*
*right and the other wrong.*

It seems to me that with Fisher and Ury's approach each party
regards the other's position as exactly opposite—and wholly inimical to—his or her own; accordingly, both parties are blind to opportunities for accommodation or compromise. The parties, in effect, see only what they want to see; they favor whatever
interpretation they regard as most compatible with their predetermined ends. They judge their own acts by a standard different from
that by which they judge their adversaries' acts; what's "one man's
meat" is *not* necessarily "another man's poison."

In sum, there *is* no universally acceptable standard of right or
wrong in any conflict. Objective criteria *do not exist*. Each party
speaks from her or his own perspective, and each has his or her
own desiderata, and who is to say that *your* desiderata are right
and mine wrong or vice-versa?

Fisher and Ury advise readers to employ rhetorical tricks to persuade opponents that certain "objective criteria" should apply in a
given situation. To wit:

*\*Ibid, pp. 84–85.

***Recast an attack on you as an attack on the problem.*** *When the other side attacks you personally—as frequently happens—resist the temptation to defend yourself or to attack them. Instead, sit back and allow them to let off steam. Listen to them, show you understand what they are saying, and when they have finished recast their attack on you as an attack on the problem. "When you say that a [teachers'] strike shows we don't care about the children, I hear your concern about the children's education. I want you to know that we share your concern: they are our children and our students. We want the strike to end so we can go back to educating them. What can we both do now to reach an agreement as quickly as possible?"\**

This patronizing and condescending approach—wherein the speaker pretends to be the possessor of all Truth, Goodness, and Light, assigned the mission of *educating* a recalcitrant opponent— might occasionally work if the opposition comprises a gaggle of dunderheads who never before encountered rhetoric. However, if you're up against someone with some experience at verbal fencing, you are apt to get a response something like this:

*Hey, fella, take that "I hear your concern" and shove it up your Orwell. Who the hell put you in charge of the agenda? I don't need my adversaries to lecture me about the importance of teamwork. If you're really interested in teamwork, stop acting like a pompous ass and start addressing the issues—specifically items two, four, and five on our complaint. You say you want to get back to educating the kids? Okay, what are you prepared to surrender on the salary proposal, and what are you prepared to surrender on the lunch hour issue, and what will you give us on the medical plan? Or do you want to have the whole thing exactly your way? Are you here to negotiate or to tell us, "Take it or leave it"? And if you're not here to negotiate, why should I waste my time talking to you?*

Fisher and Ury have a great fondness for rhetorical tricks. Consider what they term a "real-life example" of a negotiation between Mrs. Jones, a landlord's representative, and Turnbull, a tenant who believes he has been overcharged.

*Turnbull: "Mrs. Jones, I've just learned—please correct me if I'm wrong—that our apartment's under rent control. We've been told that the legal maximum rent is $233 a month. Have we been misinformed?"*

\*Ibid., pp. 116–117.

*Analysis [by Fisher and Ury]: The essence of principled negotiation
lies in remaining open to persuasion by objective facts and principles.
By cautiously treating the objective facts as possibly inaccurate and
asking Mrs. Jones to correct them, Turnbull establishes a dialogue
based on reason. He invites her to participate by either agreeing with
the facts as presented or setting them right. This game makes them
two colleagues trying to establish the facts. The confrontation is defused. If Turnbull simply asserted the facts as facts, Mrs. Jones
would feel threatened and defensive. She might deny the facts. The
negotiation would not start off constructively.\**

Wrong. Indeed, wrong, wrong, and wrong again.

First of all, assuming that Turnbull has his facts straight and
that Mrs. Jones knows her business, she knows that the legal maximum rent is $233. She also knows that Turnbull didn't pull that
figure out of his hat; obviously he has done research and is con-
fronting her with the fact that she overcharged him. When he pretends ("by cautiously treating the objective facts as possibly inaccurate") that he is inviting her to set him straight on the facts, he
is really inviting her to acknowledge that he has caught her in the
act.

He's backed Mrs. Jones into a corner, and someone who has been
backed into a corner has little choice but to fight. He knows that
she knows that she cheated him. He knows that she knows that he
knows that the legal maximum rent is $233. Does he expect her to
tell him that his figure is wrong? If so, how will that aid his cause?
And if he expects her to agree that his figure is correct (which is
presumably the purpose behind the please-correct-me-if-I'm-wrong
strategy), does he also expect her to acknowledge that she is a
cheat and volunteer to refund his money?

If he does expect these things, he's doubly naive, for he's trying
to get her to surrender at the same time that he is teasing her with
rhetorical tricks. It's bad enough to be backed into a corner, but
when you've been backed into one by a self-satisfied rhetorical
matador who now is taunting you with his flashy verbal maneuvers, you've suffered insult on top of injury.

*Ibid., p. 123.

In my opinion, the most likely way for Mrs. Jones to reply is along these lines:

> *Young man, if you want a legal opinion on the rent-control law, call a lawyer. And while you're talking to him, ask what his fee will be to defend you in an eviction proceeding, because that's exactly what you're going to face if I hear one more word about whether or not I overcharged you.*

Turnbull, I suggest, would fare much better if he put all his cards face-up on the table:

> *Look, Mrs. Jones, we've got a problem, and it could wind up costing both of us a lot of time and money in court, but I'm hoping we can avoid that, even though I'm prepared to go to the mat if you leave me no alternative. The fact is, I've found out that someone in your office apparently made a mistake about the maximum legal rent of my apartment. It's not the $300 that's in the lease; it's $233. Now, I don't want to make trouble for you or your people, and I realize that it probably was an honest mistake, and I do want to stay in the apartment provided that I can do so at the legal maximum price, so let me ask you to do this: check your records, verify that I'm right about $233 being the legal maximum, then get back to me and let me know whether you'd like to issue a refund check immediately or perhaps apply the surplus to future months' rent or however else you'd care to resolve the matter.*

If you're a purist regarding truth, you'll note that my Turnbull did not actually lie when he said, "I realize it probably was an honest mistake." It could very well have been an *honest mistake* for these crooks to think they had a sucker who wouldn't catch them in their con game.

In any event, he didn't dance around with Mrs. Jones, didn't try to come across as a cutie who ostensibly sought the truth about a matter in which he was in doubt ("Please correct me if I'm wrong"); rather, he told her where he stood and left it to her to decide how to deal with the situation.

Most importantly, by suggesting that the matter may have been an "honest mistake" by *someone in her office,* he let her off the hook. That is, he made it possible for her to give him what he sought without admitting that she had tried to cheat him.

If he had confronted her with an accusation of cheating, she would have been more likely to fight him—all in the interest of proving that the accusation was false, that she *wasn't* a cheat. By suggesting that *someone else* may have made "an honest mistake," he made it very easy for her eventually to say, "Yes, of course, you're right—it was a mistake, nothing more than an honest mistake, and someone else is responsible. Here's your money back."

Note also, please, that he gave her time to think things over. Had he demanded that she acquiesce immediately, he would have put her on the defensive. She probably would have felt that all of this was happening too fast for her, and she probably also would have been fearful that if she acquiesced she might be getting herself into trouble of some sort or other—if only by tacitly acknowledging that a "mistake" (the overcharge) had been made.

I hold out to you as an absolute rule in attempting to resolve conflicts wherein you are holding all the cards and expect unconditional—or at the very least conditional—surrender from the other party:

**Give the person time to think things over; don't try to rush the decision.**

I say that because, if a potential surrenderer feels rushed, the logical reaction is to become fearful—that is, to fear the very thing (surrender) that one feels one is being rushed into. In my experience, the tendency of people in such a circumstance is to fight—not out of a sense of conviction in the justness of one's cause, not out of confidence that one will win, but instinctively, viscerally, because when one is attacked, fighting is the normal thing to do.

As the soon-to-be conquerer, what *you* want is to let your opponent take time to come to the decision (to surrender) with full confidence that it is the right decision. The person then can accept the decision as his or her own rather than as one into which he or she has been pushed. And—always assuming that you hold all the cards—the person should feel relieved that you have provided the opportunity to get off the hook.

Consider how Mrs. Jones might react after the call from my variation on Fisher and Ury's Turnbull. I suggest the following inner monologue:

"Well, the little creep caught me in the act. Doggone. And he looked so naive, too. Just goes to show you. Well, I suppose I could refuse to give in. When he fails to pay his next month's rent in full, I could file for eviction. But there's no way I'd win once he cited the legal maximum. He's really got me over a barrel. It's like in that TV commercial. 'You can pay me now or you can pay me later.'

"On the other hand, he obviously doesn't want to go to court any more than I do, or he never would've called—he'd've just gone to court. So he's willing to settle this without a fight. He even said he'd be willing to wait for the money—let me deduct it from future payments instead of having to refund it now.

"Obviously, he likes the apartment and wants to keep living there and also wants to cooperate. Maybe I'll wait a day or two and then give him a call and invite him for a cup of coffee and tell him I found the mistake and apologize and wrap the thing up any way I can. Who knows?—maybe I can even get him to go for an extra 10 or 20 dollars under the guise of my having made some improvements to the building since the rent control law was passed."

What all of this boils down to is: When you're holding all the cards, you don't have to be cute. And when you're not holding all the cards, it's a good idea not to be cute anyway.

Most people, I suggest, can tell when you're employing rhetorical tricks. They can tell when you're doing a number on them, and they resent it. They resent having to go through the verbal motions, and they especially resent the way you have insulted their intelligence. It's far more effective, I suggest, to be straightforward and treat your adversary's intelligence with the same respect that you want shown toward your own intelligence.

All questions of rhetorical trickery aside, my main point here is that the goal of any negotiation should not be merely to get *to* yes—not merely to bend the other party to your will, by whatever means you can—but rather to get *past* yes by resolving the conflict in a way that serves the best interests of *both* parties and encourages a harmonious, long-term relationship.

Granted, not all relationships are planned as long term, and some are by their very nature unlikely to become long term. You are not thinking about long-term relationships when the conflict is between you and a police officer who has stopped you for speeding, or between you and a mechanic to whose garage you came in desperation when your car broke down 1,000 miles from your home, or between you and a telephone operator who has just told you that you cannot charge a call to your home number because there is no one there to accept the billing, and meanwhile here you are at a pay booth out in the middle of nowhere without change.

Nonetheless, I suggest, the same principles that serve you well when you are trying to resolve a conflict with someone whose relationship you intend to continue will also serve you well when you are trying to resolve a conflict with someone whom you are unlikely to see again. Moreover, in the vast majority of conflicts that you encounter during your business or personal life, your adversary will be someone with whom you *do* wish to continue a relationship—indeed, if you did not wish to continue the relationship, it would be relatively easy to resolve the conflict simply by accepting a loss: "Write off" the matter and go your way.

All of which leads me back to the three sample conflicts that I posed earlier in this chapter. We've spent enough time (you may be inclined to say more than enough time) on the one involving spouses who cannot agree on the color of a lampshade. Let's now turn briefly to the other two:

You have been late making payments on your charge account at a department store, and the store has reduced your credit line.

As I observed earlier in the chapter, it would be possible—indeed, easy—to end the conflict simply by ending the relationship. Don't shop at this store anymore. And if you are in a vindictive mood, don't even bother paying off your account. Let the store sue you, then find some excuse to file a counter claim (perhaps that the merchandise you purchased was misrepresented in the store's advertising), and then tie the thing up in court for five to 10 years.

In the end, you might very well wind up settling the bill for 50 cents on the dollar—or less.

However, the fact is that you like shopping at this store, even though you dislike the way the credit department has responded to your late payments. Moreover, you don't want to have to pay for your purchases in cash. Your goal in this particular conflict is to resolve matters in such a way that you can continue shopping at the store and enjoy the largest possible credit line. (Please make a mental note that I spoke of *your goal*. This is a subject to which I will return repeatedly in this book.)

Very well, you want to resolve the conflict and maintain or (in the best of all possible resolutions) increase your credit limit, or, at the very least, minimize the amount by which your credit limit is reduced. *That* (and do not forget it) is *your goal*. You must not let yourself be turned away from it by any intermediate goals that may develop as you pursue resolution of the conflict—for example, the intermediate goal of telling off a snooty lower-echelon manager to whom your complaint has been referred.

Now, what is the best possible way to pursue *your goal*?

Well, it may be to write a letter to the chairperson of the board of the conglomerate that owns the department store, pointing out that you have been a long-time customer and complaining that you were treated unfairly in this instance.

Or it may be to prevail upon a friend who knows the store's manager socially to arrange for an introduction so that you can present your case to the manager directly.

Or it may be to telephone the credit manager and threaten to go over his or her head if the decision to reduce your credit limit is not rescinded.

Or it may be to swallow your pride, take your lumps, and try to rebuild your relationship with the store—in other words, don't make an issue of the reduction in your credit limit; instead, make future payments on time or even ahead of time, and then, a year or so hence, apply for an increase in your credit limit, citing your excellent payment record as evidence that you deserve the increase.

□  In fact, a colleague of mine was in this very situation. He

chose to go a more or less combative route, writing to the
chairperson of the board of the conglomerate that owns the department store. He accused the credit manager and others in the credit
department of discourtesy, rudeness, and unwillingness to listen to
his explanations of why his payments had been late. He cited a
long history of dealings with the store, and he threatened that if he
did not hear from someone in a position of authority superior to
that of the credit manager, he would file suit charging discrimination under federal and state statutes relating to fair credit
practices.

☐  As it happens, my colleague is Caucasian. However, in his
letter to the chairperson, he used language that very carefully invited the inference that he was a member of a "minority group."
Thus if his credit was rejected, the store ran the risk of being attacked for discriminating against minorities; indeed, if he could
show that the store had given credit to Caucasians who were less
creditworthy than he, he would have grounds for a federal lawsuit
under the Civil Rights Act.

☐  The chairperson replied with a personal letter, and a few
days later the manager of the store telephoned to apologize. The
manager gave my friend the usual (false) song and dance about
computers not working properly. The manager also said a few
words to the effect that the credit manager was only trying to do
his job. The manager then restored my colleague's former credit
limit.

A very important element in dealing with conflict is, as I noted
some chapters ago, identifying all the parties to the conflict. In the
above situation, the conflict was principally between my friend
and the *company that owned the store*—not the credit manager at
this individual outlet. By circumventing the credit manager, my
friend *eliminated* a party to the conflict and achieved a prompt and
satisfactory resolution. You may be sure that henceforth the credit
manager will tread very carefully should my friend's account come
into dispute.

Next example:

After you enrolled your child in a private school, the school billed you for "tuition insurance." The policy guaranteed that the full year's tuition, which you paid in advance, would be refunded by the insurance company if for one reason or another your child did not finish the year. The cost of the insurance was rather small—$55.90—but you objected to *having* to pay for it, especially because no one told you beforehand that the insurance was a requirement of the school.

Okay, how do we resolve the conflict?

Well, if you want to be eminently practical about it, you'll pay the bill and say no more. A maxim among lawyers, back in the days when traffic fines usually amounted to two dollars, was, "Pay the two dollars." In other words, when the stakes are low, it's not worth the trouble that you'll have to go through to obtain redress of your grievances. You'd be better off letting your adversary win. (That is why many creditors write off relatively small loans from debtors who are deemed unlikely to pay, instead of going to court in an attempt to collect.)

Traffic fines have increased considerably in recent years, but the basic principle still applies: If you really want to keep life uncomplicated and ensure your domestic tranquility, don't get into unnecessary battles over matters of small import. Accept victimhood, and get the whole thing out of your hair. (Would you resist a gangster who threatened to kill you if you did not pay "protection" money of one cent a week? If not, at what amount would you resist? One cent a day? One dollar a day? One hundred dollars a day? One thousand dollars a day? Ten thousand dollars a day?)

However, if you want to take a stand on the matter, there are things you can do:

1. *Simply Do Not Pay the Money.* The school could continue to bill you, and you could continue to withhold the payment, and so long as the school did not take prejudicial action against your child (for example, by refusing to release the child's grades), the standoff would be working in your favor.

2. *Raise a Fuss with the School.*   In other words, telephone or visit or write someone. Use logic or threats or whatever you can muster to support your argument that the billing was unwarranted. Persist until you have won or lost.

3. *Take the Matter to an Outside Agency.*   What are the policies of your state's department of education regarding charges of this sort? Can you get help from an outside agency? Even if you can't, will the fear of an entanglement persuade the school that you should be given your way?

4. *Enlist the Intercession of a Friend Who Knows the People Who Run the School.*   If you have such a friend, and if he or she speaks on your behalf, the whole matter can be put to rest very quickly—although you probably would not want the school to drop the charge as an apparent *favor* to you when your objection was not against the amount of the charge but rather the principle of it.

5. *Sue the School.*   Seek an injunction that would prevent the school from attempting to collect the charge. Perhaps also seek some compensatory and, possibly even punitive, damages. (Of course, your legal costs, even if you handled the case yourself instead of hiring a lawyer, would be considerably greater than the school's charge; on the other hand, if you had been willing to pay the $55.90 you would not even be considering alternatives.)

There are, to be sure, quite a few more ways that you could deal with this matter. If you are in the mood for another exercise, list 10 or 20 or 30 such ways. Then rank these approaches according to their potential to bring the matter to a satisfactory conclusion.

☐   Here, meanwhile, is the way a friend of mine dealt with the problem when his daughter's school sent him a bill for $55.90 for tuition insurance that he had not ordered:

☐   First, he wrote to the school's business manager to explain why he was not paying the charge. He sent this explanation along with his check for the balance owed on his daughter's tuition, reasoning that the school might be more accommodating to a parent who had just paid the full amount of the tuition than to one who had an outstanding balance.

☐  My friend would, of course, have had more leverage if he withheld the final payment of the tuition until the dispute over the insurance was resolved; however, he really did want his daughter to attend this school, and he did not want to give the school an opportunity to cancel her enrollment for nonpayment of tuition. In sum, he wanted to *confine the issue* to the insurance, and he wanted to appear as congenial as possible with respect to every other particular of his dealings with the school, so that the school would have no way of complicating the issue by introducing examples of his intransigence in other areas of contact.

☐  His letter:

*Enclosed is my check for $1,645, which, combined with the $1,300 I have paid thus far, constitutes payment in full for $2,795 in tuition and a $150 registration fee.*

*I am not interested in the tuition refund plan. I believe that the insurance policy does not offer adequate benefits for the price. I cannot understand why the school would have any interest in whether a parent carries this plan if the parent had made full payment in tuition and fees, as I now have. In any event, the state board of education advises me that you cannot require a parent to carry this insurance.*

The letter, I suggest, was strategically sound.

My friend could have telephoned instead, but the likelihood is that he would have had to leave his message with an underling who might garble it before delivering it to the decision-maker. By writing, he was able to make his position clear, give the people at the school the opportunity to get the complete message to the decision-maker, and give the decision-maker an opportunity to think things over before responding. (I cannot overemphasize the value of giving adversaries an opportunity to think things over—especially when you are right, but even when you are wrong yet capable of exercising certain leverage: Your adversaries usually will not appreciate your leverage until they had had time to think things over.)

There is only one sentence in the letter that I find of questionable value, and that is the last. Were it true, it would be a strong argument. However, I happen to know that my friend had not consulted the state board of education before writing. He did not know whether there was any proscription against a school's requiring tuition insurance.

He could have tried to find out, but he did not want to spend that much time on the matter. He chose instead to lie, reasoning that the school's position was so illogical that the state probably would object to it and reasoning also that by being vague about his source of information ("the state board of education advises me" rather than identifying a specific person who provided this advice) he left himself plenty of opportunity to maneuver if he were challenged ("I don't remember who I spoke to at the office of education, but all this is irrelevant anyway because . . .").

Was there any *advantage* in claiming falsely to have received this advice from the board of education? Well, there may have been several advantages.

If there were indeed a proscription of the sort about which he claimed to have learned, and if the school knew about it (as the school very well might), my friend would have served notice of his superior knowledge—just as your and my mutual friend Turnbull a few pages ago served notice on Mrs. Jones by informing her of the legal maximum rent on the apartment.

Meanwhile, if there were no such proscription, the school conceivably might believe that there was one—on the basis of my friend's having said so. If so, he would have won the game, hands down. (Not all schools pay diligent attention to the regulations under which they operate.)

Finally, if the school knew or managed to find out that there was no such proscription, my friend's position would not have been damaged irreparably. True, he would *appear* to have been caught bluffing. But he could always obscure the issue by insisting that this indeed was what he had been told by someone whose name he never learned. He could then shift the focus of the argument away from the bluff in which he had been caught and toward the equities of the issue.

I do not, mind you, *advise* that you bluff under situations of this sort. Bluffing is a dangerous game—usually an unnecessarily dangerous game, akin to a trapeze artist's working without a net.

No matter how glibly you respond when you get caught bluffing, you may find that you have destroyed your credibility with your adversaries. I think my friend would have been wiser to have actually checked with the state department of education before saying that he had. My only point here is that he bluffed with the expectation that it was a low-risk maneuver, and, as things turned out, he was right.

A few days after he sent his letter, he got a call from the school's business manager. She said that the school's policy requiring tuition insurance was firm and that no exception would be made in his case.

He then asked her to refer him to her superior. She gave him the telephone number of the headmistress. He asked the business manager to telephone the headmistress and explain the situation before he called. She refused. (Obviously he was up against people who intended to play hardball.)

He now telephoned the headmistress. He could not get past her secretary. He left the secretary with the threat that if he was not informed by the headmistress within 24 hours that the charge had been rescinded, he would take action.

Twenty-four hours passed, and then 48, without his hearing from the school. He now had to take action of some sort or another or be shown to be a paper tiger.

He wrote a letter explaining in detail his grievance against the school. He addressed it to the chairperson of the state's board of education. He noted on the letter that he was sending photocopies to the state's insurance commissioner, all the senators and assemblymen on committees that dealt with insurance or education, the heads of all federal agencies that dealt with insurance or education, the congressional representatives whose committees oversaw these agencies, and the education editors and business editors of the city's newspaper. He actually mailed these letters. Then, to a copy that he sent to the headmistress, he added this note:

*You apparently considered yourself too important to take my phone call. Perhaps the enclosed letter will persuade you to revise your opinion of your own importance. I am now investigating other ways in which you may be in violation of local, state, or federal policies or statutes regarding private schools. I did not want to go to war against you, but you seem determined to leave me no choice. If you would like to negotiate a resolution of this controversy, please telephone me at your earliest opportunity.*

Two days later my friend got a telephone call, not from the school, but from the state board of education. A representative of that agency said that the agency had no control over the fees charged by private schools but had received other complaints about this school and would be pleased to counsel my friend as he proceeded to attempt to resolve his dispute. The representative also promised to send extracts from the state's Education Code that established responsibilities of private schools with respect to making available records of pupils, qualifications of teachers, licensing, and other administrative matters; my friend might use these to form an opinion about whether any other practices of the school were in violation of the law.

A day after that, my friend got a call from the headmistress, who claimed to have "just received" his letter and who said she was "distressed" that matters had reached this point. She blamed her secretary and the business manager for not having called the problem to her attention. She added that the charge for tuition insurance had been rescinded and that my friend's next statement would reflect the adjustment. She closed by urging my friend to contact her personally if ever again he had a problem regarding the school. She promised that this time he would not have any difficulty getting past her secretary.

In sum, my friend obtained unconditional surrender from the headmistress. This did not mean that he would in the future prevail in every conflict that might arise between him and the school; however, it did mean that he was in a much stronger position vis-a-vis the school than he had been before this conflict. For example, if my friend's daughter were to have a problem with a teacher, the headmistress almost certainly would listen more attentively to my friend's side of the story than to the complaint of some other parent who had not demonstrated the willingness to fight and the determination to pursue all reasonable remedies in search of redress of grievances.

You may be wondering at this point how the combative attitude of the principals in these last two examples (the father versus the school and the customer versus the credit department) can be reconciled with my principle that the primary goal of any negotiation should be not merely to get *to* yes—not merely to bend the other party to your will, by whatever means you can—but rather to get *past* yes by resolving the conflict in a way that serves the best interests of *both* parties and encourages a harmonious, long-term relationship.

Well, really, there's no dissonance.

I never said that all conflicts must be resolved to the *pleasure* of all parties. I never said that everyone *must* go away happy. Indeed, I never said that *anyone* must go away happy—although it is *better* if everyone does.

I merely said that your *goal* should be to resolve the conflict in a way that *serves the best interests of both parties and encourages a harmonious long-term relationship.*

If one of the parties is an out-and-out villain (as happens more than occasionally) and must be slapped down, then slapping down—by whatever efficacious means—is what serves the best interests of both parties and encourages a harmonious long-term relationship.

To be unabashedly cynical about it, enforced servitude—when, indeed, servitude can be enforced—is the optimum resolution to every conflict. No one ever accused Josef Stalin or Francisco Franco of not knowing how to deal with conflict. The methods of Genghis Khan also stood the test of time. Or, to borrow from Lyndon Johnson, who was much less successful at it, "If you've got them by the balls, their hearts and minds will follow."

None of this is to say that *we* should aspire toward humbling and subjugating our adversaries. A distinction must be made between the moral good and the strategic good. My only point here is that, in our study of how conflicts are successfully resolved, we must examine the whole panoply of approaches available to us and to our adversaries, lest we be surprised by an adversary who was more thorough in his or her research than we. And we should not hesitate to use any approach that we find morally acceptable against any adversary whom we cannot win over by gentler means.

In sum, I suggest that when we are dealing with people who are willing to be nice, we should also be nice. In fact, we should be nice first, and we should strive to be nicer than the next fellow. No conflict is resolved more felicitously than one in which the parties are doing their very best to be nice to each other.

On the other hand, we must recognize that there are some genuine scoundrels out there, some people who are trying to take advantage of our weaknesses in any way they can. You don't get a Josef Stalin or Francisco Franco to back off by showing him that your heart is in the right place. If you want to hold your own against the villains, you've got to be prepared to play their game.

Leo Durocher to the contrary, nice guys *don't* always finish last. In my experience, they more often than not finish first. However, there are times when you simply cannot afford to be a nice guy, and he or she who would excel at conflict resolution must learn to make the distinction between when one can and when one cannot be nice.

All of this leads to the question of power. Who has the power in a conflict? How can he or she exercise it? What should you do if you are the one without the power? The next chapter addresses these questions in some length.

# ≡10≡NEGOTIATING FROM STRENGTH

## OR HOW TO GET OTHERS TO GIVE YOU POWER TO RESOLVE A CONFLICT

---

Power cannot be seized. Even when it is demanded at gunpoint, it must be *given*, however reluctantly, by those over whom it will be exercised. Thus in any relationship between Person A and Person B, A will have power over B only to the extent that B is dependent on A for the attainment of B's goals, whatever they may be, and vice versa.

In certain situations, power and dependencies are clearly defined and not easily changed. For example, the school board's power to set teachers' salaries is well established, and teachers' dependency on their salaries (and, by extension, on the school board) is well understood. Neither situation is susceptible to quick modification.

However, the school board's power is offset to an extent by the teachers' willingness to go on strike, and the teachers' dependency may be offset to an extent by their union's abundant strike fund, by the demand of parents that the schools not close, and by a public perception that teachers are underpaid. Thus in certain circumstances, even though relationships of power and dependency may be clearly established, the balance may shift. Indeed, it is possible to envision circumstances under which a prolonged strike by teachers might incite voters to circulate a recall petition that leads ultimately to the removal from office of every member of the school board!

Even more complicated than situations of this kind are those in which power and dependencies are not clearly defined.

For example, if six airline passengers with confirmed tickets are "bumped' from a flight that has been overbooked, all six would seem to be equally powerless. However, if one of the bumped passengers is the chief executive officer of a company on which the airline depends for a great deal of business, and if she telephones someone she knows in the upper echelons of the airline's management, chances are she will get on the flight. In fact, I was a passenger when one such VIP was hustled aboard just before takeoff and—in flagrant violation of federal aviation regulations—escorted to the cockpit and given the extra seat normally used only when there is an extra pilot or aviation official aboard.

Even if none of the six passengers enjoys the rare situation of having the airline more dependent on him than on other passengers, he may be able to develop some power in the situation. For example, if he knows the pertinent federal regulations—or merely appears to—he may successfully demand boarding in place of a passenger who checked in after he did. Or if he is a friend of the ticket agent, or if he bribes someone, or if he makes enough of a fuss that the airline's employees are willing to take extraordinary measures to placate him, he may succeed in wresting away a seat from a passenger who already has been boarded.

Likewise, while a large corporation might seem invincibly powerful against an aggrieved customer, the customer's willingness to spend a great deal of time waging a lawsuit and/or a letter writing campaign to public officials may eventually wear down the resolve of those corporate officers who earlier told him, in effect, "Take it or leave it." I have abundant evidence—and will document it later in the book—of private citizens who brought major corporations to their knees in precisely this way.

Probably the ultimate in power plays is terrorism. To all appearances, a nation—any nation— is far more powerful than a band of zealots that may disagree with the nation's policies. But if the zealots are willing to take extreme measures—hijacking an airplane, claiming hostages, wreaking violence randomly on innocent citizens—the nation might be bent to the zealots' will.

By risking something that most people are unwilling to risk (their lives), the zealots claim power inordinate to their numbers and the numbers of their supporters; in effect, they make the nation dependent on them to do a certain thing (release the hostages, stop bombing churches, and so on), and this dependency gives them power over the nation—at least to the extent that the nation is unwilling to sacrifice lives by staging an all-out raid on the terrorists' stronghold or by simply saying, "Go ahead and kill them; we're not going to give in to you."

The principles of power and dependency apply to everyday problems at home and on the job no less than to larger conflicts. Let us now look at some of these powers and dependencies as they may exist within an industrial plant.

The plant's production manager has—officially, at least—a great deal of power over the plant's supervisors. The manager hires and fires supervisors. He determines which of them are to be promoted and which held back. He decides which ones are to receive perquisites, such as working the day shift rather than the night shift or being assigned to the production line with the newest equipment.

To outsiders it may seem that the manager's power over the supervisors is absolute. However, the supervisors also have considerable power over the manager. Without their support, he cannot fulfill his production quotas. He is dependent on them also for cost control and the timely completion of assigned tasks. He must rely on them to report accurately any production delays and to analyze the reasons for those delays. And the supervisors can be his best source of information regarding workers' morale. If the supervisors do not do their job for him, *he* will lose *his* job.

Thus the production manager and the supervisors are mutually dependent, and each holds a degree of power over the other. Neither can operate successfully without the support of the other. Either can interfere with the other's attainment of various important goals.

Please note that the relationship of production manager to supervisor is clearly defined. The balance of power is less obvious in a situation where two workers are not within the same chain of command—for instance, a production manager and a payroll clerk.

At first thought, it might seem that the higher-ranked employee (the manager) holds most if not all of the power over the lower-ranked employee. However, this need not be the case. Indeed, the clerk may hold considerably more power over the manager than the manager holds over the clerk.

For example, the clerk may be the person who issues the manager's paycheck. The manager will thus be dependent on the clerk for receiving his money on time. If the clerk fails to issue the check promptly, the manager may be inconvenienced. If the manager misses loan payments or other bills, he and his family may be embarrassed. If he happens to be seriously delinquent on his mortgage payment, he may face foreclosure.

The clerk, on the other hand, is not dependent on the production manager for anything. The supervision of the clerk is the job of the company's controller. The production manager does not evaluate the clerk's performance, assign the clerk responsibilities, or make a judgment about whether the clerk will get a raise. Indeed, the manager—officially, anyway—has no power whatever over the clerk.

In reality, of course, the manager has a great deal of power over the clerk. The manager, like any other employee, can complain about the clerk's poor performance. If other employees have also received their checks tardily, the clerk might be reprimanded. The manager's complaint probably will be given greater weight than complaints of other employees because of the manger's rank. If the problem is considered sufficiently serious, the clerk might be fired.

Moreover, the manager—unlike lower-ranked employees—relates as a peer to the clerk's boss. A friendly complaint, executive-to-executive, could spell serious trouble for the clerk. If the controller is not sympathetic to the manager's plight and if there have been repeated offenses by the clerk, the manager might bring the controversy before the company's executive vice president and demand that the clerk be fired.

Chances are that in the normal scheme of operations, neither the payroll clerk nor the production manager would choose to exercise power over the other. However, for the purposes of illustration let's look at an admittedly extreme example of how a conflict might develop between the two and how each might use power in an attempt to get the better of the other.

☐   The clerk, let us say, parked his car next to the manager's in the company lot. After the manager had left for the day, the clerk found a large scratch on his fender and concluded that the manager had done the damage while pulling out of his parking place. The next day he told the manager about the scratch and asked to be reimbursed for the damage. The manager replied that he definitely had not scratched the clerk's car and would not pay for repairs.

☐   Most of us, were we in the clerk's place, probably would let the matter end at that. We would recognize that the manager might be innocent, and we would realize, in any case, that we could not prove the manager's guilt. However, let us say that this particular clerk was convinced of the manager's guilt and was also very angry that the manager did not acknowledge it and offer restitution. The clerk might then vindictively decide not to process the manager's paycheck at the end of the month.

☐   As chance would have it (and as, in our scenario, chance does have it), the production manager issued a check for his current mortgage payment on the assumption that the payment would be covered by his paycheck. When he did not receive the paycheck, he complained to the controller. The controller assured the manager that he would look into the matter but added that he was unable to issue a new check until he found out what happened to the first one. When the controller discovered that the payroll clerk had never issued the first check, the production manager promptly was paid. Unfortunately, in the interim, the manager's mortgage check bounced.

☐ Incensed, the manager berated the controller at a board meeting, accusing him of running a sloppy department and not responding quickly enough to employees' complaints. The controller, having been embarrassed in front of the other executives, vented his frustration by firing the payroll clerk.

☐ The clerk, believing that he had been fired unfairly for what might indeed have been an innocent mistake, complained to the personnel director and to his union. The controller, of course, had anticipated this and was equipped with a laundry list of real or manufactured examples of the clerk's incompetence.

☐ The firing was upheld, and the clerk, feeling vengeful, circulated a companywide memo disclosing the salaries of all the senior executives—information that heretofore had been kept secret. The clerk's appetite for vengence still unassuaged, he then sent the IRS a copy of unreported "reimbursement payments," thereby subjecting some executives and sales personnel to charges of tax evasion. Finally, in a supreme act of vindictiveness, he shredded all of the corporate payroll records.

Of course, by taking any of these actions, the clerk seriously hurt his chances of ever being hired by another company, and he also ran the risk of criminal charges and a lawsuit for damages. However, by willingly accepting these consequences (or by being ignorant of them), he was able to exercise power far greater than one might expect of someone in that relatively humble job.

Moreover, the scenario need not stop here. Let us be really extravagant in our scenario writing and consider what further ramifications there may have been.

The paychecks of all employees were delayed while new records were constructed. When the assembly workers did not receive their wages, they staged a wildcat strike. Production then was halted, and orders to suppliers of parts and subassemblies were cancelled—whereupon the *suppliers* had to readjust *their* production schedules. Not only had the payroll clerk exercised power over the whole of his own company; he had even disrupted the operation of other companies. The suppliers of parts and subassemblies then had to cancel orders from their suppliers of raw materials. The suppliers of raw materials were unable to pay their bills, and their creditors forced them to declare bankruptcy.

After going bankrupt, the suppliers defaulted on their loans. . . .

The suppliers' banks, unable to carry the lost loans, folded. . . .

Depositors from other banks, fearful that their banks might also close, withdrew all their money, and the banks were then forced to turn to the Federal Deposit Insurance Corporation to fulfill the depositors' demands. . . .

Eventually, the FDIC ran out of its own funds and had to borrow from the Treasury. . . .

The Soviet Union, having observed the nation's economic crisis, decided that this was the best time to attack the United States. . . .

The Russians set off their first-strike missiles, the United States retaliated with its own missiles, and the world quickly ended—all courtesy of a disgruntled payroll clerk.

Extravagant scenarios of escalated conflict to one side, the fact remains that power inheres in every relationship *on all sides*. Every person in a relationship has—to a greater or lesser degree—power over every other person in the relationship, and most people potentially have power over a lot of others with whom they do not have a relationship.

If you can give someone something that she or he desires, you have power over that person—no matter who the person is or what it is you can offer. You also have power if you are able to withhold something that someone desires.

For example, returning to our production manager, if all the supervisors have been producing up to standard, the one who earns a promotion may be the one who is especially diligent and tells the production manager about a conveyer belt that looks like it is about to snap. That supervisor has given the production manager information that helps the manager do his job more effectively, and the manager has rewarded the supervisor by giving her what she wants, which is a promotion.

Alas, understanding what people want is not always simple. More to the point, one must make judgments about what a person *really* wants, and this may be something entirely different from what that person *says* he or she wants.

For instance, a company's director of public relations may say she wants a photocopy machine in her office because her secretary is wasting a lot of time taking material to the mail room for photocopying. That may indeed be the principal, or even the only, reason she wants the machine. However, the machine may be merely a *symbol* of what she *really* wants.

For example, if the public relations office is the only office on the senior executives' floor that does not have a photocopy machine, the director of public relations may want a machine because she wants to seem as important as every other executive on the floor. Getting photocopies promptly and efficiently may have little if anything to do with her request.

Or it may happen that a person says she wants something—even though she does not—because that thing is a means toward achieving another objective.

For example, the director of public relations may have requested new carpeting for her office. The old carpeting was perfectly adequate, and the new carpet held no significant symbolic value. (In fact, hardly anyone in the company notices new carpeting in offices, because it is always the same color.) The real reason the director of public relations ordered the unneeded new carpeting was to spend some of the money that had been budgeted for her department that year. If she did not spend all of the money in her budget, she probably would get a smaller budget for the next year. She did not want to risk "losing" that additional money, even though at present she did not need all the money she had.

The effective manager must be enough of a psychologist to *see through* stated reasons and assess what a person *really* wants. Even in cases where the apparent desideratum is a tangible and practical object, such as a typewriter, the reasons a person asks for it may be other than the obvious or stated reasons.

For example, Secretary A may say he needs a new typewriter because his old typewriter is broken. However, a *new* typewriter may not be necessary to solve his problem. What the secretary is really asking for is a *working* typewriter—not necessarily a new one. It may be possible to satisfy him simply by fixing his old typewriter.

Suppose Secretary A does get a new typewriter, and then Secretary B asks for one also. Secretary B's old typewriter may be working perfectly well, but she is the senior employee and she thinks that if anyone in the office deserves a new typewriter, she does. What Secretary B really wants is not a new typewriter but an *affirmation of her importance.* It may be possible to satisfy her by giving her a new title, such as "administrative assistant"— perhaps accompanied by additional responsibilities.

Suppose now that Secretary C also asks for a new typewriter. His old typewriter works well, and he has no interest in office politics. As a matter of fact, he hates his job and hates the company. What he really wants is to punish the company by making the purchasing department spend a thousand dollars unnecessarily. Getting the new typewriter will not satisfy him. Indeed, he probably will not be satisfied until he leaves his job.

Highest on most people's lists of desiderata is money. Almost needless to say, nearly *everyone* wants more money—if possible, a great deal more.

It is, of course, easy to understand that most people want money for what it can buy. However, money also holds a great deal of symbolic value. One might argue the merit of—but cannot deny the prevalence of—the opinion, "I make more money than you do, and therefore, I am more important than you."

The symbolic value of money apparently increases directly with the amount of money being made. For example, few people could spend more than $100,000 in a year without wasting most of the surplus. Hence, it may seem absurd for an executive vice president of marketing to argue about an extra $20,000 when renegotiating her current salary of $150,000. But if she knows that the executive vice president of finance is paid $160,000 a year, that extra $20,000 may hold more symbolic value to her than her entire $150,000 salary, and she may even quit her very desirable job over this relatively insignificant difference in pay.

The military very effectively uses symbols as rewards. Service ribbons and medals are nothing more than tangible acknowledgments of a job well done. The actual monetary value of a service ribbon or medal is rarely more than the value of the material from which it was made—if there is even that much value. Yet, to most people, the object signifies that the soldier *himself* (or *herself*) has special value, because he has *earned* the ribbon or medal by performing a praiseworthy task.

In the world of business, the equivalent of service ribbons and medals is usually bonuses or perquisites—both of which usually have considerable monetary value. However, one system in which business directly mimics the military is in awarding monetarily worthless titles.

The president has a "better" title (and, by extension, a higher rank) than the vice president. The vice president has a higher rank than the manager. The manager has a higher rank than the supervisor. And so it continues down the line.

Interestingly—and significantly—the same title may mean different things in different companies. In one company, the president may be the most powerful person—the man or woman who really runs the show. In another company, a president may report to the head of a division, who in turn answers to a vice chairperson, who reports to the chairperson.

Until recently, this broad array of corporate titles did not exist. The president ran the company and also chaired (that is, *presided* over) the meetings of the board of directors. Only in unusual circumstances would a company have both a chairperson and a president.

The separation of these positions probably came about because officers of subpresidential rank threatened to look for work elsewhere if they could not claim the coveted title of *president*. The creation of the different positions, chairperson and president—or chief executive officer and chief operating officer—solved the problem for both executives.

Not too long after this, the business world saw the creation of multiple presidencies within a single company. Instead of losing their fast-rising, ambitious executives to firms where bonafide presidencies were open, companies created more titles. The vice presidents, executive vice presidents, or senior vice presidents became presidents of their divisions. Holders of the latter titles, the presidents of divisions, became vice chairpersons of the corporation.

Nowadays in some companies the office of what had once been called "the president" is staffed by a troika of apparent equals, a group of co-presidents who report to vice chairpersons, chairpersons or executive committees, and, in a few rare cases, to the chairperson of the board.

Given the recent trend, it is conceivable that supervisors of the assembly line may one day carry the title of "president, section 23-B." And so, not surprisingly, some companies have begun to reverse the trend by *reducing* their number of titles, thereby strengthening their own titular currency. At one major distilling company (Hiram Walker), there is only one vice president, who holds the title (appropriately enough) of "The Vice President."

What substantive difference there is between business titles and "private" versus "private first class" (or "lieutenant-general" versus "general-of-the-army") is a matter for discussion in other precincts. The point here is that many institutions have recognized the value of rewarding employees with symbols—which sometimes are deemed far more desirable than mere money.

The operative word here is "desirable," and the key to gaining power in the world of business is to identify what it is that you and your co-workers desire. Yes, I said *you* must identify what *you* desire—more specifically, what you *really* desire. Just like everyone else, you may be saying (and actually believing) that you want something that you really do not.

Assess whether you are striving for what you *really* want or for merely a *symbol* of what you really want. For example, do you insist on having your own secretary because you have taken on so many new projects that you will not be able to handle all of them without someone working full time as your personal assistant? Or, are you asking for your own secretary because you feel that a person of your stature is entitled to such a status symbol?

Are you perhaps, as an entrepreneur, paying with your own hard-earned dollars for a secretary you don't need, simply because you want the appearance of a person important enough to need a secretary? I'm not saying that there's anything *wrong* with doing so; I'm saying only that it's important to understand *why* you're doing what you're doing.

I reiterate, desiring symbols of success and respect is not necessarily a bad thing. Most of us, if not all of us, want recognition for our good work. But some symbols will serve our *true* purposes better than others.

Let's return to the example of wanting a secretary because you feel that you are "important enough" to have one. You may feel that having your own secretary will show the rest of the company—and your clients and your family and friends—how important you are.

But your boss might draw a different conclusion. She might recall that everyone else who held your job was able to handle the work with only the assistance of the typing pool and a receptionist. If you are not generating more business and yet need more help than your predecessors, you probably will be perceived as someone who is unable to handle responsibility. Thus your chances of promotion could be hurt by your having a secretary. And if a promotion was what you *really* wanted all along, your request for a *symbol* of success might be what cost you the Real Thing! (A better approach for you probably would have been to ask for additional responsibility. By proving you are able to handle additional duties, you present yourself as a more attractive candidate for promotion.)

Okay, you've determined what you really want. Your next step is to look at the bigger picture. More specifically, make a list of what you want in your current position and also in the foreseeable future. Critically assess those wants. Do you want them for what they *are,* or do you want them for what they *represent?* If they *represent* something, what do they represent *to you?* Is there a better way to acquire what they represent?

After constructing your list, rank your wants in order of importance. You may want both a raise and a bigger office. You want a raise because even with your moderate style of living you hardly seem to have any money left at the end of the month. You want a bigger office because it would be more comfortable to work in and it would be more prestigious.

If prestige and comfort are not as important to you as financial security, you should rank the raise as more important. On the other hand, if you can pay your bills on time and you're not terribly concerned about putting money away, but if your office is so small and dingy that you dread going to work each day, the larger office might be your priority.

After listing and ranking what you want, the next step is to *determine who controls what you want* and *who or what stands in your way of getting it.* However, be very careful in making these determinations; just as it is easy to misjudge what you really want, it is easy to misjudge who controls it and who or what stands in your way of getting it.

For example, let us say that you have decided that you want to be a partner in the advertising agency for which you currently work. Your present title is account executive, and you report to a senior vice president, who in turn reports to the president/chief-operating-officer, who is one of the partners.

It may seem at first that what you want—partnership—is controlled by the agency's existing partners, who decide which employees of the firm get invited to join the inner circle. It may also seem that your boss, the senior vice president, is standing in the way of your being invited because, obviously enough, he wants a partnership, too, and you will not get yours until he gets his.

But wait! These conclusions may be way off base. And before you even think about how right or wrong they are, you should investigate *why* you want what you claim to want.

Does that seem silly, rather like the sort of psychobabble spouted by those colleagues of yours who pay several hundred dollars to spend a weekend in San Francisco with some self-anointed guru who will not let them use the bathroom until he has decided that they should? Trust me—at least long enough to let me tell you why I think the "why" of your desire is important.

Let us say that you want a partnership for the following reasons, in descending order of importance: (1) you want the responsibility of helping to formulate the firm's strategy rather than merely implementing decisions that someone else has made; (2) partnership means equity in the firm, which will be part of your estate and of great value to your heirs when you die; (3) there is more prestige in being a partner than in being an employee; you will gain stature in your industry, get invited to address symposia of executives at other companies, et cetera, et cetera; (4) you have been doing your present job for quite some time now, and you would like some new challenges; (5) as a partner, you will make a much higher salary.

Keep in mind that the better you understand what you want and why you want it, the better your chances will be of acquiring it. Thus before proceeding to the next phase of determining who controls what you want and who or what stands in your way of getting it, let's test the assumption that a partnership is the best way to achieve your goals.

If you want to be a partner because you want to function as a strategy-formulator rather than a day-to-day problem-solver, maybe you can achieve your goal more quickly by moving to a smaller firm where there is less regimentation and a smaller group of senior executives whom you must bypass before a partnership will be offered to you. Or if you want to be really nervy, you might start your own agency: Entrepreneurs reach the top immediately—although they often have reason to wish that they had not left the comfort and security of a previous job.

As for equity in your firm being of great value to your heirs, there is no question that this is a strong desideratum—but is partnership the only way, or even the most efficient of several ways, to create an estate? You may find that a life insurance policy that costs relatively little will provide even greater value to your heirs.

Prestige? Well, yes, partnership will enhance your stature in your industry, but there are other ways to achieve this desideratum, too. For example, if you created an especially effective campaign for one of your clients, or if you started your own agency and rapidly developed it, or if you won a particularly important account, you might achieve even more prestige more quickly.

New challenges? Well, you could get those in a variety of ways without changing your present situation: Drum up new accounts that have problems dissimilar to those of your present accounts, devise a strategy that could help your firm increase its business with a given type of client (say institutional investors or governmental agencies), or start your own part-time business, working on it evenings and weekends.

More money? That, too, may be possible without your becoming a partner. For example, if you were to recruit a major new client for the agency, you almost certainly would be able to command more money even if you were not made a partner.

None of this is to say that partnership is a *bad* idea for you or an *inefficient* way to achieve your goals. My only point is that you should look at the *why* behind what you want and make judgments about whether the thing you want is what *really* helps you achieve your goals.

Okay, let's say that you have thought about what you want and why you want it and have concluded that partnership in your firm is the most efficient way to achieve all your desiderata in the shortest possible time. Let's go back back now to those considerations of who controls what you want and who or what stands in your way of getting it. I'll repeat the premises that I expressed a few paragraphs ago and invite you to reexamine them with me:

What you want—partnership—is controlled by the agency's existing partners, who decide which employees get invited to join the inner circle.

Your boss, the senior vice president, is standing in the way of your being invited, because, obviously enough, he wants a partnership, too, and you will not get yours until he gets his.

Both of these propositions may be true, and your best approach may be simply to work your way up through the ranks—that is, help your boss do as good a job as he can, which will accelerate his rise to partnership, whereupon you can replace him and enjoy the benefits of his sponsorship as you continue your quest for partnership. But it may also be true that there are more efficient paths to your goal.

For example, working your way up the chain of command is not the only way to the top of a company. Many a chief operating officer or chief executive officer got there by a sort of zig-zag route, stepping outside the chain for a stint as executive assistant to the previous chief operating officer or chief executive officer, then stepping into the COO's post when that executive was named CEO and, finally, becoming CEO when that lady or gentleman retires.

Thus in your present circumstances, if partnership is *really* what you want (and is *paramount* among your desires—not merely one of an assortment of equally prized desiderata), you might be well advised to request an interview with your COO or CEO and express an interest in working more closely with him, even if this were to mean a temporary—but substantial—decline in pay and perquisites.

The above scenario concedes the proposition that the agency's existing partners control what you want (that is, they decide which employees get invited to join the inner circle), but it negates the proposition that your boss stands in your way (because he wants a partnership, too, and you will not get yours until he gets his). Indeed, your boss may have no interest whatever in a partnership; he may like his present situation very much and have no desire to take on the added responsibilities and pressures of sharing in the firm's policy making. In any event, it may be entirely unnecessary for you to follow him up the ladder—or leap-frog him—in the interest of securing your partnership, and it may develop that if you are sufficiently imaginative to see that there is more than one path to the same goal, you may aid your cause immeasurably by following a circuitous path and enlisting your present boss as one of your supporters.

Now let us consider the proposition that the agency's existing partners control what you want. They do, of course, in the sense that they are the people who will vote on who gets accepted as a new partner. However, the likelihood is that they do not merely cast their votes whimsically: There must be some *justification* for their voting as they do, and the justification usually will revolve around the best interests of the business.

Let us say, therefore, that you were in a position to claim the account of a major client—one whose billings amounted to a substantial percentage of your firm's existing business. Imagine how the partners would react if you were to walk in on them and say, "Gentlemen, I have in my back pocket and am prepared to deliver to you immediately the business of XYZ Corporation, which will increase this company's annual revenues by 46 percent." Would they accept as part of the deal your being named a partner? Chances are they would handcuff you to one of the chairs in the boardroom and not let you out until you deigned to accept their offer of partnership!

In this situation, while the partners still are nominally in control of what you want, the fact is that *you yourself* enjoy the greater control—by virtue of your ability to deliver the account that they want.

There's an important lesson here—one that I consider sufficiently important to warrant being stated in capital letters:

**IF THEY CONTROL WHAT YOU WANT, AND YOU CONTROL WHAT THEY WANT, THEN *YOU CONTROL WHAT YOU WANT!***

Of course, in a real—and very important—sense, you *don't* control what they want. Even if you have that account in your back pocket, someone put it there. In other words, someone or something *permitted* you to control what your partner wants.

Who or what permitted it? Well, it may be that the decision-maker at the company whose account our partners want is your father-in-law. Or it may be that you did such a good job when you were handling the account of a competing company that the decision-makers at the desired company want you on their team now. Or it may be that you were sufficiently imaginative and efficient in preparing a presentation for the desired company that the decision-makers decided that they wanted you to represent them, whether you stayed with your present firm or went somewhere else.

In all three of the above situations, your control was less than absolute. Granted, you did certain valuable things—even if only selecting the right spouse. But you had no guarantee that what you did would lead to partnership. *That* was predicated on certain people's responding to you in a certain way—something that you could *influence* but not really *control*.

Let's take this a step further:

Suppose that in your quest for the best possible way to achieve partnership you decide that you must recruit a major new client. You then assign an assistant to research companies that may be clients of competing agencies. You ask your assistant to determine which companies have been suffering a loss of market share recently and to correlate this problem to unimaginative or otherwise ineffective advertising.

Your assistant develops a list of a dozen companies, from which you select three. You then ask a copywriter and an artist to develop some ideas that you can use in a presentation to these companies. When the ideas are developed, you make your presentation, and you win an important account.

Now, tell me: Who controls your rise to partnership under these circumstances? Well, yes, the existing partners still must vote you in. And yes, you yourself had to have the gumption to go out and solicit new business. And yes, your competitors at other ad agencies had to have been doing a less-than-terrific job if the accounts that you recruited were up for grabs. But also your subordinates—the assistant who researched the accounts, and also the copywriter and artist who developed the ideas that you used in your presentation—exercised an important measure of control.

Please recall now that we began with the presumption that the agency's existing partners controlled what you want and that your boss stood in your way of getting it. Now we have come to an almost diametrically opposite point of view, wherein you and your own subordinates (perhaps aided and abetted by fate and/or your unwitting competitors) have *effective* control over the major elements that determine whether you will get what you want, and nothing stands in your way but your own gumption and determination.

As I noted earlier, dependency is a two-way street. You may be dependent on your boss for a promotion, but he is dependent on you to do the job he has assigned you. Likewise, you are dependent on your subordinates to do a good job on the work you have assigned, and they are dependent on you to hold on to their jobs.

In virtually every situation of conflict, whether in business or at home or elsewhere, you will find that there are *some* resources under your control and some resources under someone else's control. The trick is to strike a happy balance whereunder you help others achieve what they want while they help you achieve what you want.

An example:

☐   There is a fellow living in your neighborhood who wants to be the president of the neighborhood's homeowners' association. You don't especially like him, and neither do most of the other neighbors, but none of you wants to take on the responsibilities of the presidency.

☐   He asks you to support his candidacy. Instead of telling him that you think he is a pompous and praise-seeking idiot, you ask him how he feels about a proposal by City Council to fence off the portion of a nearby playground that is being used by children under age seven.

☐   Truth is, he does not care at all about whether this portion of the playground is fenced off, for he is not a parent. However, he knows that you have two daughters under age seven, and that you favor the proposal, and that many other neighbors do also. He therefore tells you that he is strongly in favor of the proposal. You reply that you will vote for him if he promises to support the proposal vigorously whenever City Council seeks an opinion from the homeowners' association. He agrees. You vote for him.

Okay, nobody ever said you had to like the guy. The point is, you controlled something that he wanted—a vote for the presidency of the association—and you were able to trade it for something that he controlled—advocacy of your position regarding the fence. One hand, as the old saying goes, washes the other.

No matter who you are or where you are, there are resources that you control. This applies in familial settings, social situations, and business. It applies *especially* in business, where familial loyalties, social standing, and other peripheral factors are not present to confuse the issue. And it applies no matter how low or how high your position on the business' totem pole.

Consider this: Even if your only responsibility is to work on an assembly line screwing nuts into bolts, you control that portion of the line. You determine how quickly the nuts will be screwed into the bolts and how tightly. Of course, you are limited by a variety of factors, among which are the ability of the human body to perform certain operations and the ability of machines to respond to the control of their operators. However, while there may be an up-side limit to what you can do, there is no down-side limit. You can stop working at any time you wish.

Of course, if your work is not up to required standards, you may not control your portion of the assembly line for very long. However, for as long as you remain in your job, you have the ability to stop the progress of the entire assembly line—at least temporarily.

To reiterate, dependency is a two-way street, and you— whatever your situation—are in control of certain resources that can be beneficial to other people.

All of this brings us to yet another proposition—the penultimate one in this chapter: The next step, after you have determined what you really want and who controls it, is to assess what resources *you* control.

Let us say that you are a bookkeeper, responsible for recording in a journal which checks have been okayed by certain officers of the company. You control how accurately and how quickly entries are made. You also are the best source of information about entries in the journal.

Obvious enough? Okay. But you may also control some resources that are not quite so obvious to you. For example, you spend all day looking at checks and invoices. If you're astute, you probably know as much about how your company uses its cash as anyone else in the organization. You also may be the first person to find irregularities in how that money is being spent.

Suppose that you notice that an inordinately large number of checks is being written to a particular supplier of paper. Although the checks are accompanied by what appear to be legitimate invoices, you cannot imagine corporate headquarters going through that many cartons of paper in a single week. Your suspicions are confirmed when you inspect previous year's journals and find that this year the company is spending 10 times as much for paper as it did in previous years. You then pull out the suspicious purchase orders and see that they all have been requisitioned by the same person.

You report your findings to the vice president of finance, and your discovery of the embezzler earns you not only a raise but also a promotion to junior accountant. Meanwhile, the vice president of finance was not the only person in your company who was interested in the resource (that is, information about the embezzlement) that you controlled.

This brings us to the final step in how to have others give you power:

After you assess what resources you control, *identify who wants what you control.*

Returning to our example, a number of people at your company would have been interested in the information about the bogus purchases of paper. Your supervisor was one: She could have used the information as much as you. If you had told your supervisor, and she passed the news along to the vice president of finance, both you *and* the supervisor might have been rewarded.

At first thought, it may seem to you that the better course would be to go directly to the vice president of finance and not share the reward. However, inasmuch as your supervisor is in direct control of your work, you might have been better off to share the glory with her—with the prospect that she would reward you commensurately at some point in the future.

Of course, there is also the possibility that your supervisor might have taken the information and used it for her own benefit, claiming all credit that should have gone to you. On the other side of this particular coin is the prospect that, had your supervisor done this, you would have certain leverage over her, for in the future you would be able to reveal that your supervisor had claimed credit for what you had done.

Yet another person who would have been interested in this resource (information) that you controlled was the embezzler. Had you confronted this individual before telling anyone else, he or she may have offered you a bribe in exchange for your silence.

None of this is to say that you should or should not have taken one of the above approaches. My only point is that you should recognize the resources that you control as well as the resources controlled by others, and that you should also recognize who wants the resources that you control.

And that, in a rather large nutshell, is how to negotiate from strength by getting others to give you power to resolve a conflict. Before proceeding further, let me reiterate and summarize the main points of this chapter:

**Power Grows Out of Someone Else's Dependency.**  *If you can give someone something that he desires, you have power over that person—no matter who he is or what it is that you can give him. You also have power if you are able to* **withhold** *something that someone desires.*

**Understanding What People Want Is Not Always Simple.**  *You must make judgments about what a person* **really** wants, and this may be something entirely different from what he **says** *he wants.*

**The Key to Gaining Power Is to Identify What You and Other People Really Desire.**  Assess whether you are striving for what you *really* want or for merely a *symbol* of what you really want.

**When You've Decided That You Want Something, Look at the Bigger Picture.**  More specifically, *make a list of what you want in your current situation and also in the foreseeable future.* Critically assess those wants. *Do you want them for what they* **are,** *or do you want them for what they* **represent?** If they *represent* something, what do they represent *to you? Is there a better way to acquire what they represent?*

**Rank Your Wants in Order of Importance.**  Recognize that you may have to sacrifice the less important to gain the more important. Next—

**Determine Who Controls What You Want and Who or What Stands in Your Way of Getting It.**  Keep in mind that the better you understand what you want and why you want it, the better your chances will be of acquiring it. Explore alternate ways to get what you want; they may be much more effective—and easy—than what at first appeared to be the *only* way.

### Identify the Resources That You Control and the People Who Want These Resources.

Once you've done all this, the rest is relatively easy. All you've got to do is trade what you've got for what the other person has that you may want.

One more example will illustrate the power you can have even in your relationships with large corporations. A close friend whose business involved extensive travel experienced a near bankruptcy during the Reagan recession of the early 1980s. He owed bills to three airlines: Eastern, American, and United. He chose to fight his way back to solvency rather than to declare bankruptcy— during which time, of course, all his bills became long overdue.

When he could afford to pay some bills, he wrote checks for one-half of the outstanding amounts and mailed these to the airlines with letters explaining his circumstances and promising full payment upon hearing from each on two requests—reinstatement of his account and a promise to rescind any negative credit reporting. The results:

Eastern referred the amount to a hard-nose collection agency in Orange County, California. My friend took them on by sending copies of his correspondence with Eastern to the collection agency and to the state agency governing collection agencies. He never heard from the agency or from Eastern again. Eastern *did* receive one half of the amount due it.

American responded with a form letter request for additional information. My friend returned it with the remaining balance. He never did hear from American again. American, though, *did* receive the *full* amount due it.

United responded with a letter reinstating credit under certain conditions. United, of course, got the *full* amount due it *and* a loyal customer—one who sells United to his friends and who discourages friends from flying Eastern and American. Additionally, my friend is recovering financially now and is traveling again—on United.

He also plans to expand into the travel industry. Who do you think will get his business?

If I seem flip about this, let me quickly backtrack. I never intended to imply that there is no skill in making such arrangements. I said, please note, *"relatively* easy!"

The task of negotiating a resolution of conflicts, a resolution in which each of the parties goes away content (in other words, a resolution that does not merely get *to* yes but *past* yes), may be extremely difficult. But I suggest to you that the difficulties are all mechanical . . . technical . . . matters of mere nuts and bolts. Once the parties in a conflict have come to appreciate the desires of each other and the capacity of each to contribute to the satisfaction of the desires of the other, the battle is more than half won.

At the risk of seeming to summarize a summary, let me state in conclusion: The point of this chapter is that parties to a conflict will aid their cause greatly if they first *assay* and then *display* their strengths. What resources do you control? Who wants what you control? What do you want? Who controls those resources?

Only if you persuade your adversaries that you have at least as much to offer them (by way of incentive *or* deterrence) as they have to offer you can you exercise any power in resolving your conflict. And once you've accomplished this, all the rest is negotiation. Of course we all negotiate, but in the next chapter you'll discover how professional negotiators really operate.

# ≡11≡HOW PROFESSIONAL NEGOTIATORS OPERATE

## POSITIONAL BARGAINING VERSUS INTEREST BARGAINING

Civilians often fail to differentiate between negotiation and debate. In debate, viewpoints are diametrically opposite and the adversaries seek to defeat each other. (Unconditional surrender is the best of all possible resolutions.) In negotiations, viewpoints also may be diametrically opposite—at least initially—but the adversaries are searching for compromise.

In debate, and in what used to pass for negotiations some years ago, there are fixed positions: Side A and Side B both seek to demonstrate that they are "right." Practitioners of *positional bargaining* operate in fundamentally the same way.

Positional bargainers articulate certain demands (their "positions"), and they measure their success in terms of those demands to which opponents accede. In positional bargaining, either I win or you win; either a majority of your "positions" prevail, or a majority of mine do. The closest we can come to a compromise is a situation in which we each win a certain number of points and we "split the difference" on those points remaining in dispute.

Practitioners of interest bargaining, meanwhile, investigate the *real*—as opposed to stated—desires of opponents. They ask themselves, "Now that we know what these people *say* they want, what do they *really* want? What will make them happy?" Interest bargainers then seek ways to satisfy their opponents' desires—by, among other approaches, offering desiderata that they themselves control in exchange for desiderata that their opponents control.

For example, an employee may demand a raise, and the employer may feel that one is not warranted or that it cannot be given without creating undesirable precedents.

As a positional bargainer, the employer would express her reasons for not granting the raise and would then either compromise with a smaller raise or would steadfastly refuse any increase whatever. The employee, meanwhile, would either quit or grudgingly accept what was given—and perhaps malinger or otherwise deliver less than maximum performance in the future.

However matters turned out, both parties probably would feel aggrieved—the employer because she was paying more than she felt she should, the employee because he felt he was being underpaid.

Of course, seasoned positional bargainers might anticipate an outcome of this sort and might attempt to turn the situation to their advantage by exaggerating their positions. Thus the employee who wants a 10 percent raise might demand 20 percent, reasoning that after he and the employer have split the difference he will wind up with what he originally wanted.

But two can play this game. If the employer feels that she is being "high-balled," she can respond with a "low-ball": Instead of offering a smaller raise than the employee wants, she can demand that the employee take a *cut* in pay of 20 percent, supporting her arguments with complaints about a downturn in business, low productivity, et cetera; then she can offer to split the difference, and both parties will be back at square one.

Whatever the eventual resolution, I suggest that both parties in this example of positional bargaining—and in most others—are likely to feel aggrieved. Each considered his own needs, not the needs of the other; one party attacked, the other defended, neither sought to make the other happy, and neither ended up with what he wanted.

Now let's look at how the employer might handle the situation if she were an interest bargainer.

She first would attempt to determine *why* the employee asked for a raise. Was it strictly a question of needing more money to keep up with inflation? Or was there some special reason the money was needed—for example, tuition for a child about to enter college.

Was the requested raise sought mainly as a *symbol*—a way of keeping up with others whom the employee regards as less hard working but more amply rewarded? Or was it seen as a way to compensate for other desiderata that the employee was not receiving—for example, a title, a more attractive office, or a longer vacation?

Once the employer knew what the employee *really* wanted, the employer might be able to provide it—or an acceptable substitute—without creating any of the problems that would result if the employee's request for a raise were granted.

For example, let us say that the employer determined that the employee really needed more money to keep up with inflation. At the same time, the employer was not in a position to offer a raise. If she did so, she would have to give a raise to all other workers in the employee's job category, and this would raise the cost of what was being produced without raising the quality of the product or providing any other justification for charging customers more money for it.

Moreover, the employee, despite a greater *need* for money, had not demonstrated a greater *entitlement* to it. In other words, the employee was not working better or faster or more skillfully than other employees. In sum, the employee did not—in comparison to other employees—*deserve* a raise.

We could, if we chose, make the employer's task much simpler by positing the availability of a large pool of replacements. And indeed, if there were a great many other people who were available to do the job as well as the protesting employee and for less money, the employer would not have all that much of a conflict, except insofar as her sense of charity would impel her to want to "take care" of her long-standing employee. She could resolve the conflict (or, if you will, pseudoconflict) simply by replacing the disgruntled employee with someone who was willing—nay, eager—to work for much less.

But let's not make things so easy for the employer. Let's say that this particular employee is uniquely valuable. Let's say that the employee could not be replaced except at prohibitive cost: To recruit and train a replacement would entail at least as much expense, when amortized over five years, as the employer would spend acceding to the employee's request.

Let's also say that the employer is not being chintzy; she is paying the employee all she believes she can realistically afford for the work being done: If she had to pay more for this type of work, she would have no choice but to stop doing business, for she could not realistically raise prices commensurately and still remain competitive with other producers. Let us, finally, say that the employer sincerely *cares* about this employee and wants to do what is *best* for the employee, apart from any consideration of the employee's contribution to the business.

Allright, let us, as interest bargainers, turn our attention not to *what* the employee requested but *why*.

The employee, you may recall, asked for a raise—by definition, an increase in the amount of money paid for a given amount of work. But wait! Is that what the employee *really* wanted? Or did the employee merely want *more money*?

You don't see a difference?

Then please think about it for a moment.

A raise involves more money for the same amount of work. Is it possible that the employee would have been happy to have the opportunity to do more work—and, in the process, earn more money?

In other words, might this particular employee be satisfied if the employer offered the opportunity to work a greater number of hours, perhaps with time and a half for overtime? Would the employee have been satisfied to receive an incentive bonus for production exceeding a certain level? Would the employee accept an arrangement whereunder a commission was paid for certain sales generated from contacts that the employee developed?

Please note that all of these approaches would provide, without unduly burdensome cost to the employer, what the employee *really* wanted—that is, more money (to keep up with inflation)—while not being part of what the employee *said* he wanted (a "raise"). Had the employer not been an interest bargainer who sought to determine *why* the employee asked for a raise, she might have missed the opportunity to serve both the employee's best interests and her own.

Let's move now to the second of the questions that I raised some paragraphs ago about why the employee might have asked for a raise: Was there some special reason the money was needed—for example, tuition for a child about to enter college? If so, there might be vehicles other than a raise to achieve that objective.

For example, the employer might have contacts with collegiate administrators who could help arrange a scholarship for the employee's child. Or the employer might establish a plan whereunder children of employees would receive low-interest tuition loans that the children could repay from earnings once they had been graduated from college.

If the *real* concern of an employee was paying for a child's tuition, it might be possible to provide a host of solutions to that problem without ever once having to give what the employee asked for—a raise.

Easier still to provide, of course, are the symbolic rewards that an employee might seek—a title, a more prestigious office, et cetera. But the employer would not have any idea of what rewards might satisfy the employee unless the employer looked *behind* the employee's request and made a judgment about what the employee *really* wanted.

All too often, I think, most of us make judgments about what people want based on what they *say* they want without ever looking to the *interests* that underlie their requests. And all too often we lose valuable employees or otherwise sever valuable relationships because we take people's declarations at face value.

☐ I am thinking now of a friend who publishes newsletters and who had as his personal assistant a brilliant young woman of exceptional ability who could not—alas!—get along with anyone else in the office. Indeed, she fought with everyone from the receptionist to the printer, the building superintendent to the graphic designer, the reporters to the mailing room employees.

☐ Many of us might, in the situation of my friend, simply assume that the woman had a personality problem that was too severe to warrant our further interest. We would, therefore, fire her—and deprive ourselves of the further benefits of her talents.

☐ The positional bargainer might examine the situation and attempt to entice her to improve her behavior—perhaps by some sort of trade-off. In other words, the positional bargainer might say, in effect, "If you'll stop giving everyone a hard time, I'll give you a raise of X dollars a week and also buy you a new desk, chair, and typewriter."

☐ The interest bargainer, meanwhile, would investigate the *reasons* for the assistant's behavior and seek a way to eliminate whatever it was that stimulated the undesired behavior.

☐ For example, it might turn out that the assistant had some duties that she felt were demeaning: making coffee in the morning, opening the mail, or taking telephone messages for someone who was outside her chain of command. If my friend found some way to eliminate these duties, he might have helped her feel better about her work and, in the process, motivated her to get along better with the other people in the office.

☐ If my friend could not have eliminated conveniently all of the onerous duties, he might have eliminated several of them, or at least *one* of them, and, in the process, given his assistant an incentive to change.

☐ As chance would have it, he was a positional bargainer, and he instead gave her an ultimatum: She would either shape up or ship out. She shipped out. Everyone in the office was happy except him; while he succeeded in ridding himself of a person who was a source of irritation and discord, he also lost someone who had been making a very important contribution to his business.

Might he have turned her around? Could she have been motivated to get along with others? Perhaps. The trick, I suggest, lies in not *demanding* change but rather in *creating motivation to change*. And that, of course, requires an understanding of the *why* behind the problem—in other words, determining the *interests* of the people with whom you are bargaining.

Let me give you another example of interest bargaining, based on the experience of yet another of my friends, a lawyer:

☐ Unlike most people in his profession, this attorney was not a member of a firm. Rather, he had his own small office, staffed only by himself and a secretary, and he did a lot of "public interest" work (that is, cases deemed beneficial to the public but usually providing little if any monetary reward).

☐ His secretary asked for a raise. She was a positional bargainer, and she came well prepared to support her position. In the manner suggested by Fisher and Ury (see Chapter 9), she introduced "objective" data, pointing out that most legal secretaries in that city earned 30 to 50 percent more than she did. She also came equipped with calculations of how long it would take my friend to train a satisfactory replacement and how much of his own time he would lose in the process. The thrust of her argument was that if she stopped working for him, he would have to spend the equivalent of *three years' worth* of her raise simply to recover from her departure and get back to the point where he had been when she left.

☐ Her arguments were, of course, logical. There was no question that she could make more money working for another lawyer, and there was no question that my friend would lose quite a bit of time and money—to say nothing of the pleasure of a relationship with a very competent and efficient subordinate.

☐ Had my friend been a positional bargainer, he might have attempted to build a case in opposition to hers.

☐ He could point out, for example, that he had hired her directly out of high school and had invested quite a bit of time (and, by extension, money) in training her; this being so, he could argue, she *owed* him something that the typical legal secretary does not owe her boss. In addition to attempting thus to appeal to her sense of loyalty, he could appeal to her sense of civic responsibility, pointing out (truthfully) that he could not do the same amount of pro bono work that he now did if he had to pay her what most legal secretaries were paid.

☐ He could further play on her guilt by pointing out that he had done some free legal work for her parents. And he could appeal to her sense of the practical by reminding her that his office was very close to where she lived; if she took a job with another lawyer, chances were she would spend a good portion of the additional money for travel and parking—to say nothing of the time that she would waste in transit. He might also remind her of the comforts and conveniences that she enjoyed in his office; for example, she was allowed to wear jeans and other casual attire rather than the usual business clothing, and she was permitted to store her lunch in his refrigerator.

☐ But these arguments probably would carry little if any weight with her. She probably had considered many if not all of them before asking for the raise. In any event, all such arguments are irrelevant: Whether she was "right" or my friend was "right," the fact remained that he could *not* pay her the money she had asked for unless he changed the way he worked, taking on fewer pro bono cases and more financially rewarding cases.

☐ As a positional bargainer, my friend might very well use all his arguments on her and then when they failed, throw up his hands and say, in effect, "Look, I'm paying you all I can. Take it or leave it."

☐ As an interest bargainer, however, he learned—by the very simple tactic of asking her questions—that she was having a hard time getting by on her present salary and that she really needed *more money* (as opposed to "a raise"). He also learned that she liked her present job very much, did not really want to leave it, and would like very much to be able to work more hours if the opportunity were available.

☐ He promptly arranged for her to do part-time work—on *his* word processor—for another attorney. He also offered her free use of his office and his word processor for any freelance work that she might develop on her own.

☐ As a freelancer who, in effect, provided her "own" word-processing equipment, she was able to charge quintuple the hourly rate he was paying her (and triple the hourly rate she would receive at other law firms). By working every second Saturday, she was able to earn a monthly gross that exceeded by far the additional amount of money she had requested as a raise. Concurrently, she was able to maintain all the desiderata of a job that she had always like and never wanted to relinquish. Meanwhile, my friend was able to continue doing business as he had long done, and when his cash flow improved to a point that he was able to offer her more money, he very quickly did.

What all of the above boils down to is simply this: Any fool can say, "Take it or leave it." And you don't have to be much smarter to say, "Let's split the difference." What separates the professional negotiator from the amateur—or from the non-negotiator—is the professional's ability to find *creative solutions* that help *all parties* obtain their interests.

Let's apply this principle to a situation that has some elements in common with the beige-lampshade/peach-lampshade controversy of a few chapters ago. You and I want to start a business together. You want the headquarters to be in New York City, and I want it to be in Los Angeles.

If we were positional bargainers, each of us would itemize the reasons he believed he was "right." Then each would try to persuade the other, and, failing this, we would "split the difference." All other things being equal, splitting the difference would mean locating the business somewhere around Kansas City—midway between the two preferred locations.

Levity aside, let's look at the conflict as an interest bargainer might:

Step 1 is to ask why. (Step 1 is *always* to ask why!) More specifically, why do you want the headquarters to be in New York City, and why do I want it to be in Los Angeles? Also, is there some reason why you do *not* want the headquarters to be in Los Angeles or why I do *not* want it to be in New York? (I might be arguing for Los Angeles not because I really want our headquarters there but because I definitely do *not* want our headquarters in New York and feel I must provide an alternative. I might very well be equally happy with Houston, New Orleans, or Miami.)

I may say—and sincerely believe—that I want Los Angeles because that city is our company's largest market and also is the best source of skilled workers. But are these my *real* reasons? Or am I insisting on Los Angeles because I like the life style and am looking for an excuse to justify my living there? Or, on the other side of this latter coin, may I be resisting New York because I have always found the city abrasive and overly expensive?

Likewise, you may say—and sincerely believe—that you favor New York because it is the nation's banking center and is also more convenient to the industrial cities where most of our suppliers are located. But are these your *real* reasons? Or are you insisting on New York because you currently teach part-time at Columbia University and do not wish to give up that extremely fulfilling activity? Or because your mother-in-law lives in nearby Connecticut and you'd have a hard time persuading your wife to move so far away from her? Or because your mother-in-law lives in Laguna Beach and you cannot stand the thought of living so close to her?

Step 2 as a professional negotiator is to consider letting the other fellow have his way. That's right, I'm advocating that you consider unconditional surrender—not because your adversary enjoys a position of superior power but simply because surrender may be in your best interest.

Let's return for a moment to the situation in which an employee requests a raise. If you think about the request and the arguments pro and con, you may decide that the employee really does need a raise (not merely an opportunity to make more money) *and* deserves it *and* can be given it without creating any serious problem. Indeed, you may recognize that you should have offered the raise before the employee asked for it.

Well, go ahead and give the raise. Don't feel compelled to negotiate simply for the sake of not "giving in." Except in cases where you fear creating an undesirable precedent, you'll usually be wise to accede to every reasonable request—or even to be more generous than the petitioner asked you to be, as the following case illustrates:

☐   A friend of mine who makes his living as a writer had written several books during the early 1960s for Paperback Library, which since has become Warner Books. The publisher of Paperback Library at that time was one Hy Steirman, now a legendary figure in paperback publishing.

☐   Steirman had invited my friend to develop a proposal for a series of novels. My friend presented the proposal, and Steirman invited him to lunch.

☐   "I think we may be able to do business on these books," Steirman said. "What kind of advance [against royalties] would you want?"

☐   For earlier books, Steirman had paid my friend advances ranging between $1,500 and $2,000. Assuming that Steirman would not have asked the question if he did not intend to pay a larger advance than these amounts, my friend asked for $2,500.

☐   "I think I can do better than that for you," Steirman said. "Let's make it $3,000."

☐   My friend recalls today:

*No one ever accused Hy Steirman of being dumb or an ineffective negotiator. But he wasn't the sort of guy who tries to squeeze every last drop of juice out of the lemon, and he also recognized the value of paying a fair price for what he wanted. He knew that an advance of $3,000 would enable me to spend more time on the books than an advance of $2,500, and he trusted me to write better books because I was receiving more money.*

☐   My friend continues:

*Of course, there was no guarantee that I wouldn't take the extra money, go on vacation, then come back and do the books as quickly as I could. But Steirman had faith in me as a result of having dealt with me on earlier books and knowing how I work. The extra 20 percent that he volunteered as an advance got him much more than an additional 20 percent of quality in the book.*

Here is another example of the value of unconditional surrender:

☐   Speaking of Columbia University (as we were some paragraphs ago), a story is told about the time during the late 1940s when Dwight D. Eisenhower was president there. Students, it seemed, were ignoring signs that commanded, "Keep off the Grass." No matter how many times the grass was replanted, no matter how large the signs, no matter what other measures administrators took to protect the grass—erecting small fences, et cetera—the students invariably avoided the sidewalks and took the most direct routes from one building to another. Paths were worn along the routes, and administrators despaired that grass would never grow there.

☐   After every other attempt to deal with the problem had failed, Eisenhower was consulted. "The answer," he said, "is simple. Put sidewalks where the paths now are and plant grass where the sidewalks now are."

☐   In sum, Eisenhower recognized that the best solution to this conflict was unconditional surrender to the students, who had determined routes from one building to another that were more efficient than the routes established by the engineers and other planners who installed the first sidewalks.

When your team is "wrong," and sometimes even when it isn't—but when practicality favors acting as if it were—unconditional surrender may be a very good idea. To borrow again from Chapter 9, "Pay the two dollars." In other words, when the stakes are low, it's usually not worth the trouble you'll have to go through to obtain redress of your grievances; you'd be better off letting your adversaries win. And if your adversaries are "right"—as Eisenhower decided the students were in choosing paths that represented the shortest distance between two points—do not let your desire to "win" prevent you from choosing the most expeditious solution to a problem. Things may work out in such a way that what the other guy *really* wants is not at all incompatible with what you *really* want, even though your original positions may appear to be antithetical.

Now let's return to the situation in which you and I are partners who want to locate our corporate headquarters in different places—you in New York City, I in Los Angeles. Is it possible that I can—Step 2—win by losing (that is, serve my best interests by letting you have your way)?

Maybe it is. Maybe, on reflection, I will conclude that the business can be headquartered in New York City at least as well as in Los Angeles. By asking *myself* what *I* really wanted, I may have been able to recognize that my opposition to your idea grew from personal objectives rather than from the objectives of the business. I may now say, "Partner, you were 'right'—let's set up shop in New York."

I might surrender directly, or I might attempt to milk the situation for some strategic advantage—for example, by not acknowledging the "rightness" of your position but rather by appearing to acquiesce and perhaps implying that I expect some sort of payback: "Okay, partner, I thing you're wrong about New York, but I can see that it means a lot to you, so I'll go along with you this time. Just remember how cooperative I've been the next time we have a disagreement of this kind."

However I handle the situation, the point is that it is possible to serve one's own best interests by giving the other fellow *exactly* what he asks for. Unconditional surrender is not always a "defeat." It may be the best way to resolve your conflict.

Let us, however, say that unconditional surrender is not the best answer to a given problem. Then we must proceed from Step 1 (find out why) and Step 2 (consider letting the other fellow have his way) to Step 3: Find some other way to give him what he really wants. This usually will be the most felicitous solution to any conflict.

I once was negotiating on behalf of a manufacturer who was being sued by an inventor who claimed that the manufacturer had stolen one of his ideas. The inventor had filed his lawsuit pro se— that is, without employing a lawyer—alleging patent infringement and seeking both compensatory and punitive damages.

In my experience, the do-it-yourself litigator is always a zealot—someone who is so convinced that he has been wronged that he is willing to do whatever he must (including incurring the considerable costs and extraordinary inconveniences of dealing with the maze that is our nation's court system) to ensure that "justice" will "prevail" (that is, to ensure that he will get his way—or, at the very least, get "even" by inflicting "punishment" on an adversary that he deems fitting to the "crime").

When I was brought into the case, litigation had been in progress for more than four years. The inventor, a man in his late thirties who had never finished high school and had become an inventor after taking several electronics courses while in the U.S. Air Force, had argued successfully against several of my client's attempts to get the case dismissed. A judge had appointed a "master"—that is, a court officer who can become more actively involved in a case than a judge, serving more as a mediator than a referee—and the master had ruled that the case should go to trial.

I was satisfied that my client was both morally and legally "right." That is to say, my client had not infringed on the inventor's patent but rather had developed—independently and slightly ahead of the inventor—a closely similar but significantly different mechanism for accomplishing the same purpose. However, my mission as an interest bargainer was not to "win" the negotiation by forcing my adversary to surrender; my mission was to resolve the controversy by developing a solution that would make everyone as happy as possible.

My first question, therefore, was: What does this guy *really* want? More precisely, what was there that was sufficiently important to him that would persuade him to spend hundreds if not thousands of hours trying to machete his way through the legal jungle to bring the corporation that I represented to its knees?

Did he really believe that the company had stolen his invention? If so, did he hope to get rich from court-enforced royalty payments, perhaps augmented by punitive damages? Or was he more interested in a "moral" victory? Did he want to "punish" the company that he believed had ripped off his invention? Did he want to thumb his nose at the lawyers who had been making his life so difficult over the past four years? Did he want to force my client—and perhaps, by extension, the world—to acknowledge that he was an inventor whose work merited acclaim?

Did he want *all* of the above?

In search of an answer, I invited him to dinner. He did not attempt to conceal his astonishment. Heretofore, every representative of my client with whom he had dealt treated him as a nuisance and as an inferior. *We* (my client and its representatives) were the Big Corporation, the cold, imperious entity that would not let human considerations get between us and our beloved bottom-line. *He* was Don Quixote, trying to score a victory on behalf of the small man.

*We,* in his view, were the villains, and *he* was the hero. And the truth was that everything we had done thus far had encouraged him to feel this way and to want to punish us—perhaps as much for our imperiousness and lack of humanity as for our transgressions (real or imagined) upon his patent.

At dinner I tried first to establish a conversational bond that related to matters other than those in controversy. In other words, I wanted to know something about *him,* apart from his relationship with my client.

What sort of person was he? What were his likes and dislikes? Was he an athlete? An outdoorsman? A fan of mystery novels? A chess player? A parent? A religious man? A man of strong political opinions? What was his personal background? What did he want out of life?

I learned that he was the oldest of seven children in a blue-collar family and now the father of three children of his own. He ran his own TV repair shop and made a very comfortable living. He spent most of his evenings working on his inventions. He enjoyed the company of his wife and children but spent much more time alone in his workshop. He described himself as a "loner" who would rather "tinker with things" than do anything else. He confided that he probably would not have had the stomach to continue doing legal battle with my client were it not that he got great satisfaction from figuring out the different steps he had to take and the ways he could handle each step most effectively. "It's like looking at a motor," he said, "and figuring out what makes it work."

What he most wanted out of life, I eventually concluded, was respect for his intelligence. He disliked being thought of as a "mere" technician, a (in his words) "skilled laborer rather than a man who uses his brain." At one point during the evening he remarked, "People who have a college education sometimes act as though nobody else is as smart as they are. Being a lawyer can't be any harder than being a TV repairman. It's just that you do different things." Smiling, he added, "I proved I can handle myself with the best lawyers. You have guys that get paid a couple of hundred dollars an hour. They tried to get the case dismissed, but I won. I'd like to see them try to figure out a schematic for a Sony."

Also high on his list of desiderata was the opportunity to do challenging work and be paid fairly for it. He *loved* his work. It was *because* he loved it that he felt so aggrieved that my client (allegedly) had ripped off his invention. He loved his work so much that he could not bear the idea that someone else would take credit for it.

Money was much less important to him than recognition. Indeed, he had substantial savings, the result of his long hours of hard work and his frugality. He did not want especially to change his life style or to enjoy a greater number of material comforts. He simply wanted to continue living as he did, but to be afforded recognition for his accomplishments, beyond the recognition he got from customers as a person who knew how to fix a broken television set.

I reiterate that he was, in my opinion, "wrong" in the lawsuit against my client; that is, he was both morally and legally incorrect in claiming that my client had stolen his idea. But he was a *good* man, the sort of man my client could profitably employ. And that was what he *really* wanted—someone (whether my client or another company) to *hire* him to invent things, to pay him a salary and give him an office (or even a corner) in which to work and free him of the burden of having to market his inventions when all he really wanted to do was create them.

After several meetings, I told him that I would arrange an introduction to my client's director of research and development. He was pleased—no, thrilled—to have this opportunity. Their meeting went well, and the director of R & D told me that he would like very much to hire the man—provided, of course, that the hiring could be accomplished without jeopardizing my client's interest in the litigation.

The man took the job, discontinued the lawsuit, and has been working for my client ever since. I get a card from him every Christmas. He never forgets to tell me how happy he is in his new job and to thank me for my efforts on his behalf. He absolutely refuses to accept my assurance that I was merely doing my job—and doing my client a favor by recruiting someone so valuable to work for the company.

This story has a happy ending not because I'm such a bright guy or a keen judge of human character or a great humanitarian; it has a happy ending simply because I am not so stupid as to get locked into a positional bargaining debate of the sort that my client's lawyers had been carrying on over the previous four years with the man and because I undertook the very simple task of investigating what he really wanted.

Let's now return once again to our earlier hypothetical example wherein you desire to locate our company's headquarters in New York and I wish to locate it in Los Angeles. Let us further hypothesize that you have discovered that I *really* favor Los Angeles because I like the life style there, and I have discovered that you *really* favor New York because you teach at Columbia and your mother-in-law lives in Connecticut.

How can you prevail and yet give me what I really want?

Well, you might learn that part of what I like about the L.A. lifestyle is year-'round tennis. You might then introduce me to some friends who play year-'round tennis—indoors—in New York.

Are beaches important to me? Well, New York has beaches, too. You might invite me to spend a weekend in the Hamptons and another at Fire Island. Perhaps I can be made to appreciate that I can enjoy beaches from June through September in New York and then vacation in Florida or Los Angeles for three or four weeks during the rest of the year. All told, I may be able to achieve a greater total of enjoyable days on the beach if our business were headquartered in New York than if it were headquartered in Los Angeles—especially if the greater profits that result from headquartering in New York afford me more beach-time than I now am getting in Los Angeles (as well they may).

Sell me on this, and you'll have persuaded me to establish our headquarters in New York—persuaded me through interest bargaining. Did you "win" the negotiations? Yes, but so did I: we both will benefit from my acquiescence to your preferences.

I repeat, always investigate the *why* behind the other person's position. "Why" is the most important word in any interest bargainer's vocabulary.

Do I want Los Angeles for reasons of life style rather than for the reasons I've stated? Then forget what I've stated, and find a way to give me what I *really* want—the "Southern California life style," perhaps *more* of it, effectively speaking, while I am living in New York than I ever got while living in Los Angeles!

Meanwhile, what about your real wants?

Do you *really* want to stay in New York because you enjoy teaching part-time at Columbia? Then perhpas I can show you that you'd get the same satisfaction from teaching part-time at USC or UCLA. If I introduce you to people at these universities who can help you explore developing your own teaching position there, I may make it very easy for you to find in Los Angeles the very thing that you deem most attractive about remaining in New York.

Or do you want to remain in New York because your mother-in-law lives in nearby Connecticut and you'd have a hard time persuading your wife to move so far away from her? Well, how about inviting your mother-in-law to visit Los Angeles? She might like Toluca Lake even better than she likes Darien, or she might like Hancock Park even more than she likes Stamford. Bring Mohammed to the mountain, and you may find that you'll get everything you ever wanted in your original "positional" negotiations.

The more imaginative you can be in determining a person's real wants and the ways of satisfying them, the greater the likelihood that you'll develop a resolution to a given conflict that pleases your adversaries as much as it pleases you. Once again—I'll risk boring you—the operative questions are:

### What do these people *really* want? And why?

In positional bargaining, negotiations are seen as a contest from which one side will emerge victorious and the other will be defeated. In interest bargaining, each side strives to help the other achieve its goals.

# 12 THE MINI-MAX STRATEGY

## OR WHAT SHOULD I GIVE
## AND WHAT SHOULD I GET?

Ideally, of course, all parties in a conflict will be adroit practitioners of interest bargaining, and each will give an abundance of real desiderata unto others before the others even get around to asking for anything. Ideally also, there will be a veritable cornucopia of desiderata to spread around. Alas, in reality, things rarely happen that way.

Let us say that you are an interest bargainer. Let us also say that you have become a master at determining what people really want and why. Let us say further that you've become very adroit at the next two steps of interest bargaining: knowing when to let the other fellow have his way and finding some alternate means of giving him what he really wants.

Suppose it still doesn't work.

Suppose that you have determined that the secretary who asked for a raise really wants exactly that: More money for the amount of time that she is now working—not merely the opportunity to make more money by working a greater number of hours. Suppose also that you cannot pay that amount of money, or do not feel that you should, and cannot devise an alternate approach that the secretary finds acceptable.

Another example:

☐   Suppose that you've been late making payments on an unsecured loan and the bank has been dunning you. You'd like to pay—you really would—but you do not have the money.

☐   What now?

☐   Well, first of all, *don't* assume that the conflict *cannot* be resolved. No matter how difficult and/or obstinate your adversary seems to be, there usually will be a way to achieve some sort of accord.

☐   Maybe you were not quite as skillful as you might have been in determining your adversary's real wants and ways of satisfying them. Or maybe your adversary is a positional bargainer who will happily settle for much less than she has led you to believe.

☐   Whatever your perception of the situation, *don't* throw up your hands in despair. The conflict may still be negotiable. There may still be a possibility of pursuing trade-offs. And if you employ the mini-max strategy, chances are that you will come out in much better shape than seemed likely when you were thinking about throwing up your hands in despair.

Mini-max is a favorite of professional negotiators. It is based on the simple premise that most people are willing to give up something in order to get—or keep—something else.

Granted, not everyone who is in a conflict wants to resolve the conflict. Granted, some people get satisfaction simply from *being* in conflict. But most people—or so goes the theory (and I subscribe to it)—would really prefer to resolve the conflict and turn their energies to other matters.

This means that the secretary who wants—*really* wants—a raise may happily accept a smaller raise than she originally sought, especially if you can find some way to help her realize most if not all of her other interests.

It also means that the bank may be amenable to a pay-back arrangement that deviates from the ostensibly sacrosanct terms of your note. In other words, if you cannot make the payments as scheduled, maybe you can talk the banker into changing the schedule or making some other adjustment.

Mini-max is an approach to achieving trade-offs that adversaries will find acceptable. Maybe none of the adversaries will get *all* that they want, but all of the adversaries should get *enough* of what they want to let them walk away from the negotiations feeling satisfied.

Negotiators who employ mini-max do not begin negotiating until they have resolved four questions:

1. What is the minimum that I can accept?
2. What is the maximum I can ask for without getting laughed out of the room?
3. What is the maximum I can give away?
4. What is the least I can offer without getting laughed out of the room?

☐   In the interest of putting these questions into perspective, let's return to the situation of the secretary who wants a raise. For the purposes of this illustration, I shall play the secretary and you the boss.

☐   I definitely want a raise—*not* merely the opportunity to make more money, but an out-and-out, more-money-for-the-same-amount-of-work raise. I am resolved that if I do not get a raise I will quit.

☐   Before I approach you about the raise, I should ask myself the four mini-max questions:

## 1. What is the minimum that I can accept?

☐   In other words, I must make a distinction between what I *would like* and what I *require*.

☐  This leads to a concept that is an indispensable element in negotiations, a concept that is the very foundation of the mini-max strategy: the concept of BATANA, or *Best Alternative To A Negotiated Agreement*.

☐  It's all good and well to talk about why I *should* have a raise, but what will happen if I can't persuade you to give me one?

☐  If you flatly refuse me, and I remain on the job, I will have considerably less leverage with you than I now have. On the other hand, if you refuse the raise and I quit, what are my prospects of improving my situation in another job?

☐  Will it be easy for me to find another job that pays more money? An equally desirable job? Will I perhaps have to add an hour of commuting time to my schedule? Will I have to start at the bottom of a new totem pole rather than enjoying my present position in the middle of your totem pole?

☐  After considering my alternatives, I will decide that I would be better off staying where I am, even without a raise. If that's the case, I shouldn't attempt to negotiate. My best option is— remember Chapter 11—unconditional surrender; more precisely, I should count my blessings and not make a pest of myself.

☐  This doesn't mean that I cannot improve my situation. I can let you know that I feel I am not making as much financial progress as I would like. I can ask your advice about how I might make myself more valuable to you and, in the process, merit more money.

☐  But this approach does not entail negotiation. It involves a request, not a demand. You are free to grant or deny my request. I have no leverage in our discussion.

☐  This situation is not necessarily intolerable. If you are a reasonable employer, you probably will appreciate my desire to better my lot in life, and you probably will be pleased that I approached you as I did. Unless you are a conscienceless scoundrel who wishes only to exploit me, you will answer my question by telling me how I might make myself more valuable to you, and you will reward me once I have demonstrated my additional value. Once again, however, this approach does not entail negotiation—the process has more in common with prayer.

Conversely, I may find, on considering my alternatives, that I have much more going for me than I realized. I may find that people who perform the same work that I do earn 30 or 40 percent more and enjoy perquisites at least as good and in some cases better. I may also find that there are quite a few jobs of this kind that entail even less of a commute than my present job and offer a variety of additional conveniences or other advantages.

☐ On investigating the market for my skills, I may conclude that I have been wasting my time working for you. Indeed, I may decide that instead of asking you for a raise I should simply seek a job somewhere else.

☐ If I don't make that decision, it is still advantageous for me to know that I have the option of working elsewhere. Indeed, it changes the game completely. I am ready now not merely to *ask* for a raise but to *demand* one.

☐ If I want to be a wise guy (a posture that usually is ill-advised), I can saunter into your office and say, "Look, pal, the people down the street have offered me $X as opposed to your $.75X. As an act of kindness, I'm giving you an opportunity to top their offer."

☐ Or, if I want to be tactful, I can approach you thus: "Boss, I've really enjoyed working with you over the years, and I've learned a lot from you, and I like you very much, and I really don't want to leave. But some opportunities have arisen, and rather than simply deciding to take advantage of them without consulting you, I thought we might talk about how I could achieve the same benefits here."

☐ However I express it, the fact remains that I'm dealing from strength, and there is now quite a bit of room for negotiation. I am not a supplicant; I am someone with a much-desired service (my work) to offer to the highest bidder.

☐ Please note the *essential* difference between the two situations that I have described: *power*. In the first situation, I am at your mercy, and there is nothing to negotiate. In the latter situation, I have considerable strength—all growing out of the fact that I have a highly desirable *alternative* to a negotiated settlement.

☐ (There is, of course, yet a third situation, in which you

would be at my mercy because I am indispensable—or nearly indispensable—and you will do whatever you must to accommodate me. In this situation, as in the one first described, there is nothing to negotiate; I can simply tell you what I want, and you'll have no choice but to accommodate me.)

☐ Very well, I have determined my BATANA (*Best Alternative To A Negotiated Agreement*), and that gives me a basis for determining my *minimum acceptable settlement*. By definition, my *minimum* is the smallest offer that I will accept—no matter what the circumstances.

☐ Let us say that I now earn $X per hour. Let us say that I know I can find work elsewhere for $1.5X per hour. Given the desirability of remaining in my present job (with all its conveniences, comforts, et cetera), I am willing to accept less here than elsewhere—let's say $1.4X an hour.

☐ Okay, that is the *minimum* figure that will be in my mind as negotiations get under way.

☐ It is *not* the amount of money for which I will ask. It is *not* the amount of money I *would like*. It is *not* the amount money I think I *deserve*. It is the *minimum I will accept*.

☐ In other words, if the negotiations end with your offering me 1.39X an hour, I will walk away.

☐ Is it facetious to contrast $1.39X to $1.4X? No. Then how a bout to contrast $1.39999999999X to 1.4X? No again. The *minimum,* under the mini-max strategy of negotiating, must be *exactly that*. It is the demand *below which you refuse to deal*.

☐ Therefore, before entering the negotiations, determine your minimum—your *absolute* minimum—and be prepared to walk out if you do not get it.

☐ What if you are not prepared to walk out? Then mini-max is not for you. If you do not actually *have* a minimum, you have no basis for negotiating. You may bluster, and you may beg, and you may even get everything you've asked for, but your success will not depend on your negotiating skills, for, if you are not prepared to walk out, you are not negotiating, you are merely bluffing or praying.

## 2. What is the maximum that I can ask for without getting laughed out of the room?

☐   How much do I want? Well, ideally, of course, I'd like to be paid as well as the chairman of General Motors—$1+ million a year including bonuses, plus perquisites galore. Realistically, however, I must admit that this is beyond reach. You, my boss, do not earn even a fraction of this remuneration.

☐   Okay, I'd *like* $1+ mil a year. I'd like the *sky,* if you'd give it to me. But if I asked for the sky, you'd look at me as if I were crazy, and then you'd probably tell me that we didn't really have very much to talk about. Then you'd hire someone else.

☐   How, then, do I find a realistic point somewhere between my acceptable minimum and the sky? In other words, if my present hourly rate is $X, could I ask for $10X? Probably not. $4X? Again, probably not. Then how much? What is the highest figure that I could ask for without seeming ridiculous?

☐   Usually, of course, it is very difficult to ask for a significantly higher figure without in some way changing the parameters of what is being negotiated. In other words, if I am now working as an eight-hour-per-day secretary at $X per hour, it is extremely unlikely that I will persuade you to pay me $2X for doing *exactly the same work that I am doing now.*

☐   Probably the best that I can hope for is a percentual increase based on the rate of inflation, perhaps coupled with a bit more money that represents my gain in efficiency since I have been on the job. Also, if the work I am doing is fairly complicated, I might garner leverage from whatever it might cost you to replace me should I quit.

☐   Let's put some numbers on these justifications for a raise.

☐   Rate of inflation? For easy calculation, let us say that it is 10 percent. Gain in productivity? Let's say that I am doing 20 percent more work per hour now than I was a year ago. That's $X plus $.1X plus $.2X, or $1.3X.

☐   Your cost to replace me? Let's say that you could hire a trainee at $.75X to produce half my current output. Let's also say that it would take that trainee three years to reach my present level of productivity; therefore, you would be losing $.5X per hour at the start of the trainee's period of employment, but you eventually would be ahead of the game if you raised the trainee's pay by 10 percent per year ($.75X+$.075X=$.82X+$.082X=$.92X versus my $X).

☐ To avoid wandering into the deep waters of higher mathematics, let's simply say that it would cost you another $.2X per hour for the first year, what with the trainee's lower productivity and the amount of your time that would be necessary to train him or her, versus my already knowing the job and performing it well.

☐ Okay, $X (my present hourly rate) plus $.1X (one year's inflation at 10 percent) plus $.2X (my gain in productivity) plus $.2X (the replacement factor) equals $1.5X. I could make a good case that this is what my salary should be.

☐ Please note that this amounts to a 50 percent raise. Perhaps, to leave some room for haggling, we might add another 10 percent, giving us a total of $1.65X.

☐ That's quite a bit more money for the same work, but we are, after all, looking for a *maximum*. All other things being equal—more specifically, my duties going unchanged under the new order of things—I may decide that this is the *most* I can ask for without getting laughed out of the room.

### 3. What is the maximum I can give away?

☐ Very rarely do negotiations revolve around a situation in which one party will get more for doing exactly the same as before. Usually there is a change of some sort on each side, or else there is very little to negotiate.

☐ I've seized on the situation of a secretary seeking a salary increase because its simplicity is most conducive to my making the points I want to make. More often, however, mini-max negotiators will be involved with a myriad of issues.

☐ For example, a food processor may be negotiating the purchase of certain stainless steel tanks. The manufacturer of the tanks may have established a certain price, and the food processor may have been unable to obtain more than a nominal discount. However, by changing the specifications of the desired tanks, the food processor might lower the price considerably. Likewise, by paying cash instead of insisting on supplier-provided financing, the food processor may obtain concessions.

☐ The operative question here is, how much can the food processor afford to give away? If the ideal quality of the tanks is X, can the processor accept X minus 5? X minus 6? X minus 10?

☐ Once a maximum giveaway has been established regarding quality, what other areas are there in which accommodation may be possible? Will the supplier of tanks make concessions in price in return for prompt payment of cash? For delayed delivery of the merchandise? For the buyer's willingness to endorse the product in advertising?

☐ Obviously, the greater the number of elements in any negotiation, the greater the leeway of the negotiators to wheel and deal. However, in even the simplest negotiations, there is usually some opportunity to make adjustments.

☐ Returning to the example in which I am a secretary seeking a raise, what, if anything, can I offer to make you, my boss, willing to pay me more money?

☐ Have I been inflexible about overtime? Perhaps I can, in the language of poker players, "sweeten the pot" by promising that, if I get the raise, I will work as many as three hours of overtime in any given day, so long as I am given compensatory time during the same month.

☐ Am I aware of some situation in the office in which I can make an unsolicited contribution? For example, do I have an idea about how to reorganize the mail room in a way that will save the company quite a bit of money? Then perhaps I can use the promise of doing this as a bargaining chip in our negotiations.

☐ Whatever the case, the operative question is, *what do I have that I can give you*? The next question is, *what is the maximum that I can (or am willing) to give in return for what I want?*

### 4. What is the least I can offer without getting laughed out of the room?

☐   Once again, the probability is that I will be asked for something in return for my being given something—especially if I seek a raise of more than the approximately 50 percent that can be explained away by inflation, productivity, and the nuisance-cost of your hiring my replacement.

☐   Very well, what will you ask? And what am I prepared to give?

Do you want me to take on additional responsibilities? Allright, what is the smallest number of new responsibilities that I will accept for the amount of money that is involved? What is the least I can accept and still give you (or appear to give you) your money's worth?

None of the above is to say that negotiators should strive to get the most in return for giving the least. While many negotiators do, I think it's a bad idea—for reasons I'll discuss later. My only point here is that you should *know,* going into negotiations, what you are *willing* to give, what you are *able* to give (albeit reluctantly), what benefits you realistically can *expect,* and what benefits you ultimately will *accept* (albeit reluctantly).

When all of this has been worked out, you are ready to enter negotiations, asking for something *reasonable* and having a *realistic* possibility of getting it.

In the next chapter, I will discuss ways to determine your opponent's minimum and to structure your offer in a way that your opponent will find most appealing. Meanwhile, let's turn to the second of the hypothetical examples that I introduced at the beginning of this chapter, involving an unsecured loan that is overdue at a bank.

At first thought, it may seem that there is nothing to negotiate. Bankers would certainly like you to think that there is nothing to negotiate, and they print all sorts of fancy forms that are designed to intimidate you into believing that your contract is nonnegotiable.

But wait! What would happen if you simply did not have the

money to pay? Obviously, the bank would lose the unpaid balance of your note, plus whatever it spent attempting unsuccessfully to collect. Also, the bank would "lose" whatever you might have paid in interest if you had not stopped making payments.

Your banker realizes that these possibilities exist. You should also realize that they exist—and you should realize that your banker realizes it. The truth of the matter is that if your bank antagonizes you to a point where you simply refuse to pay, the bank will have taken what was *your* problem (paying off the loan) and made it *its own* problem (collecting the money).

This brings us back to BATANA, or *Best Alternative To A Negotiated Agreement*. We spoke earlier of *your* BATANA, but what of your opponent's? What is the *bank's* best alternative if you cannot (or simply refuse to) pay?

Well, the bank could sue you for the money. Given that there is no dispute about the legitimacy of the debt, the bank almost certainly would "win" the suit—that is, obtain a judgment allowing the attachment of your assets to satisfy your indebtedness.

But what would the bank have to do to obtain such a judgment?

The bank would have to pay lawyers to go to court. Some institutions would like you to think that this is no big deal. They would like you to think that they have a staff of lawyers sitting around with nothing better to do than chase after troublesome customers. The truth is, of course, that all lawyers cost money—even if they are on staff rather than retained as out-of-house counsel. Therefore, the bank cannot attempt to collect its money without spending some additional money.

It is also true, of course, that the bank, if it prevails in court, could obtain as part of the judgment reimbursement for its costs in suing you. Under certain circumstances, the bank might even obtain additional—or "punitive"—reimbursement.

If you are wealthy, this could be a frightening prospect. But suppose you have no money. Suppose you are on the brink of insolvency and possess no real estate or other property that could be attached by the bank in an attempt to obtain reimbursement.

Under such circumstances, the *bank* may very well be at *your* mercy.

Indeed, a friend of mine was in approximately these circumstances when he decided to take a stand against a bank that was dunning him for payment:

☐ My friend had a vast collection of credit cards—five separate ones from one bank, three from another bank, two from yet another, and one apiece from about five other banks. He had accumulated the collection over two decades, always remitting promptly whatever his minimum monthly payment might be. As a result, his name appeared on computer-generated lists of "good" credit prospects, and banks fell over each other in their rush to add him to their lists of people who pay circa 20 percent annually for the use of money which the bank obtains from depositors at an interest rate of less than one third that amount.

☐ Everything went swimmingly until my friend suffered some business reverses. For a while, he was able to continue making payments by drawing "cash advances" on the very same credit cards. Then, as his fortunes continued to decline, he found that he had exhausted his credit limits and could pay from ordinary income only a fraction of the amounts that were due.

☐ When he missed several payments in succession at one of the banks, the bank revoked his cards. He then stopped paying that bank entirely, reasoning that he would be wiser to use his limited funds to nourish the relationships with the banks that had not revoked his cards.

☐ The neglected bank then began to dun him. Collectors telephoned him, both at home and at work, demanding payment. Initially he attempted to negotiate an expansion of his credit limits, but he quickly learned that the collectors did not have the authority to negotiate. Moreover, the collectors would not transfer him to an officer who did have the authority to negotiate. They stated flatly—presumably under orders from a superior—that any question of expanding his credit limits would have to wait until he had brought his accounts up to date.

☐ Angered at what he regarded as cavalier treatment, my friend stopped accepting the collectors' telephone calls. He then wrote a letter to the chief executive officer of the bank, complaining of the way he was being dunned. He accused the collectors (whether rightly or wrongly, we shall not address here) of being discourteous, abusive, and unwilling to listen to reason. He also threatened to sue the bank for violating the federal Fair Credit Practices Reporting Act. And he said he would not even consider repayment until he had established a relationship with an officer of the bank who had the authority to negotiate a settlement of these accounts.

☐ In an act demonstrative of both his panache and his understanding of how corporate structures operate, he concluded his letter: "I will accept no further communications from anyone within your organization below the rank of vice president."

☐ He soon was contacted by an assistant vice president. He refused to speak to that junior officer. A few days later, he was telephoned by a full vice president.

☐ My friend said, in effect: "When I tried to be a nice guy, you people treated me as a mendicant. I attempted to make my payments, and you cut off my credit, and you even had the effrontery to order the flunkies in your collection department to harass me in the evening at my home. Now you've put me in a position where I'd just as soon go bankrupt as continue to take the kind of pressure you've been giving me. Do you want to go to court? Fine, go ahead. The first time you or any of my other banks sues me, I'll file for bankruptcy. Then all of you can stand in line with your hats in your hands, and you'll get nothing, because there's nothing there other than what's already spoken for by first and second mortgages and other secured loans. Meanwhile, if you really *do* want to get some money back, you're going to have to make some attempt to treat me like a human being and take into account the reversal of my fortunes. You want your money? Okay, you'll have to reopen my accounts—enlarge the credit limit, reduce the monthly payments. It's either that or no deal."

☐ In effect, my friend was telling the vice president that accommodating him would be better than the bank's own BATANA (*Best Alternative To A Negotiated Agreement*). If the bank did not accommodate him, they would have to go to court. The bank might obtain a judgment, but it would be costly (in terms of legal fees, among other expenses) and there was little likelihood of collecting any money.

□ The vice president at first blustered and lectured and threatened and in other ways generally made himself unpleasant. My friend stuck to his guns. In the process, he got specific about what the bank would have to do if it was to collect any money. He said he would not pay penny one unless the bank immediately suspended interest charges on his payments. (He did not pull this idea out of thin air; he had learned, via an article in a magazine, that banks sometimes suspend interest charges for customers who are having difficulty paying.) He also demanded that the bank not report him to credit bureaus as delinquent. And he insisted that there be no additional dunning phone calls, whether during business hours or in the evening.

□ The vice president pretended to be appalled, but he did not terminate the conversation. Soon he allowed as how he might be willing to make some adjustments if my friend made a sincere attempt to pay. Eventually he acceded to all of my friend's conditions. All that was left to negotiate was the amount by which my friend would reduce his principal each month.

□ The two men settled on a sum that averaged out to roughly three quarters of my friend's previous monthly payments. The crucial difference, of course, was that the full payment now would be credited against principal rather than mostly against interest.

My friend won, I suggest, because he fully understood—if only instinctively—the principles of mini-max. Let's review their application to this case before we move on:

## 1. What is the minimum I can accept?

My friend was seeking concessions. That is, he did not really want to fall back on his BATANA and declare himself bankrupt, but neither was he *able* to surrender unconditionally and bring his payment schedule up to date, for he simply did not have the money. What he wanted—nay, *needed*—was some sort of relaxation of the demands on him.

In a sense, the *minimum* that he could *accept* was tied to the *maximum* that he could *give away*. He had to persuade the bank to reduce his schedule of payments to a bearable amount—the amount equal to the *maximum* that he could pay.

Of course, he would *seek* a great deal more than this. But this was his minimum.

### 2. What is the maximum I can ask for without getting laughed out of the room?

Given a magic wand, my friend could have found no end of desiderata to seek. He could seek outright forgiveness of his debt. He could also seek an apology from the bank's chief executive officer for the way his case had been handled, plus reprimands for the collectors who irritated him, and perhaps a luncheon invitation to the private dining room that is reserved for the bank's senior executives.

Realistically, however, he could ask for none of these things without being dismissed as a crackpot. Indeed, had he even voiced such wishes, the vice president might very well conclude that this was a person with whom it would be impossible to negotiate and that the case therefore should be turned over to lawyers for collection.

Accordingly, my friend asked for quite a bit—but nothing that was *unrealistic*. Initially he asked that the bank enlarge his credit limit and reduce his monthly payments. When he was turned down, he took a fall-back position, demanding suspension of interest, no unfavorable credit report, and termination of dunning phone calls.

The important demand, of course, was suspension of interest. Indeed, the other two might just have been thrown in as pseudo-issues from which he could retreat in a trade-off for concessions on the suspension of interest.

Connected with suspension of interest was the schedule of repayment of principal. For instance, if my friend had volunteered to repay the full principal immediately, there would be no conflict—for this would amount to surrender. Conversely, if my friend refused to pay more than one penny per month, there would have been no possibility that the bank would accede. He would have to pay an amount that would seem *reasonable* to the bank, an amount that would bring the matter to an end as soon as was reasonably possible.

As things worked out in the negotiations, the vice president linked this issue to the suspension of interest charges. He did not say to my friend, "Okay, we'll suspend your interest charges. By the way, how soon do you think you'll be able to start paying off the principal?" Rather, he said, in effect, "Well, if we do agree to suspend your interest charges, do you think you'll be able to make payments of $X per month against the principal?" (There'll be a lot more discussion of linking issues in a future chapter.)

What my friend did, in sum, was seize on every *reasonable* demand he could make, then bargain against the vice president's counterdemands.

### 3. What is the maximum I can give away?

As I noted earlier, this was tied to the minimum that my friend could accept: It was dictated by his resources. In other words, his maximum giveaway was whatever he could pay at the time.

Of course, the figure was not absolute: If the success of the negotiations hinged on an additional $10 a month, he probably could have found room in his budget to accommodate the bank, whether by delaying payments to other creditors or by foregoing lunch one day a week or by suffering some other abstinence.

But there was, objectively speaking, a figure above which he could not go. The figure was somewhere below his existing aggregate of monthly payments; else he would not have stopped making those payments. And it presumably was no lower than the figure on which he finally settled—three quarters of those payments.

### 4. What is the least I can offer without getting laughed out of the room?

This, of course, relates to the schedule of repayment. Let us say that the bank's original schedule called for monthly payments on the loan amounting to 5 percent of the outstanding balance, with 1.9 percent applied as interest (a common figure in transactions of this kind) and the remaining 3.1 percent applied to the principal.

If the bank were willing to forgo the interest, payments of 3.1 percent of the outstanding balance would retire the loan on schedule. However, the bank might feel it was entitled to an accelerated retirement in exchange for its willingness to forego the interest.

If I were negotiating this transaction, I would start rather low—let's say with an offer of 2 percent. This would be 40 percent of the original payment, and it would amount to one tenth of a percentage point above the level of interest.

The bank presumably would dismiss this as wholly unacceptable. Then I would offer to sweeten the pot in exchange for concessions on other points. ("Do I have your assurance that there will be no unfavorable credit report? Do you promise me that there will be no dunning phone calls? Very well, what do you think would be a realistic figure instead of my 2 percent?")

As things worked out, my friend and the vice president settled on payments of about three quarters of the previous monthly payments—that is, three quarters of 5 percent, or .375 percent, some .65 percent more than the original schedule called for as payment against principal—all in all, not a bad deal.

Let me state emphatically that two of the four mini-max questions must be answered independently of what your estimate may be of the other side's strengths in a negotiation: *What is the minimum I can accept, and what is the maximum I can give away?*

The issue here is *not* what you think the other side would tolerate but rather what *you yourself* can tolerate. Your levels of tolerance exist wholly independently of your adversary's situation.

Conversely, the other two questions—regarding what you can offer and what you can ask for without getting laughed out of the room—relate to your adversary's circumstances. In the next chapter, we'll discuss ways that you can assess his or her position and determine how he or she answers mini-max's crucial four questions.

# ≣13≣DETERMINING YOUR OPPONENT'S MINI-MAX

Allright, you've determined the minimum you can accept and the maximum you can give away. What is your adversary's situation? How can you assess his or her minimum and maximum—which, of course, may be quite different from what your adversary *says* they are?

Rule one is:

**Never assume that the other guy will be reasonable (that is, will do what you would under the same circumstances).**

A minimum or maximum need not make sense to anyone except the person who subscribes to it.

For example, a convict was holding hostages at a prison in the Northeast. He had articulated a number of demands, among which was that the governor of the state come personally to the prison to negotiate with him.

The warden wisely called in a colleague of mine, a professional negotiator. I say "wisely" not only because professionals are likely to possess skills that nonprofessionals do not but also because the convict probably would mistrust the warden himself or other officials of the prison. If they attempted to negotiate, the convict might become irritated and vent his anger on the hostages.

My colleague first contacted the governor's office. He did this only in part because he felt that the governor should be informed of the situation. (Aware of the facts, the governor might establish guidelines for the negotiations or might even choose to go to the prison as a way of ensuring the hostages' safety.) A second reason that my colleague contacted the governor's office was so that he could truthfully say to the convict that he was acting for the governor.

Having discussed the situation with an aide of the governor, my colleague now went to the section of the prison where the hostages were being held. The convict had taken command of a cell block, the entrance to which was barred. The negotiator stood outside the bars and called to the convict, who presumably was nearby but could not be seen. The convict refused to let the negotiator inside the cell block, saying that he would speak only to the governor. The negotiator replied that he might be able to arrange that but had to speak to the convict first. The convict insisted that no one but the governor himself would enter the cell block.

It might seem, on the basis of what I've described thus far, that the convict's absolute minimum was an appearance by the governor. That certainly was what he *said* was his minimum. But people often bluff about a minimum or can be persuaded that a sincerely stated minimum is unrealistic and should be changed.

Over the next several hours, calling through the bars, my colleague tried to learn what the convict *really* wanted. He used the convict's insistence on a visit by the governor as a device to continue the dialogue. The negotiator said that the governor's office had been informed of the convict's demands and wanted some additional information so that the governor, should he agree to come to the prison, would be prepared to deal expeditiously with the situation.

The convict resisted at first, then began providing information about his grievances. One of the grievances, my colleague eventually learned, had to do with butterflies. The convict complained that he was besieged by butterflies—so many of them that he was having a hard time concentrating on the discussion.

My colleague realized quickly that the convict was hallucinating. There was no way for butterflies to get into the cell block, and, in any event, there were no butterflies in there at that time of year.

My colleague asked if the convict would agree to release some of the hostages in exchange for the prison's erecting a net that would keep butterflies out of the cell block. The convict said that he would consider releasing the hostages after the net was erected. Sure enough, when a net was placed over the entrance to the cell block, the convict released several hostages. He also permitted my colleague to enter the cell block and begin discussions that led ultimately to the release—unharmed—of the remaining hostages.

In sum, the convict's *real* minimum at this stage of the negotiations was *not,* as he stated, a visit by the governor; it was the relief—or the promise of relief—from his hallucinations.

I repeat rule one: *Never assume that the other guy will be reasonable.*

Of course, the convict was literally *un*reasonable, the victim of a psychiatric condition. However, many people who are certifiably sane will behave during negotiations in ways that their adversaries will regard as "unreasonable"—that is, in ways contrary to the ways the adversaries themselves would behave.

Have you ever known or heard of a father whose family suffered because he gambled away his paycheck? Or because he drank it away?

Have you ever known or heard of someone who walked out on a very good job—and, in effect, threw away a whole career—because a boss or some colleague made a thoughtless remark?

Have you ever known or heard of someone who risked financial loss, bodily injury, or even death simply to prove that he was not afraid of something?

To most of us, such behavior is unreasonable. Yet people behave that way all the time. Your adversaries in a negotiation may be among those people.

That leads us to closely allied rule two:

**Do not assume that your adversary's values are the same as what yours would be if you were in his or her position.**

This may seem rather obvious, and yet, in the course of negotiating, I often encounter adversaries who—to their detriment—assume that their values and mine (or the values of their clients and my clients) are identical.

One of my favorite illustrations of this point involves a concept that is expressed by the Chinese words, *mein tzu,* which translate roughly as "loss of face." A long-standing tradition in China and among many Chinese immigrants places "loss of face" (that is, shame, embarrassment, ridicule) very high on the list of personal tragedies. To be perceived as dishonorable, to be caught cheating or bluffing, to be revealed publicly as a fool—these are phenomena to be avoided at all costs. Indeed, many Chinese have seized upon suicide as the only honorable escape from a situation in which the sole alternative seemed to be *mein tzu.*

The concept of *mein tzu,* I hasten to add, is not restricted to the Chinese. "Death before dishonor" is a saying of Anglo-Saxon origin, and the Italians have their *delitto del onore,* or "crime of honor." Until fairly recently in Italy, there was a maximum—I repeat, *maximum*—prison sentence of seven years for a husband convicted of killing a wife who had been caught committing adultery.

Indeed, most civilizations—possibly *all* civilizations—have had a concept of personal honor that was, if not inviolable, certainly very important. At the same time, honor—or prestige, or "face," or whatever we choose to call it—means different things to different people, and sometimes what is dishonorable to one person is a badge of achievement to another.

For example, many of us believe that it is morally impermissible to take advantage of another person's weakness. Those of us who share this value probably would be appalled by some fast-talking hustler who obtains thousands of dollars each week selling bogus insurance policies to illiterate indigents.

Conversely, certain people admire the ability to recognize and exploit a victim. To people of this persuasion, the seller of bogus insurance policies is worthy of admiration. Just as one man's meat is another's poison, one man's scandal is another's scam.

Very well, picture a situation in which two men have been arrested for working as a team selling bogus insurance policies to illiterate indigents. Man 1 is a member of a social group that condemns the exploitation of another person's weakness, and Man 2 is a member of a social group that admires such "shrewdness."

How would these men react if you caught them in flagrante delicto and threatened to expose them? Man 1, I suggest, would do virtually anything to "get off the hook" and spare himself the shame of his arrest, whereas Man 2 would at worst have mixed emotions—discomfort about having been caught, but pride about being revealed as a participant in this clever scheme.

All of this brings me back to my earlier-promised illustration of adversaries in negotiations who assumed—to their detriment— that their values and mine (or the values of their clients and my clients) coincided.

☐   I represented a company whose president had made disparaging personal remarks about the president of a labor union. Journalists had been present and reprinted the remarks, and the president of the union was enraged. Accordingly, the union's negotiator held out as a "nonnegotiable demand" that the president of the company make a public apology.

☐   Now, the truth was that the president of the company realized that he had spoken injudiciously and was fully prepared to make a public apology. However, the union's president and/or negotiator apparently regarded a public apology as shameful and believed the president of the company would resist making one.

☐   If the union had not made a big deal of the apology, but rather had requested one *en passant* after the major issues of the negotiations had been settled, the union probably would have fared much better in the negotiations. However, by identifying the matter as important—more specifically, a "nonnegotiable demand"—the union's negotiator gave me ammunition that I otherwise would not have. Every time the issue arose, I was able to say, "Look, I'll do what I can for you on this—I realize how important it is to your president—but I can't guarantee anything. Meanwhile, if you want me to go to bat for you on this issue, you'll have to cooperate with me on others."

☐   And I also was able to say, "If I can get him to apologize, will you go along with me on Issues X and Y?"

☐   I extracted quite a few concessions for the company simply because the union's president had put his negotiator in a position where the negotiator *had* to extract from me a concession about which my client could hardly care less!

☐   Let me repeat: The union's president weakened his negotiator's position immeasurably because, in my opinion, the union's president looked on a public apology as a great indignity—one that he wanted to inflict on the company's president in punishment for the latter's injudicious remarks. The company's president, meanwhile did not share this value; to him, a public apology was not an indignity, not a source of shame, but rather a reasonable response in circumstances where one has made an error of this sort.

☐   In effect, the attitude of the company's president permitted me to pay in a coin that was absolutely worthless to my client for concessions that were worth a great deal. The recipient of this payment regained "face," but at an extravagant cost in wages and benefits for the workers whose well-being supposedly was paramount to him.

One other illustration of differences in values:

☐   I once represented a university that wanted to strengthen its English department. The dean decided to create three visiting professorships that would be filled by internationally reputed writers.

☐   The dean developed a list of several dozen writers whom he deemed most desirable and sent each a letter inviting him to apply for one of the professorships. In attempting to make the positions extremely appealing, the dean offered a substantial stipend, a generous benefits package, and an assortment of other inducements, ranging from complimentary membership in the faculty club to the services of three—yes, not one, not two, but three—teaching assistants.

☐  A month after the dean's letter had been posted, only a handful of the writers had applied for a visiting professorship. Interestingly, these were the people at the very bottom of the dean's list of desirable prospects. The more highly desired writers either had declined or had not even bothered to reply.

☐  The dean now obtained permission to increase the attractiveness of the visiting professorships. The stipend was raised, the benefits package fattened, the other perquisites augmented. Another letter went out seeking applications, and once again the most ardently desired writers either declined or did not respond.

☐  That's when I was asked to take a look at the situation. I telephoned several of the writers who had not responded and immediately learned why. The writers were offended that they would have to *apply* for a position and might, after expressing their interest, be rejected.

☐  Complained one: "Who does your dean think he is to ask a man of my experience to beg for a job?"

☐  Groused another: "I don't apply to universities; universities apply to me."

☐  To the dean, of course, the word "apply" did not have a negative connotation. In academia, positions are routinely filled by search committees that invite "candidates" to "apply." To have been "accepted" even as a "candidate" is considered something of an honor, for many other invitees were turned away and many other people were never invited in the first place.

☐  To the writers, however, the word, "apply," was like a red flag waved in front of a bull. The connotation was that the writer was being put on trial and might very well be judged inadequate. The irony of being "invited" to be deemed "unworthy" was not lost on these wordsmiths, most of whom refused to play the game.

☐   At my suggestion, the dean discarded the idea of seeking applications and instead chose the three writers that he most wanted on his faculty. He invited them to *accept* guest professorships. One of them did; two others graciously declined because of conflicting commitments. The dean then invited two others. Eventually the three guest professorships were filled with writers from the upper portion of the original list—but this would not have happened if the dean had not been able to see the difference between the writers' values ("apply" is a dirty word) and his own.

☐   In effect, when the dean initially issued his "invitations" to prospective "applicants," he misjudged the writers' mini-max positions. He thought that the writers would be most interested in the size of their salaries and benefits packages and an abundance of perquisites. In fact, the writers were *most* interested in *avoiding* what they perceived as an indignity: being asked to risk rejection.

How can a negotiator determine what are an adversary's hot buttons and avoid pressing them? How can a negotiator learn what *really* is important to the adversary?

That brings us to rule three:

**Do research.**

This may seem so basic that it need not be stated. Yet I frequently encounter adversaries who have no idea of how my clients have responded in similar situations in the past, and I frequently encounter clients who have no idea of how adversaries have responded.

Does the lender who is hounding you for a past-due payment have a history of taking debtors to court?

How did the boss from whom you requested a raise react when other employees requested one?

How did the zoning commission vote the last time someone sought a variance similar to the one that you now seek?

How have courts ruled in cases that involve controversies similar to the one in which you now find yourself?

What kind of deal did the used-car dealer offer your friend who traded in a model in the same condition as the one that you now want to trade?

The more information that you have, the better equipped you'll be to determine your adversary's mini-max positions. If, for example, you know that the used-car dealer last week offered a trade-in of $X for a car identical to your own, you can be fairly confident that the dealer will be amenable today—no matter what he may say to the contrary—to a similar price for your car.

Much information of the sort you seek may be obtained simply by questioning other people who have been in your circumstances. Still other information is a matter of public record—for example, the rulings of courts or other governmental bodies.

If you do not explore the available information *before* you enter negotiations, you obviously will be unnecessarily handicapped while negotiating.

Rule four:

## Ask questions of your adversary.

I never cease to be amazed at people who attempt to negotiate simply by stating their positions and never inquiring into an opponent's desiderata. Actually, one of the very best sources of information about what will satisfy your adversary is your adversary him- or herself.

Does your adversary insist on speaking personally to the governor? *Why* does he insist on speaking personally to the governor? ("Look, if you really insist on this, I may be able to get it for you, but, before I do, let me tell you, the governor isn't involved personally in any of the policies of the Bureau of Prisons. All the rules and regulations come from the Superintendent of Prisons. So, if your main concerns are the food in the mess hall and the way the warden is now screening your mail, the guy to talk to is the Superintendent of Prisons, *not* the governor. . . .")

Does the president of the union want a public apology from the president of the company? *Why* does he want a public apology? Will he settle for a private apology? What is he willing to trade for an apology? ("I can understand that your guy feels my guy should apologize, but let's face it, both of our guys have very strong egos. If I go to my guy and tell him there's no way we can make a deal without his apologizing, he's liable to say, 'Forget the whole thing, let's shut down the plant.' If the apology is really important to you, give me something I can take to my guy as a trade.")

Do the writers object to *applying* for the visiting professorships? Very well, what arrangement would they prefer? Is there *any* way that the university can attract them as teachers? Given a magic wand, what would they create as the ideal relationship between them and the university?

Does the person who is suing the insurance company claim damages for loss of earnings? How much did she lose? Under what circumstances? How can these losses be traced to the injuries that she claims to have suffered?

Does the secretary who wants a raise feel that he is making a greater contribution to the company now than he was a year ago? What additional contribution is he making? What does he believe is this contribution's worth to the company?

Such questions, I state emphatically, should *not* be cast at an adversary as challenges. They are not rhetorical questions being posed during the course of a debate. ("Brutus claims that he loved Caesar; yet what evidence has he given us of this love?") Rather, they are sincere attempts to determine exactly what it is that your adversary wants and why he feels he is entitled to it.

I cannot be too emphatic about the importance of "why." Only when you have obtained an answer to this question—or, better yet, quite a few answers—will you be able to address your adversary's *interests* rather than his *positions*. By extension, only when you have addressed his interests can you hope to achieve a resolution that satisfies both him and you.

Rule five:

**Use silence.**

One of the most formidable weapons of professional negotiators is silence. Most people hate silence and will attempt to fill it up with information—which is exactly what you want.

Your opponent says, "I cannot guarantee that this price will be available to you after the first of the month."

You remain silent.

Your opponent says, "You do expect to order more of these after the first of the month, don't you?"

You remain silent.

Your opponent says, "Look, the company has got a big price increase planned. If you give me your order now, I'll give you a price that you'll find very attractive. I won't be able to do this after the first of the month."

Of course, seasoned negotiators realize the value of silence and also realize that other seasoned negotiators realize the value of silence. Neither you nor I am likely to go up against a seasoned negotiator and extract a lot of information simply by being silent. (Your opponent says, "Look, if you're just going to sit there and not say anything, stop wasting my time. Come back when you have something to say.")

All the same, newcomers to negotiation often reveal far more than they intended to—and far more than they should have revealed—simply because an opponent created a silence that the newcomer could not resist filling with an extra detail, an extra argument, or an extra attempt at persuasion.

Rule six:

## Mirror back tentative understandings.

Every time your adversary gives you a significant piece of information, verify that you understand it correctly by paraphrasing it and asking him or her to ascertain that your paraphrase is correct.

For example, your adversary might say, "We can't go along with this unless we get payment of one third of the bill by the first of next month and the balance within three months."

Mirror this back to her by saying something to the effect of, "Let me make sure I understand you. You want to be paid one third of the full amount by the first of next month. Then you want the remaining two thirds within three months of the first payment."

The purposes of this mirroring back are several:

You really *do* make sure, by paraphrasing, that you and your adversary are talking about the same thing.

You impress on your adversary's memory the understanding that she just expressed. (People sometimes forget offers they have made unless someone reinforces their memory.)

You invite your adversary to eliminate ambiguities. ("I didn't say I want the remaining two thirds within three months of the first payment; I want it within three months of today.")

In paraphrasing, you may be tempted to distort your adversary's tentative offer. ("You want to be paid one third of the *past-due balance* by the first of next month and the remainder in equal payments over a period of three months, after which we can talk about retiring the principal of the debt.")

You also may be tempted, for rhetorical effect, to mirror back a parody of your adversary's position. ("In other words, you're telling me that you don't care whether I starve, so long as I get you your money within three months.")

Please resist these temptations. You are not—or should not be—mirroring back tentative understandings for rhetorical effect or to con your adversary into accepting something that he had not intended. You are seeking to verify the boundaries of a preliminary agreement, *not* to introduce bases for further disagreement.

Of all the above rules, the most important is to ask questions. Begin with open-ended questions. Then probe with follow-up questions. Keep asking until you learn everything that you want to know—or until your opponent grows weary of answering.

The purpose—don't lose sight of it!—is to determine your opponent's mini-max position. What is the *least* he can accept? What is the *most* he can offer?

# ≣14≣UNPACKING

A̲s I noted in Chapter 5, there is never only one source of conflict: Every dispute has at least two matters in controversy and may have dozens.

For example, the buyer of a photocopying machine may complain that it is "no good." What does she mean? That it breaks down too frequently? Or that when it does break down, however infrequently, service calls are too costly? Or that service calls, whatever their cost, are insufficiently prompt? Or that the machine never breaks down but consistently makes copies of low quality?

Each of these is a separate problem. Only the first and last of them might "reasonably" (to you and me) be regarded as evidence that the machine is "no good." But if the buyer regards the ma-

**229**

chine as "no good," whatever her reason(s), the seller has a problem.

Of course, the seller could—on the theory that the customer has no recourse now that the sale has been made and the machine paid for—refuse even to listen to complaints. In that case, the customer might lick her wounds and create no further problems. The greater likelihood, however, is that a disgruntled customer will tell other people about her bad experience and perhaps persuade some people not to buy *any* of the company's products.

Under extraordinary circumstances, an aggrieved customer might take extreme measures that would be far costlier to the company than any mollifying action. For example, she might sue (costly to the company in legal fees, even if the customer loses), might file a complaint with a governmental agency (also potentially quite costly, even if the company is right), or even perform an act of sabotage, such as dynamiting the company's headquarters.

The seller would be far wiser to seek an amicable resolution of the controversy, even if he believes that the customer is "wrong." And, in terms of the seller's values, the customer may very well be "wrong." That is, the machine may be functioning as well as any competing model in the same price range. It may "require servicing" (the company's way of saying "break down") only because the customer is giving it far heavier use than it was designed to receive. The service calls may be less expensive than those of competing companies and far more prompt.

If the seller "gives in" on any of these points, he is apt to feel cheated and, in any event, will not significantly aid his own cause. On the other hand, if he inquires into the customer's full range of complaints, he may learn that a major part of the problem has nothing to do with what the *buyer* identified as the problem. For example, one telephone operator in the seller's service department may be discourteous; were it not for unpleasant dealings with this one operator, the buyer might be satisfied with both the machine and the manner in which it was being serviced.

The seller may also learn that the buyer has a friend who purchased a similar photocopier from a different company at a lower price and now feels gypped for having paid the higher price for this machine. However the seller might deal with this problem, it has nothing whatever to do with the (allegedly) frequent breakdowns that the buyer uses to justify her claim that the machine is "no good."

And the seller may learn that the buyer has been using her photocopier in a way that it was not designed to be used—for example, by making an extraordinarily large number of two-sided copies, which cause breakdowns because the toner from the "down" side of a two-sided copy transfers to the rollers and clogs the machine.

By "unpacking" the buyer's complaints—that is, by identifying *all* the sources of dissatisfaction and by dealing with them as *separate issues*—the seller may be able to devise an approach that will satisfy the buyer without entailing a significant sacrifice on the seller's part.

For example, the seller might institute changes that ensure that customers making service calls are not treated discourteously by telephone operators (a worthwhile move under any circumstances—the seller should be grateful to the buyer for calling the problem to his attention). If the seller wants to go a few extra steps to satisfy this buyer, he might say, "Not only am I going to get this situation straightened out immediately, but I also want to give you my private telephone number. Should you ever be treated discourteously again by one of my operators, I want you to take his name, then let me know what happened. I assure you that I will see to it personally that you get nothing but the best care from my service department in the future." (All this apparent largess will cost nothing if the seller really does his job and gets the service department on the ball.)

The seller might also point out the features on his machine that are superior to those on the machine that the customer's friend bought at a lower price. ("Your friend may have a good machine for the money, but it can't do a fraction of what your machine can do, and it wouldn't hold up under your volume for more than a day or two at a time.")

And the seller might further persuade the customer to spend a relatively small additional sum for a machine that is far better suited to the customer's need of two-sided copies. ("If you intend to continue doing that kind of photocopying, I can set you up with a machine that'll give you a lot more speed, a higher-quality image, and even such features as automatic collating and stapling. It'll cost you twice as much as your present machine, but it'll cut your operating time in half and your down-time to near zero. I can take your present machine on trade and give you credit for the full purchase price. That means you wouldn't have to come up with a penny in cash; you could keep your present schedule of payments, increasing them just enough to cover the difference in price between the two machines.")

Had the seller not "unpacked" the customer's original complaint that the machine was "no good," the seller would have gained (and learned) nothing and might have made an enemy for life. By determining the full range of complaints and addressing them individually, the seller satisfied the customer, sold a higher-priced machine, and probably cultivated a source of future business.

In every negotiation, I suggest, it is prudent to "unpack" an adversary's grievances—that is, determine *all* the components of a given disagreement and thereby change single-issue conflict into multiple-issue conflict.

Until this has been done, the tendency of adversaries will be to take a do-or-die stand on the single issue. Either you are "wrong," or I am "wrong." Either you will "win," or I will "win." Meanwhile, when multiple issues have been identified, it becomes possible to link movement (that is, concessions) on Issue A with movement on Issues B, C, D, et cetera. And that is what negotiating is all about.

This point is so important that I am going to state it again, in capital letters:

**WHEN MULTIPLE ISSUES HAVE BEEN IDENTIFIED, IT BECOMES POSSIBLE TO LINK MOVEMENT ON ISSUE A WITH MOVEMENT ON ISSUES B, C, D, ET CETERA. AND THAT IS WHAT NEGOTIATING IS ALL ABOUT.**

If you are not yet persuaded of the importance of this point, consider once again that single-issue conflict can only be resolved with a "loss" by one or both parties. In multiple-issue conflict, however, adversaries have an opportunity to *trade concessions* and otherwise assist each other in achieving various aims. Operating under this attitude, negotiators are not combatants but rather collaborators, each trying to help the other get a good deal. Thus they *search for points of agreement* rather than merely exchanging rhetoric about a single point of *disagreement.*

And let me state emphatically that the attitude cannot be a mere pose, a pretense of the desire to accommodate when in truth what you want is to nail your adversary to the wall and take him or her for all you can. If you intend to negotiate effectively—whether on your own behalf or someone else's—you must recognize that you're *not* going to "win" it all, at least not consistently, and when you do "win" everything, it will usually if not always be at prohibitively high cost.

The trick is to *help your adversary get a good deal.* Then everyone goes away content, and there often is an opportunity to continue the relationship to the mutual profit of all parties.

For a better idea of how all of this works, let's look again at the photocopier-related conflict—this time noting what might occur when adversaries take the single-issue approach and when they take the multiple-issue approach.

## SINGLE-ISSUE APPROACH

BUYER: This photocopier you sold me is no good.

SELLER: It's as good as anything on the market. Go drown yourself.

BUYER: If you don't give me my money back, I'll sue.

SELLER: Go ahead and sue. I'll countersue for defamation of character.

At this point, of course, the buyer may merely walk away and never return. In perhaps nine of 10 cases, the worst that will happen to the seller is that there will be one more person on the street spreading bad word-of-mouth. This is, of course, undesirable, as is the fact that the seller will continue to remain ignorant of certain operations of his service department that are antagonizing customers (to wit, the rude telephone operator); however, such problems rarely if ever prove catastrophic. What can and sometimes does prove catastrophic is what happens in that ninth case out of 10, when an adversary decides on a vendetta and files a lawsuit or complains to a governmental agency or takes some action aimed at punishing you for not treating her in a way she finds acceptable.

☐ I know well of one such case involving a bank and a borrower. The borrower was having financial problems and was frequently late with his mortgage payments. If a payment was 15 days late, the bank was authorized by federal law to apply a late charge. If a payment was 30 days late, the bank was authorized to initiate foreclosure proceedings, which called for the borrower to pay the full amount of the mortgage or suffer the sale of the house by the bank.

☐ In practice, the bank never initiated foreclosure proceedings before the loan was 60 days overdue. Usually, even after 60 days, the bank would attempt to avoid foreclosure by working out an agreement under which the borrower would have several months to bring the payments current. Rarely did the bank actually initiate foreclosure proceedings until a payment was 90 days overdue, and even more rarely did the bank actually foreclose on a mortgage and sell the borrower's house. However, whenever a payment was 60 days overdue, the bank did send out a pink slip of paper headlined, "Final Notice—Foreclosure."

☐ The borrower in this story had received perhaps a dozen such notices over the five years that the bank had held the mortgage. The first few times, he telephoned the loan service officer and asked her to understand his problem. She agreed not to initiate foreclosure proceedings if the note was brought current within 30 days.

☐ Then the bank changed loan service officers, and the new

one had a patronizing manner that irritated the borrower. He perceived her as condescending, unfriendly, uncooperative, and even slightly sadistic—as if she took pleasure in his plight. I hasten to add that he may have been "wrong" in perceiving her this way; she may have been the sweetest, most cooperative, most helpful person imaginable: But the borrower *did* perceive her this way, and these perceptions are important to this story.

☐ After a number of exchanges with this loan service officer over payments that the borrower managed to bring current within 30 days, he got a foreclosure notice on the twenty-ninth (rather than the sixtieth) day that his payment was overdue. He telephoned the loan service officer and told her that someone at the bank had made a mistake. She replied that the notice was issued properly and that he had 30 days to bring his payments current. Angry, he telephoned her boss—the vice president in charge of the bank's mortgage division. The boss would not accept the phone call.

☐ Now not merely angry but furious, the borrower wrote a letter of complaint to the bank's chairman. Realizing that he would serve his purposes best by reporting not just one grievance but several, he gave the matter some thought and came up with the following items:

1. The bank was practicing discrimination by serving notice of foreclosure on him sooner than on other borrowers. (He did not have information that his account was being treated differently from the accounts of other borrowers, but this was his conjecture. If his accusation proved erroneous, he could always back off without diminishing his other grievances—discourtesy, inconsiderateness, et cetera.)

2. The bank sought to force him into foreclosure because he had atypically high equity in his house—more than 50 percent, this a result of a very large down payment plus rapid appreciation in the house's market value. If the bank could force him into foreclosure, the bank would quickly recoup its principal, and an attentive officer of the bank or someone connected to an officer of the

bank might purchase the house dirt cheap at the foreclosure sale, then turn around and sell it quickly at a substantial profit. (As with the allegation of discrimination, he really had no information that anything of this sort was going on at the bank, but the scenario was plausible and the borrower could always abandon the allegation without diminishing his other grievances.)

3.   The bank, by issuing foreclosure notices prematurely, was harassing and vexing him, causing him emotional distress, and making it difficult for him to concentrate on his work. Thus if matters were not resolved promptly and to his complete satisfaction, he would sue the bank and the chairman personally for compensatory and punitive damages. (The likelihood that such a lawsuit would be sustained, let alone won, was very slim; yet the chairman was being put on notice that this borrower knew the way to the courthouse and that there might be reprisals if something was not done to mollify him.)

☐   The chairman wisely took action on the letter, instructing a senior vice-president to contact the borrower and attempt to make peace. The senior vice president telephoned, acknowledged that the most recent foreclosure notice had been issued improperly, and apologized—not only for the improper handling of the account but also for the manner in which the borrower had been treated by the loan service officer and the vice president in charge of the mortgage division (who had refused to accept the borrower's telephone call). The senior vice president added that he would instruct the people in the mortgage department to be more careful with the account in the future, and he invited the borrower to telephone him personally if any problems arose.

☐   The borrower went away satisfied, and the whole matter might have been put to rest there. Unfortunately for the bank, some six months later the borrower received another premature foreclosure notice. He promptly telephoned the office of the senior vice president, only to learn that the man no longer worked for the bank. His replacement? The former vice president of the mortgage division, who had refused to take the borrower's call during the first incident.

☐ The borrower did not even attempt to talk to him this time. He placed a call instead to the chairman—who happened to be out of town. The borrower then filed an in-person lawsuit in federal court, alleging everything that he had threatened in his original letter to the chairman.

☐ Had the bank's lawyers thought and acted swiftly, they probably could have settled the matter with a token payment (or perhaps no payment at all), an apology, and the assurance that the borrower would have no further problems. Unfortunately for the bank, the lawyers did not think and act swiftly: They filed an answer denying the allegations and a motion to dismiss the lawsuit.

☐ Meanwhile, the lawsuit caught the attention of an attorney who specializes in "class actions" (legal proceedings in which one plaintiff is designated as the representative of a large group of people who are similarly situated and who will share in any recovery that the original plaintiff may achieve). This lawyer took the borrower's case on contingency and amended the complaint so that the suit became a class action, thereby increasing the bank's exposure many hundredfold. The lawyer then was able, under a legal process called "discovery," to question officers of the bank under oath about matters related to the complaint.

☐ The lawyer was not able to determine that the borrower's account had been handled differently from other accounts or that the bank made special efforts to foreclose on houses in which borrowers had high equity. However, one of the arrows that the borrower had fired indiscriminately into the air did come to rest on the bull's-eye of a very important target: The lawyer learned that the son-in-law of one officer of the bank had made considerable profit by purchasing houses on which the bank had foreclosed, then reselling them.

☐ In short order, the following events occurred:

The bank settled the lawsuit for a sum of more than one million dollars, one third of which was awarded to the lawyer as a contingency fee, the balance of which was divided among the plaintiffs.

Criminal charges were filed against the officer whose son-in-law had purchased the foreclosed properties; under the law, the officer was not entitled to profit from or enable others to profit from whatever information he might have about foreclosed properties. The officer also was forced to resign.

The one-time vice president of the mortgage division, subsequently senior vice president, was fired, as was the loan service officer.

The borrower received enough in the settlement of the lawsuit that he was able to pay off most of his loan.


☐ Thus was a conflict escalated—and eventually resolved at great expense to the bank—when it might easily have been defused if only the people at the bank showed a little understanding for and courtesy to the borrower. The conflict was permitted to escalate in part because some of the people at the bank were officious martinets but in larger part because they did not see beyond the ostensible single issue (the borrower's payments were late) and attempt to satisfy him on such other issues as accessibility of officers when he wanted to discuss his mortgage. (For want of a nail, the shoe was lost; for want of the shoe, the horse was lost. . . .)

Let us now return to the photocopier-related conflict as it might be addressed by a practitioner of the multiple-issue approach.

## MULTIPLE-ISSUE APPROACH


BUYER: This photocopier you sold me is no good.

SELLER: Gee, I'm sorry to hear that you feel that way. What's wrong with it?

BUYER: It breaks down too often.

SELLER: Gee, I'm sorry to hear that, too. Do you mean that it actually breaks down in the sense that parts need replacement, or just that the copier requires servicing? [Note, please, that the seller is not challenging the buyer's perceptions, although he is setting the stage to persuade the buyer that there is a difference between the two types of problems that the buyer might be regarding as "breakdowns."]

BUYER: Don't give me that double talk. If the machine won't run, I call it broken down. I don't care what you call it. [Note that the buyer refuses to get drawn into a discussion that she perceives as potentially weakening to her cause. This may or may not be a good strategy, depending on how the seller responds. Some sellers, more strongly convinced that the buyer is irritated, might take greater pains to appease her. Other sellers might become irritated themselves and abandon any desire to come to terms with the buyer.]

SELLER: Okay, I see your point. How often does this happen—these breakdowns, or whatever you want to call them? [The seller—wisely, in my view—refuses to become ruffled and also refuses to be sidetracked by something that really is not very important to his purposes.]

BUYER: I don't know. Every few weeks or so.

SELLER: Every few weeks, huh? That's pretty often. [Note that the seller is still not challenging the buyer's perceptions; indeed, the seller is telling the buyer, in effect, "Unless there's some explanation for this, you've got a legitimate grievance and it's my responsibility to satisfy you." This can hardly fail to put the buyer in a more amicable frame of mind—even though the seller has *not* acknowledged that there is something wrong with the copier, let alone that the seller is responsible.] How many copies would you say that represents? Does the machine break down approximately every hundred copies or every thousand copies or every ten thousand copies or every hundred thousand copies?

BUYER: I would say approximately every ten thousand copies.

SELLER: Well, I can understand that this upsets you, especially if you've got a very important job that you're running at the time, but, believe it or not, one service call every ten thousand copies is extremely low for a machine in this one's price range. In fact, Consumer's Union did a survey of copiers selling below $X—which is one and a half times the price of your machine—and the average number of copies between service calls was only three thousand. The machine that you have, which tested out at Consumer's Union with an average of one service call every seven thousand copies, got the highest rating in the survey. And your machine's performance is almost 50 percent better than that!

BUYER: Look, save the sales talk for someone else. The machine breaks down more than it should. [The seller, in my opinion, has effectively disarmed the buyer of any justification for a complaint about the machine's alleged breakdowns. The buyer remains hostile, dismissing the rebuttal as "sales talk." The seller could, like the bankers in the earlier illustration, treat this as a single-issue conflict and declare himself the winner. Instead—]

SELLER: I'll make a deal with you. If you show me service records to the effect that your machine requires service no more than once every ten thousand copies, I'll buy the machine back from you for exactly what you paid for it, even though it's used. But before we talk any more about that, I'd like to know more about your complaint. What's the most common cause of the breakdowns? Paper jamming? Skipped copies? [The seller obviously is taking something of a chance here. If the buyer takes him up on the offer to buy back the machine at full cost, the seller obviously will lose money. However, he is confident that his ploy will work, because he believes that what the buyer *really* wants is not a refund but reassurance that the seller will work with him to achieve satisfactory operation of the machine. If the seller refunded the buyer's money, the buyer would have to go out and buy another machine. The shopping alone would take a lot of (presumably costly) time, and the buyer might still not get a good value as the machine she now owns—a prospect that should be fresh in her mind after the seller's recent speech about the Consumer's Union survey.]

BUYER: Well, there are some paper jams, not too many skipped copies. Sometimes the machine just stops running. Also, there's a lot of wrinkling.

SELLER: On two-sided copies only, or on one-sided copies also?

BUYER: Mainly on two-sided. Maybe entirely on two-sided. [Note, please, how the mood of this dialogue has changed. The seller has assumed the role of an eager-to-be-helpful diagnostician, and the buyer has fallen neatly into the role of describer-of-symptoms.]

SELLER: Gee, I wish I'd had a chance to speak with you before you bought the machine. It's really not designed to do a lot of two-sided copying. Didn't my salesman tell you that?

BUYER: No. Of course, I don't remember saying that I intended to do a lot of two-sided copying, so I guess he's not at fault. [Note, please, that the seller *invited* the inference that the salesman was at fault; the seller is not being at all defensive, and his apparent willingness to accept blame can hardly fail to persuade the buyer that the seller is a reasonable person.]

SELLER: Well, whatever his representations, I intend to stand behind my machine completely. But before we talk any more about that, I'd like to know more about your complaint. Do you have a service contract with us?

BUYER: Yes.

SELLER: I see. So your complaint, then, is not about the cost of the service calls, since you pay the same amount no matter how many calls we make. What you're most concerned about is that your operation gets disrupted when you have down-time.

BUYER: Exactly.

SELLER: How quickly do we usually respond? Four hours? Six?

BUYER: Somewhere around there.

SELLER: In other words, the same day—unless you place the call after noon.

BUYER: Usually.

SELLER: Did we *ever* not get a service representative to you on the same day if you called before noon?

BUYER: Maybe once or twice at most. I don't recall a specific instance right now of that ever happening.

SELLER: Okay, how about the shortest time? Do we ever get there within two or three hours?

BUYER: Sometimes.

SELLER: Would you say about half of the time, a third of the time?

BUYER: Maybe a third of the time.

SELLER: Well, I can't get mad at my people over that. All in all, their response is as fast as anyone's I know in the industry. Short of having your own in-house technician, you're not going to get a service call in less than two hours with any consistency. How about after-hours service? In other words, if you place a service call after noon and the rep doesn't get to you before you close at five, would you be interested in a contract that provides emergency after-hours service? The rep would certainly get there sometime during the night so that your machine would be up again by nine the next morning.

BUYER: No, I wouldn't be interested in that. There'd be nobody here to let your guy in. [Note, please, the continuation of the amiable tone of the dialogue. Note also that the seller and buyer now do indeed seem to be *working together* to try to devise ways of dealing with the problem.]

SELLER: Okay, let me make sure that I understand the full range of your problems before I try to suggest some solutions. Are the service reps courteous and helpful?

BUYER: They're okay. I have no problems here. But you've got one telephone operator who needs some manners put on him.

SELLER: Tell me about him.

BUYER: He's a real wise guy. He always has some sarcastic comment to make. And he's a goof-off, too. I can't tell you how many times he's put me on hold—sometimes for three or four minutes.

SELLER: Well, I'm certainly going to investigate that. I won't have any customer addressed sarcastically by one of my employees. As for being put on hold, well, occasionally it's unavoidable, but it shouldn't happen every time, and you certainly shouldn't be kept waiting for three or four minutes. I wonder if my operator is making personal calls on company time. Either that or I need more people in that department. I'll have to look into that. By the way, do you happen to have the name of the operator who gives you so much trouble? [Note that the seller has, in effect, appointed himself a judge of the buyer's complaints—taking full responsibility for some, dismissing others. This is a risky tactic—it may antagonize many adversaries, especially those who recognize it as a tactic—but it seems to be working here.]

BUYER: I never asked him his name.

SELLER: Well, do me a favor. If this ever happens again, get his name, will you? Then telephone me directly with it. I'd really appreciate the opportunity to get to the bottom of this. Now, how about any other problems you may have had with us—can you think of any others? [By inference, if the buyer cannot think of any other problems, there *are* no other problems.]

BUYER: Not at the moment, I can't. [The buyer is too smart to get hooked by the inference; thus, she qualifies with "at the moment."]

SELLER: Well, if you do think of any, will you let me know personally—just as soon as you think of them? [By inference, "If I don't hear from you, there are no other problems."]

BUYER: That's a promise. [There was no reasonable way to escape getting hooked by this inference.]

SELLER: Thanks. Now, let's see if I can summarize your problems and what we've agreed to do about them. You've told me that you've been treated discourteously by one of my telephone operators, and we've agreed that I'm going to deal with that. We've also got the problem of your being put on hold too frequently and for periods of time that are too long, and I'm going to take care of that. I've offered to eliminate overnight down-time by arranging for your machine to be serviced after hours, but you're not interested in that because there's no one in your office at that time. You want to make a lot of two-sided copies, and the copier simply isn't designed for that, and we haven't decided yet how we're going to deal with this. Also, the machine simply is not designed to take your volume of work without requiring servicing more frequently than you wish, and we still haven't solved this problem, either. Have I covered everything? [By inference, "Speak now or forever hold your peace."]

BUYER: Yeah, I guess those are all the major problems. [She still won't accept the inference, so she qualifies with "major." The seller could attempt to nail her down by asking her to identify the other problems, but the seller—wisely, in my view—doesn't pursue this point because the buyer seems close to being won over and might be antagonized unnecessarily by being cajoled into providing other complaints or admitting that there are none. What's most important here is that the seller unpacked the original, single-issue complaint into four complaints and is now ready to link his own movement on some with the buyer's movement on others.]

SELLER: Okay, the two areas where I haven't satisfied you involve two-sided copies and the frequency of service calls that are necessitated by your high volume of work. [Inference: "You've accepted my concessions on the other points, so now it's your turn to be cooperative."] Well, Ms. Buyer, I'm afraid there's no way that the machine you have is ever going to perform any better than it does now in either of these departments. So here's what I'm going to ask you to do: Look around at other machines that sell for up to 50 percent more, and then get back to me. If you find a machine that gives you more than you're now getting, and if I can't offer you a machine that gives you even more than that one—but at a better price—I'll buy my machine back from you, full price, and that'll be the end of it. Meanwhile, I'd really like to have you stop into the showroom and check out some of the machines I have now—somewhat more expensive than yours, but with quite a bit more performance. I think I can set you up with a machine that will meet your needs in every way. And if I'm wrong, I'm willing to put my money where my mouth is and buy back your present machine. Will you give me a call after you've looked over some other machines, so that we can arrange an appointment?

BUYER: Well, uh, I don't really feel the need to look at other machines right now. You seem like a reasonable fellow, and I think we get along pretty well. Let me stop by your place and see what your other machines are like. [Truth be told, the last thing in the world that the buyer wants is to waste several days looking at competitors' photocopiers—and the seller suspected this from the start.]

SELLER: Very well, let's set an appointment. How's next Tuesday morning?

To see how unpacking works on the scale of international diplomacy, let's return to the example—discussed in earlier chapters—of France's dispute with South Korea over France's plan to open diplomatic relations with North Korea.

☐ When France made known its plan, South Korea did not simply say, "That's a bad idea, and we oppose it." Nor did South Korea say, "If you go ahead with your plan, we will suspend diplomatic relations with you." South Korea knew that France would be aware of South Korea's opposition, and South Korea had no intention of suspending diplomatic relations with France. How, then, should South Korea deal with the matter? By introducing other issues—and linking movement on some with France's movement on others.

☐ South Korea did exactly that. Its negotiators threatened that if France opened diplomatic relations with North Korea, the South Korean government would create (unspecified) problems for French companies that were bidding to sell South Koreans a high-speed train for the Seoul-Pusan railway, a subway system for Pusan, two nuclear reactors, and certain sophisticated equipment for generating electricity from ocean tides.

☐ All of a sudden, there was not just one issue; there was a table full of issues. And how did France respond? By promising some dire consequence if South Korea carried out its threat?

☐ No. That would have accomplished little if anything. Instead, France made a counter-offer, stating, in effect, "Look, Seoul-brothers, there's no way we can continue to resist opening diplomatic relations with North Korea. We know you don't like it, and there are more than a few people in our own government who don't like it, but the whole thrust of our foreign policy over the past decade has favored expansion rather than contraction of diplomatic relations. So, no matter what you threaten, there is no way that we are going to be able to accede to your demands. And if you carry out your threats, you will leave us with no choice but to retaliate. We haven't at the moment developed a laundry list of retaliatory measures, but please trust our well-known Gallic ingenuity: We will come up with measures that are at least as onerous to you as your threatened measures will be to us. But there may be a way to avoid all of this counterproductive unpleasantness. Consider this: You guys have been saying for quite some time now that you want to be recognized diplomatically by some Soviet-bloc nations. If you will back off on your threats, we will persuade at least one Soviet-bloc nation to recognize you."

☐ South Korea found this offer appealing in principle but hoped to get as much mileage from it as possible. Obviously, to be recognized by one of the small-fry among Soviet-bloc soft-liners (such as Rumania) was not as valuable as being recognized by one of the big-fry (Russia herself or perhaps Poland) or one of the larger soft-liners (Yugoslavia, let us say) or one of the smaller hard-liners (Albania).

☐ South Korea, practicing mini-max, thought big and said that it would accept the arrangement only if recognition were accorded by Russia or China. France, of course, could not deliver either, and so the negotiators' task was to determine an acceptable substitute for one of these nations.

☐ As I write this, the negotiations have not been completed, but that is of little moment to the point I want to make. The point is that the negotiators had converted what could have been a win-or-lose single-issue conflict into a multiple-issue conflict and now were actively searching for mutually acceptable ways of resolving these issues. By linking the issues, they made it possible for one side's concessions on one issue to be repaid by the other side's concessions on another issue.

☐ What will it take to achieve a mutually acceptable resolution? Well, if France cannot come up with a satisfactory substitute for Russia or China, perhaps South Korea would accept a deal whereunder an independent desideratum was thrown into the pot. In other words, France might say, "We can't give you Russia or China, but we can give you Czechoslovakia, plus we can relax our restrictions on importation by French clothiers of textiles made in South Korea."

☐ South Korea might counter, "We'd like Czechoslovakia, but we'd need something more than a relaxation of the restrictions on textiles. We'd have to get something that would make our people believe we are punishing you. So, let's try it this way: You give us Czechoslovakia and you relax the restrictions on textiles, and then we will prevent one of your companies from getting work on a major project—either the Seoul-Pusan train or the Pusan subway, take your pick."

☐ France: "Well, we could probably live with that, but both of those jobs are pretty major. Would you trade one of them for the equipment that will generate electricity from ocean tides? Or possibly we could give you not only Czechoslovakia but also Bulgaria."

☐ South Korea: "Well, throw in Bulgaria and that makes it a

whole new ballgame. We could then very comfortably accept the relaxation of restrictions on textiles. We wouldn't have to give you a hard time about any of the industrial projects. . . ."

☐ And so it might go, resulting ultimately in a mutually acceptable agreement, and all because the negotiators learned how to unpack a single-issue conflict and link concessions on certain issues with concessions on other issues.

# 15 UNDOING, TOKENING, BONE-THROWING, ISSUE-SUBSTITUTION

## AND OTHER PATHS TO PACIFICATION

O nce a conflict has been analyzed and broken into its various parts (from single-issue conflict to multiple-issue conflict), many options may—and usually will—present themselves as means by which to satisfy an adversary who at first might have seemed unsatisfiable.

Let us look now at some of these options.

## UNDOING

The easiest way to resolve any conflict is to learn an adversary's real grievances and then *undo* the source of grievance. Often this can be accomplished at rather low cost, and frequently it can be accomplished without sacrificing anything important.

For example, an employee who requests a transfer from one department to another may not *really* want to change departments; he may merely object to a situation in his present department. For instance, he may now have the responsibility for telephoning delinquent accounts to request payment. A shy person who hates to confront people about things of this sort, he may like everything about his present job but this one duty—and he may dislike this duty so much that, in order to escape it, he is willing to throw over all the benefits he now enjoys.

By taking the interest bargainer's approach and learning what the employee's *real* grievances are, we may find that we can make him happy simply by assigning the telephone calls to someone else in the department who does not mind—and may even enjoy—making them. Eliminate the grievance, and you'll have eliminated the conflict—every time.

Another example of *undoing* can be found in the preceding chapter's illustration about the photocopier-related conflict. One of the buyer's grievances (as the seller quickly learned when he "unpacked" the grievances) had to do with the attitude of a telephone operator and another had to do with being placed "on hold" when phoning for service. The seller promised to *undo* the problem, and the buyer was satisfied.

## TOKENING

In *tokening*, we give something that is inexpensive or—better yet—free to us but dear to the recipient, in order to avoid giving something that is expensive to us, though perhaps no more dear to the recipient.

For example, the senior mechanic in the service department of an automobile agency may resent the fact that a less-senior mechanic receives the same hourly wage. Seeking a badge of distinction over the other mechanic, the senior might ask for a raise or for extra vacation days or such other perquisites as a company car.

A boss who is not attuned to interest bargaining might take these requests at face value and assume that this is what the mechanic really wants. However, a practitioner of interest bargaining would explore *why* the mechanic says she wants these things.

If the interest bargainer concludes that what the mechanic seeks is merely an ego-massage, it would be possible to offer her a satisfactory *token*—for example, the title of "assistant service manager" or an extra-large locker in the room where employees change. Either token may satisfy her, and neither would prove nearly as costly as giving her what she requested.

Another example of tokening:

☐ The headmaster at a private school was antagonizing parents by not being very friendly to them and by not taking prompt action on their complaints. The members of the school board, having decided to replace him at the end of the semester, voted to begin an immediate search for his replacement. Before the president of the board could inform the headmaster of the decision, one of the members who opposed his dismissal telephoned him with the news. The headmaster promptly quit, refusing to spend even another day in the school.

☐ The board now was faced with the problem of appointing an interim headmaster. It was an especially thorny problem, because the departed headmaster, unpopular though he was among parents, was extremely popular among teachers. Members of the board feared that if they did not handle the matter extremely adroitly, they might face a walk-out by the majority of the teachers—a serious problem under any circumstances but an especially serious problem in midsemester.

☐ There was no time to conduct a search outside the school for an interim headmaster. The occupant of that position would have to be chosen from among the present faculty. The board favored a seventh-grade teacher who had excellent credentials and also excellent rapport with parents but who was rather unpopular with other teachers. The problem was, how to appoint her without provoking a walk-out?

☐     The president of the board, a woman with exceptional skills as a manager of conflict, approached the problem in three stages.

☐     The first stage involved a private discussion with each teacher. In the discussion, the president explained what had happened with the old headmaster. The president then spoke of the necessity of naming a current faculty member as interim headmaster and asked if the teacher had any suggestions.

☐     Several teachers suggested the seventh-grade teacher—who already was the board's first choice. The president gave these teachers no indication that the board shared their opinion; she merely expressed thanks for the suggestion and said she would take it under advisement. She knew, of course, that when she announced the appointment, these teachers were likely to assume that their suggestion had been taken, and they probably would be pleased if not also flattered.

☐     Other teachers made other suggestions or said that they had no suggestions. The president gave them no indication that the board had someone in mind for the job. Instead, she said that *some parents* favored the seventh-grade teacher. (The statement was literally true, in that all of the members of the board were parents of the school's pupils.) The president asked the teachers if they approved of this choice.

☐     Quite a few teachers expressed disapproval. The president took note of their sentiments and promised to be in touch after the board had met. The president and other members of the board then assessed the situation and decided that the opposition to the seventh-grade teacher's appointment was not strong enough to warrant a change in plan.

☐     The president now brought the problem into stage two by calling a meeting of all the teachers. In substance, she addressed them as follows:

☐     "We have solicited your opinions about whom to appoint as interim headmaster. We hoped that it would be possible to establish some sort of consensus about the best person for the job, but we found that there is considerable difference of opinion among you.

We recognize, as you do, that the most important thing is to continue running the school as well as we can. If parents decide that we cannot run this school as well as competing schools are being run, the parents may withdraw their children, and the school will have to close, and all of you will be out of jobs. Therefore, it is essential that we, the members of the board, make a decision, even if it does meet with the disapproval of some of you. Our choice is X, one of our seventh-grade teachers. I will ask her to leave the room now, and then I will ask any of you who oppose the appointment to state the reasons of your opposition."

☐ Please note that the president did not ask for a vote to *ratify* the appointment. She announced the appointment as a fait accompli, then invited opponents to speak their piece. She was, in effect, conceding *nothing* to the opponents. However, by inviting them to express the reasons for their opposition, she was giving them a *token*—the chance to be heard, to let off steam, to express hostility toward the appointee, *even though the appointment had been made!*

☐ Many teachers spoke against the appointment. The president of the board gave each speaker a full hearing, sometimes seeking amplification of complaints, as if the details might in some way affect the future course of events. However, the president was careful not to challenge the perceptions or arguments of any complainant; she wisely resisted what would have been to most people a strong temptation to rebut someone's case against the appointee. She did not want a *debate* or even the *appearance* of a debate. She wanted to occupy the high ground and let the opponents exhaust themselves down below.

☐ After all the complainants had been heard, the president tallied their number. Some 40 percent of the faculty had spoken in opposition to the appointment, and the likelihood was that another 20 to 30 percent shared these sentiments but refrained from expressing them.

☐ The president now spoke to this effect: "Well, I see that a substantial minority opposes our decision. Of course, this is an administrative matter, not an election, so, even if a majority of you opposed the decision, we would not necessarily change our minds.

However, the members of the board and I are extremely eager to maintain good relations with all of you and to have the benefit of your opinions about how the school should be run. Therefore, we will not make our decision final at this time. Instead, we will appoint X as acting headmaster, and we will have another meeting within the next two weeks. After that meeting, we will let you know what we have decided."

☐   To all appearances, she was being extremely accommodating, but, once again, she had conceded *nothing*. The decision had been made, and it would not be changed; but as a *token* to those who opposed the appointment, she announced—ostensibly magnanimously—that the decision would not be *made final* at this time. (In fact, *no* decision is *ever* made final unless it involves an act that is irrevocable.) Meanwhile, of course, school would be in session, the teachers would continue teaching, the seventh-grade teacher would serve as interim headmaster, and other teachers could hardly justify staging a walk-out when the board was being "so reasonable" in taking their opinions into account.

☐   Over the next two weeks, the president carried out stage three of her plan: She phoned each of the opponents and said, in substance, "I wanted to discuss this with you privately before I brought it up at the formal meeting, because your opinion is very important to me. We've decided to keep X as interim headmaster, but we are limiting her appointment to the remainder of this school year. We will not decide until the summer whether or not to renew her for next year. We will not, of course, tell her of your opposition to her, and, in fact, we encourage you to help us guide her in doing as good a job as possible. If you have any ideas about policies that she should establish or ways that she should deal with the problems that you have complained about, please jot down your suggestions and pass them along to me, and I will take them up with her without letting her know where they came from."

☐   Now the task was complete. The president had not merely imposed the board's will on the teachers; she also had put the opponents in a position where they would be seen as disloyal if they did not support the choice—a posture that was reinforced by the president's pledge of confidentiality regarding complaints. Moreover, the president was putting opponents in a position where, if they did not offer suggestions about how the interim headmaster should deal with certain problems, they would have no defense if the problems continued. (It is not insignificant that the president asked that these suggestions be put into writing; most of us find it more bothersome to write than to talk, and many of us will abandon a grievance or a goal if we are forced to take the time and trouble to write about it.)

☐ Please note that the president need not have gone through any of this if she were willing to risk a walk-out by the teachers. She could have simply announced the decision and let the chips fall where they may. But she *defused* the opposition and ensured there would be no walk-out by giving the teachers a *token*—the *illusion* of their having contributed to the decision and to the resolution of the problem.

☐ By the way, when the summer came, the interim headmaster's appointment was made permanent. There was no announcement of the decision, and there was no opposition to it. The board did not solicit opinions about how to handle the matter, and none of the teachers volunteered any—*or* reminded the board that the appointment had been temporary. By this time, the teachers had grown used to working for the new headmaster; none, apparently, wanted to make waves.

Many companies and other organizations use suggestion boxes, gripe sessions, and similar solicitations of members' opinions as tokens. If an occasional suggestion is followed, the organization seems to be sincerely interested in what the members think.

Some organizations, of course, are sincerely interested in what members think. These organizations may be totally unconcerned about the tokening value of meetings, suggestion boxes, et cetera. However, that value exists, whether or not it is an organization's purpose.

Some organizations also use meetings and similar sources of input for a purpose that most members would regard as nefarious: to find out who the troublemakers are (and, in the process, to assess how others in the organization respond to the troublemakers).

# BONE-THROWING

Closely akin to tokening is bone-throwing, wherein one gives an adversary something of relatively little worth to compensate for a major loss. Often this is done to assuage feelings when one has triumphed on a conflict in which one issue was dominant. In the manner of the master who throws a bone to a dog, the winner gives the loser an offering of some sort so that the loser does not go away empty handed.

An example:

☐   I have sued you for damages because you failed to deliver certain materials that I ordered. I am dead wrong: Our contract contains an escape clause that exonerates you if your supplier failed to deliver the materials to you. There is no way that I will get a court to find against you; however, I am angry because this is the third time that you've failed to deliver one of my orders and perhaps also because your collection department has been relentless in pursuing me when my payments are late.

☐   One way that you could address the problem—indeed, the way most companies probably would address it—is to have your lawyer seek a dismissal of my lawsuit or, failing to achieve that, harass me with depositions, interrogatories, and other legal proceedings. Eventually the case would be thrown out of court or I would lose my will to fight.

☐   This, however, would cost you money (anything involving lawyers costs *lots* of money) and wouldn't accomplish anything other than getting rid of a nuisance. Consider, instead, inviting me to lunch and approaching me along these lines: "Look, I realize that you wouldn't have sued unless you were really upset, but my lawyers tell me that there is no way you are going to win. Whether they're right or wrong, you and I both will spend a lot of money on the lawsuit, and we both have better uses for it. Now, you know and I know that I'd've delivered the materials on time if I could've obtained them from my suppliers. I'm sorry that I couldn't do it, but I was helpless. If you maintain this lawsuit, we'll stop doing business together, and you're going to have the same problems with delivery from other companies that you had with me, only maybe a little worse, because they might not be as conscientious as I. We've done business for a long time, and by and large it's been a satisfactory relationship for both of us, so how about considering this: Discontinue the lawsuit, and I promise you I'll take personal charge of your orders in the future and do my very best to get them delivered on time. Not only that, I'll also speak to those people in my collection department—I realize they've been giving you a hard time—and we'll be a little more relaxed about your payments. Maybe we can work things out so that we don't start hounding you for money until you're 45 days later rather than 30 days late, the way we've been doing lately."

☐ Probably none of this would work if I sincerely believed that I was going to win the lawsuit or if I was so angry at you that I wanted to punish you, whatever the cost to me. However, very few people seek pyrrhic victories, and approximately half of all litigants are going to lose. So the probability is that I will back off on the lawsuit *if you throw me a bone.* A promise to ease up on collections is just such a bone.

Another example, this one not hypothetical:

☐ Several dozen journalists were invited to a product announcement luncheon. The goal of the producer—and of the public relations firm that arranged the luncheon—was to present the new product as attractively as possible, so that the journalists would write about it favorably.

☐ So-called "press" luncheons are extremely common—and usually extremely lavish. Perhaps in the most ideal of all possible journalistic worlds, no one would accept an invitation to such an event, for the host obviously is attempting to curry journalists' favor and journalists are supposedly unbuyable. However, in the real world, there are many such events, and, if you want the attention of the press, you have a better chance of getting it when you offer a free meal than when you don't.

☐   Allright, after the luncheon mentioned two paragraphs ago, one of the journalists who attended wrote a negative story about the new product. An inept public relations executive might mistakenly assume that the journalist (1) had atypical integrity and (2) honestly believed the product to be bad. This is indeed one possibility, but it is only one. An astute public relations executive would inquire further.

☐   The public relations executive who supplied me with this story did inquire further. He did not approach the journalist directly; rather, he approached a mutual friend, who revealed that the journalist resented being assigned to a secondary table when other journalists whom he regarded as his inferiors sat at the table with the guest of honor—the president of the company that introduced the product.

☐   Of course, neither the journalist nor the mutual friend stated specifically that the journalist's disgruntlement over the seating arrangement led him to write negatively about the new product. But there was certainly an opportunity to draw the inference that the journalist's pique about the seating arrangement had interfered with his ability to *appreciate* the product.

☐   Apprised of the journalist's pique, the public relations executive arranged a private luncheon for the journalist and the president of the company. Not one word was spoken about the previous luncheon. Instead, the president behaved as if the luncheon were purely social. Only when the journalist brought up the product did the president discuss it, and, even then, the president made no reference to the journalist's negative review. Rather, he listened to the journalist's opinions about the product and thanked him for them, promising to take them into account when a later model was introduced.

☐   A short time after this private luncheon, the journalist referred again to the product—this time in a way that was not wholly positive but that lacked the negativism of the earlier story. And a short time after that, the journalist wrote of the product positively—even though the product had not been changed in any way.

# ISSUE-SUBSTITUTION

In issue-substitution, we seize an issue that is important to our adversary and trade a concession on it for a concession on an issue that is important to us. This assumes, of course, that not all issues are of equal importance to all parties—but the truth is, they rarely are.

Even in the most highly structured negotiations, personalities and personal preferences play a large part. Please remember that during the Vietnam war one of the main reasons expressed by the United States for not withdrawing was that doing so would entail *losing face*. I repeat, this was an *expressed* reason, not merely one that was held in the back of someone's mind. The leaders of our nation *acknowledged* that they would not end the war because they *feared appearing foolish!*

There are countless parallels in everyday life where people take a stand on issues that really are not important to them. Here are three for-instances:

☐   The landlord of my office building announces a rent increase. I recognize that the increase is in line with those in comparable buildings, but I oppose the increase anyway—because I have some other grievance against the landlord. (I don't like the way the building manager had her secretary handle my last complaint instead of dealing with it personally.)

☐   The president of my neighborhood's homeowner's association tries to persuade members to support a zoning variance for a nearby development. I don't have an opinion one way or the other about the variance—indeed, I don't even know why it's being sought or why it's being opposed. However, I oppose it because I dislike the president.

☐   A European nation that exports quite a bit of a certain product to the United States has erected barriers against importation of the same product. American producers of the product, through their trade association, demand that these barriers be lifted. In fact, if the barriers were lifted, the nation probably would not

import any of the product from the United States, for the local supply is abundant, cheaper, and better suited to the tastes of the population. However, the nation maintains the (unnecessary) trade
barriers as a sop to local producers. Meanwhile, Americans clamor
for removal of the barriers, even though they know (or should
know) that they will sell little if any of their product there.

The key in issue-substitution is to seize upon issues of this sort
and substitute concessions on them for concessions on issues that
are important to you.

For example, let us say that the product under consideration in
the last example was wine—which indeed was a subject of controversy between the United States and certain European nations
during the early 1980s. As European wines continued to gain market share in the United States while locally made wines enjoyed
relatively little sales growth, American producers asked the government to intervene, blocking imports unless certain European
nations lowered their barriers against American wines.

It would have been very easy for the European nations to disarm
the American producers. All they would have had to do was eliminate their barriers against wines that their citizens would not
have bought anyway. Had they done so, they would have gained a
bargaining chip in other trade-related negotiations with the
United States. ("Okay, you guys, we've given you the green light
on wines—sell our people whatever you can. Now we want your
help on something else [phosphate, automobiles, fresh fruit,
take-your-pick].")

The Europeans, however, were not smart enough to do this, and,
consequently, a problem that could have been defused at the vir-
tual snap of a finger persisted for a number of years—and continues as I write this.

☐   For a successful use of issue-substitution, consider a conflict
that I arbitrated between two neighbors over a hedge on the common boundary of their properties.

☐   The neighbor that grew the hedge (hereinafter, Mr. A)
pointed out that the entire hedge was on his side of the boundary.

He added that he wanted the hedge for privacy and also to block his view of Mr. B's back yard, which Mr. A deemed unsightly because Mr. B was an amateur mechanic who had several junked automobiles in the yard.

☐ Mr. B said he wanted the hedge cut down because it blocked his view of the street when he was trying to pull his car out of the driveway and also because it blocked the sun for much of the day. He also said, *en passant,* that he thought Mr. A was snobbish and "trying to be something that he's not" by attempting to make his house resemble the walled-in estate of a rich person.

☐ I was able quickly to assess that Mr. B's main objection to the hedge was neither that it blocked the sun nor that it blocked his view of the street but rather that he regarded it as Mr. A's attempt to *snub him*. In other words, the hedge was—to Mr. B—Mr. A's way of saying, "I'm better than you. In fact, I'm so much better that I don't even want to have to look at you."

☐ In talking privately with Mr. B, I learned that his feelings about Mr. A grew in part from an incident 10 years before when Mr. B, who is a scoutmaster, solicited a donation from Mr. A for the Boy Scout troop and was refused. In a sense, Mr. B's opposition to the hedge had nothing whatever to do with the hedge itself but was merely an excuse to get back at Mr. A for what Mr. B perceived as a personal slight when Mr. A refused to make a donation to the Scouts.

☐ I discussed the matter privately with Mr. A, who had long forgotten the request for the donation. On reflection, he calculated that he had been asked at a time when he was financially pressed. He had refused not out of any sense of snobbishness or low esteem for the Scouts or Mr. B's involvement with them but simply because he did not have the money.

☐ I suggested that Mr. A make some gesture that would convince Mr. B of (1) Mr. A's good feelings toward the Scouts and (2) Mr. A's respect for Mr. B. After some thought, Mr. A, whose financial situation had improved considerably over the decade, suggested that he underwrite a week of summer camp for a needy member of Mr. B's troop.

☐ Mr. B loved the idea, and not another word was exchanged

between the neighbors about the hedge—which was a bogus issue from the very start and easily resolvable once a substitute-issue was found.

For another successful use of issue-substitution, let's look again at the diplomatic fracas between France and South Korea that I discussed in the previous chapter.

After France had revealed its intention to open diplomatic relations with North Korea, South Korea threatened to refuse to accept bids fom French companies for a high-speed train, two nuclear reactors, and some sophisticated equipment that generates electricity from ocean tides. Truth was, South Korea had no bonafide reason for wanting to block French companies from obtaining this business; South Korea had merely seized upon an issue to substitute for what it regarded as a more important issue—its place in the diplomatic world. France, by volunteering to convince a major Soviet-bloc nation to open diplomatic relations with South Korea, found yet another issue to substitute for the issue of whether French companies should be permitted to bid on the construction projects that South Korea threatened to block.

# ≡16≡THE HARDBALL NEGOTIATOR

## OR HOW TO FIGHT DIRTY WHEN YOU HAVE TO

I n the best of all possible negotiating worlds, you would never have to fight dirty. Everyone would practice win-win negotiating, in which each adversary does her or his best to help the other guy get a good deal.

Alas, we do not live in the best of all possible negotiating worlds, and some of the most outspoken champions of win-win negotiating would nail you to the wall if that would help them get an iota of advantage over you. Thus while I strongly recommend entering a negotiation intent on being agreeable and cooperative and helpful, I also caution you not to assume that the other guy will be as nice as you. Expect—or, at the very least, do not rule out—that the other guy will try to take advantage of you, and be prepared to defend against ploys that will give him or her an *unfair* advantage.

Following are some of the more common ploys and some of the more effective ways of dealing with them.

## "THERE'S NOTHING TO NEGOTIATE," DEFENSIVE VARIATION

When you approach a hardball negotiator with a request or demand, expect him to turn his back, as if there were nothing to negotiate.

You may be an employee seeking a raise. You may be a customer who feels she has been overcharged. You may be Belgium and have discovered that Moscow is installing missiles along your border.

The hardball negotiator shoos you away with no more apparent respect than he would show to an irksome insect.

"You want a raise? You must be crazy."

"What do you mean, overcharged? My prices are the fairest in town."

"Move the missiles? Don't be ridiculous!"

Sometimes the hardballer will simply tell you no. Other times, he'll not say anything at all, or he'll say merely that he'll think about it. And if he says he'll think about it, chances are you won't hear from him again unless you phone, in which case he probably won't take your call, but, if he does take your call, he'll tell you no. Or he'll tell you to put your request/demand in writing, backing it up with all the facts you can assemble; and *then* you won't hear from him again unless you phone, in which case, if he eventually takes your call, he'll tell you no.

What the hardballer is gambling on is the well-known fact that most people do not want to fight—in fact, they want so much *not* to fight that they will let others take advantage of them time after time after time.

Perhaps eight in 10 people on whom the hardballer turns his

back will never bother him again. The remaining two, or so he hopes, will he happy enough to have finally gotten his attention that they will settle for less than they originally would have if he had not stonewalled them.

Of course, the other side to this picture involves the guy who got stonewalled and was so angry that he set out on a vendetta— remember the fellow in Chapter 14 who sued the bank? And we can't forget the ill will that the hardliner engenders among those with whom he deals. How many employees got turned down for a raise and, without giving the hardliner a chance to relent, took another job? How many customers got stonewalled on a complaint and never bought at the store again?

Please keep in mind that I never said hardballing is a *good idea*. Throughout this book, I have advised strongly against it. I think hardballing is far more costly in the long run than win-win negotiating, and, even if that were not true, being a hardballer goes against my moral code.

All the same, people employ that style of negotiating, and you have to be prepared to deal with them.

Sometimes, hardballers operate on orders from above. For example, it's no secret that you can resolve a complaint much more easily with IBM, whose management practices a win-win philosophy, than with AT&T, where, from the very top down, the propensity is to tell you, "That's our policy." (Translation: "Go drown yourself.")

At other times, you'll counter a *sua sponte* hardballer who hasn't yet been weeded out of an organization whose orientation is win-win. A friend of mine encountered such a hardballer in IBM's credit department. When he objected to her request for more information in support of his application, she responded with a lot of gobbledegook to the effect of, "That's our policy."

My friend, who had been doing business with IBM for more than two decades and knew the company's philosophy well, hung up on her and wrote to IBM's chairman. Within a few days, several senior officers of IBM telephoned to apologize, and, before the end of the week, IBM's top-ranked regional executive visited my friend at his office. My friend got the credit. If the lady in the credit department didn't get fired, you can be sure she got assigned to a course in customer relations.

"That's our policy"—those are not only fighting words, they're words of consummate arrogance and defiance. If the person who utters them is working for someone else, forget about rhetoric or other means of persuasion; you've got to go to the boss. And if the person who utters the words *is* the boss, you've got to put a knife to his throat—figuratively, of course—and bring him to his knees before you can expect to reason with him.

How do you bring such a person to his knees?

Most of the ways are obvious, although few people have the patience, financial resources, and/or gumption to carry them out.

**Sue.**   Yes, it's costly if you use a lawyer. But in every jurisdiction in the nation, a person is allowed to bring a lawsuit without a lawyer. You may spend a great deal of time figuring out such mundane matters as what line on the page is acceptable for the first line of the caption in a complaint, but, if you are willing to endure such drudgery, you can force your adversary to defend himself before a judge and jury—or to settle in the interest of avoiding that fate.

Generally, the lower the court, the easier the procedures will be for the do-it-yourself lawyer. However, there is an offsetting generality: The lower the court, the lower the amount of potential recovery, and therefore the lower the exposure of the defendant, and therefore the lower the stakes for your adversary. When I sue, I sue in the highest court of competent jurisdiction—federal court, if my case qualifies, or the highest pertinent state court if the case cannot meet the standards of the federal courts.

**Complain to a Governmental Agency.**   Most businesses and other organizations are subject to governmental regulation of one sort or another. Find out the different agencies that regulate your adversary, then file a complaint with each of them. The worst that will happen to you is nothing—that is, the agency will not take action on your complaint. But even if that is the case, you will have added another complaint to the agency's file on your adversary, and, if enough complaints accumulate, your adversary will suffer as a result. Meanwhile, you may hit the jackpot and come upon a governmental regulator who champions your cause.

**Complain to a Professional Society or Other Association.** Virtually every business or other organization is a member of an association that can be a source of pressure on a recalcitrant. Physicians and dentists, in addition to being licensed by the states in which they practice, are members of professional societies that usually respond to every complaint. Retail businesses are often members of the Better Business Bureau, the Chamber of Commerce, or some similar organization, or, even if not members, are subject to pressure from such organizations. To be sure, the pressure is not nearly as great as that from governmental regulators. All the same, if enough complaints accumulate, the object of the complaints will suffer inconvenience to one degree or another.

**Make the Matter Public Through the Media.** Virtually every major newspaper or television or radio station nowadays has a "consumer reporter" or some similar staffer who investigates complaints about people or organizations within the community. If you can interest a journalist in writing a story about your complaint—or even in making a telephone call to your adversary about a possible story that may never get written—you will be putting your adversary under a sort of pressure that he or she cannot fail to find oppressive. (The more theatrical reader may find this prospect so appealing that he will telephone his adversary, or prevail upon an acquaintance to do so, pretending to be a journalist. Obviously, I counsel against this and mention the technique here only in the interest of being comprehensive!)

**Make a Pest of Yourself in Other Ways.** Depending on how much time you want to devote to the matter and how much visibility you are willing to accept, you can do anything from complaining repeatedly via telephone to picketing the organization's headquarters (or any other site). The more flamboyant you are willing to be, the greater are your chances of shaming, cajoling, and/or intimidating your adversary into listening to you.

***Threaten to Do One or More of the Above.*** It's generally a
bad idea to threaten unless you're prepared to follow through if
your bluff is called. In these circumstances, however, there's not
much that you can lose—other than credibility with your
adversary—if you threaten and do not follow through. And if
you've reached the "go drown yourself" point, you may have to *buy*
credibility but you don't really *have* any to lose.

Let me restate most emphatically that extreme measures rarely
will be necessary to bring your adversary to the bargaining table.
With most adversaries, once you've given any indication that you
are prepared to fight, you'll immediately be afforded new respect.
And the larger an organization, the greater the likelihood that
you'll get action simply by sending a letter of complaint to the chief
executive, for that officer usually will channel the complaint
through the organization, and any number of middle-managers
may be criticized for letting the complained-about situation come
into being.

A case in point:

☐   A friend of mine bought a washer and dryer from Sears, the
nation's largest retailer. The machines were delivered but not installed. The salesperson explained that different personnel handled the delivery and installation. My friend was told that the installation department would soon be in touch.

☐   The department phoned within a few days and reported that
a service person would install the machines on a certain day the
following week.

☐   My friend said, "Great, let me get out my calendar, and we
can schedule an appointment."

☐   The department replied, in effect, "We can't schedule appointments, because we don't know how long each installation will
take. We can only tell you the day."

☐   My friend said, "You mean that you expect me to stay home
all day waiting around for your mechanic simply because he can't
organize his time?"

☐   The department said, "We're sorry, but we do not schedule
appointments for specific times—only for specific days."

☐ My friend railed and ranted for a while, asked to speak to a supervisor, went through the same routine with him, asked to speak to the regional manager, and finally was told by the manager's assistant that the company's policy was to schedule dates but not hours for installation.

☐ My friend now wrote to Sears' Chicago-based chief executive:

> *Your attention is invited to the enclosed invoice for a washer and dryer. Despite numerous attempts over a period of several weeks, I have not been able to persuade anyone at your San Francisco store to schedule an appointment to install the machines.*
>
> *The machines are useless to me uninstalled, so I have made arrangements to buy the same items from another company.*
>
> *Please instruct your local subordinates to make an appointment with my office to reclaim your machines.*
>
> *Judging from your most recent earnings report, Sears certainly is in no position to chase away paying customers with cavalier treatment of the sort I've received. I expect that your shareholders will be very interested in my recent experience with Sears. Perhaps I'll tell my story at your next annual meeting.*

☐ A few days later, my friend got this letter from the company's director of consumer relations:

> *I have been asked to answer your letter addressed to [the chief executive officer] dated XXXX and appreciate your comments, which are being carefully reviewed, concerning a washer-dryer purchase.*
>
> *A representative of our company will be in touch with you promptly on the points you have raised.*
>
> *Thank you for taking the time to bring this matter to our attention.*

☐ A few days later, my friend was telephoned by one of Sears's local executives, who said, in effect, "We're sorry you had this trouble, and we'll do what we can to straighten things out. You said in your letter that you made arrangements to buy the same items from another company. If you haven't already completed that transaction and you still want our washer and dryer, I'll arrange to have someone come out and install them at your convenience. If you want the other company's machines, I'll send someone to pick up ours—again, at your convenience."

A complete turn-around, was it not? And all because of a letter to the boss.

Now, far be it from me to say that Sears' chief executive quaked at the prospect that my friend would show up at the next annual meeting and harangue the chairperson in the presence of the stockholders. Maybe the CEO was appalled to learn how the San Francisco office was treating its customers and decided to take prompt corrective action. Or maybe he gathered, from the tone of my friend's letter, that here was a nut-job who could be very troublesome if not placated. Maybe the CEO didn't even see the letter; maybe it got intercepted by some assistant who took action for either or both of the above reasons or any of a dozen others.

Whatever the case, my friend got exactly what he wanted after the entire chain of command in the San Francisco office had told him, in effect, that there was nothing to negotiate.

## "THERE'S NOTHING TO NEGOTIATE," OFFENSIVE VARIATION

In the above example, the hardballer was on the defense. Or, to mix metaphorical spheres, the ball was in the consumer's court. In other words, the consumer—representative of the little guy (namely, you and me)—was the party with a request, and the hardballer was the one who denied the request.

You may find yourself in the reverse situation—namely, where the big guy makes a request or demand of you and, on being told no (or "let's negotiate"), employs hardball strategies to bring you to your knees.

To wit:

☐   Your child falls on the sidewalk, cutting his brow on the curb. You rush him to the emergency room of the nearest hospital, where a doctor puts in a couple of stitches, applies a bandage, and sends you on your way. A few days later you get a bill, and it takes your breath away. The hospital wants $XXXXX, and, even though you know medical costs have gone crazy lately, you can't for the life of you imagine how anyone could justify $XXXXX for the five-minute procedure of putting a couple of stitches in a child's forehead.

☐ What are your options? If you're like most people, you'll gripe about doctors and hospitals having a license to steal, and then you'll pay the bill—maybe a little late, maybe not all at once, but you'll pay.

☐ And if you don't pay? Then, most probably, the following sequence of events will occur:

1. You will get a number of dunning letters and perhaps a phone call or two. You'll be threatened with damage to your credit rating if you don't pay immediately.

2. The case will be turned over to a collection agency, which will do some more dunning by phone and/or mail, probably being a little nastier about it, especially if the dunner perceives you to be ignorant of your rights. (You may, for example, be told that your bank account will be attached if you don't pay—which, under certain circumstances, could be true after a judgment was won in court but certainly is not within the province of any collection agency.)

3. The case will be turned over to a lawyer, who will dun some more and finally (except in cases where the money is considered too small to bother with) sue you.

4. There will be an assortment of legal maneuvers by your adversary, designed to get a judge to declare a winner without even trying the case. In some jurisdictions, these maneuvers include such devices as a "notice to admit," whereunder you are sent a list of allegations against you and, if you do not deny certain crucial ones, you've lost the case. (If you don't respond within a certain time, you've lost the case, too—and many people, not knowing any better don't respond at all.)

5. The case will go to trial and, if you cannot persuade the judge or jury that you do not owe the money, your adversary will get a judgment against you. The judgment may include not only the amount of the original bill but also interest, lawyers' fees, and court costs.

6. Your adversary will obtain a court order allowing the attachment of certain of your possessions, possibly including bank accounts, to whatever extent is necessary to satisfy the judgment.

7. If you do not turn over your possessions voluntarily, they will be seized by law-enforcement officers.

Obviously, this is a pretty grim scenario, and the prospect of having all of these things happen might impel you to pay the bill even if you feel the amount is outrageous. That, of course, is what your adversary is counting on. The system, by effect if not also by design, steamrollers the little guy. Therefore, your adversary can sit back and let events take their inexorable course; to borrow from a well-known TV commercial, you can pay him now or you can pay him later.

But wait a minute. Suppose the charge really *is* outrageous. Suppose the bill is a *mistake*. Maybe you got *someone else's* bill. Are the above-described events really inexorable, or is there some way you can stop them?

There are, of course, many ways you can stop them. In court, you can persuade a judge or jury that the charges are unwarranted. And at any earlier stage, you can persuade your adversaries of their error.

And if the bill is not in error but *is,* nonetheless, too high, you can negotiate.

Negotiate with a *hospital?* Aren't hospital bills sacrosanct? *How* does one *negotiate* with a *hospital?*

Your adversary would like you to think that there's nothing to negotiate. In fact, except when you are dealing with a crazy person—and sometimes even then—just about every dispute can be negotiated.

How do you get a hospital to negotiate? Use the same techniques

I described in the previous section, "There's Nothing to Negotiate," Defensive Variation. That is, locate someone within the organization who has the authority to settle the case, and then make known your grievance. If you get no satisfaction, go over that person's head. If you must, go to the chief executive—perhaps pointing out that you are prepared to sue and that you intend to name him as an individual defendant in addition to naming the organization as a corporate defendant. And, if you still get no satisfaction, do what you must to bring the organization to its knees—sue, complain to a governmental agency, et cetera, et cetera.

Usually, you won't have to go beyond a few letters or phone calls—especially if your grievance is legitimate, but sometimes even if it isn't. If there is one thing hardballers understand, it is the threat of someone who understands hardballers!

How, *more specifically,* do you get a hospital to negotiate? Let me call once again upon the experiences of one of my friends, a fellow whom I call The Great Litigator. He is not a lawyer, and he has never even been to law school. But he gets very upset when he believes people are trying to take advantage of him, and he has made it a point to learn certain things about the law, and he has brought in-person lawsuits against quite a few people, and he has never lost a case. (Several of his victories were jury trials, but the vast majority were settled out-of-court.)

☐　It was the Great Litigator whose two-year-old daughter fell on the sidewalk, cutting her brow on the curb, and was rushed to the hospital, as I described at the start of this section. Many hospitals now require advance payment for emergency room treatment (a practice of questionable legality, in my opinion, and I look forward to the day it is tested in court by someone who was damaged after being denied care for not paying), but the hospital to which The Great Litigator brought his daughter admitted her without a prepayment.

☐　The Great Litigator then received the bill that I have reproduced below. This happened in 1982, and I want to emphasize the year because, given the unrelenting rise in hospital costs, the charges may seem much less outrageous today than they did then.

| | |
|---|---:|
| Emergency Room Fee | 90.00 |
| Laceration of Sutures | 65.50 |
| Tac Solution | 10.00 |
| Suture Pack | 4.50 |
| Suture Set | 26.50 |
| | $196.50 |

☐ The Great Litigator took one look at the bill and hit the proverbial ceiling. Then he forced himself to sit and relax for a few moments and have a nice, calming cup of chamomile tea so that when he telephoned the hospital to protest he would not seem like a raving maniac. Then he phoned a physician friend and got some opinions on the legitimacy of some of the charges on the bill.

☐ Finally he telephoned the hospital and asked to speak to the administrator. (The administrator, as The Great Litigator knew—because he makes it a point to be informed about such things—is the senior officer at a hospital who has authority over billing. There are a chief of staff and other authorities with authority over medical matters, but no one—not even the chairperson of a hospital's board—overrules the administrator on matters concerning billing.)

☐ As he expected, The Great Litigator was not put through to the administrator but to an underling. The Great Litigator said he believed he was being overcharged and asked if the underling had the authority to settle the controversy. The underling asked for more details, but The Great Litigator refused to provide them "except to someone who has the authority to settle." (For why he was adamant about this, see the next section of this chapter.)

☐ The underling put The Great Litigator on hold, then switched him to another underling, who asked more questions but eventually acknowledged that he did not have the authority to settle. The Great Litigator insisted on speaking to someone with such authority, and the underling told him, in effect, "Go drown yourself."

☐ The Great Litigator now wrote the following letter, dated July 27, 1982, to the administrator:

*Dear XXXXXXX:*

*I have received your invoice dated July 9, 1982, a photocopy of which is enclosed. Not only are the sums therein scandalous, but I have learned that they are far in excess of what you charge Blue Cross and other third-party payers. Please have someone telephone me who has authority to negotiate and enter into a settlement of this matter.*

☐ He did not, in fact, have evidence that the hospital had a different price for third-party payers. He was ad-libbing, based on the opinion of his physician friend that some of the charges on the bill were unreasonably high. He *assumed* that third-party payers wouldn't accept such charges.

☐ He promptly received a letter, dated July 29, from the hospital's "business office manager." It read, in pertinent part:

*There must be some misunderstanding on your part regarding how XXXXXXX Medical Center handles the billing of patient accounts. To my knowledge, as the Business Office Manager for this facility, the charges generated from the various departments within the hospital are the same for all patients regardless of whether the patient is paying cash or whether the hospital is billing their insurance; there is no differentiation made whatsoever.*

*I am sorry that you have received incorrect information in this regard. If there is anything further that I can explain to you, please feel free to call.*

☐ Obviously, the hospital was playing hardball. The administrator referred the letter to a subordinate, who did not address the allegation that the sums in the bill were scandalous but rather told The Great Litigator that he *misunderstood* and had received *incorrect information*. The subordinate then volunteered to *explain* but not to negotiate a settlement. Translation: Go drown yourself.

☐ The Great Litigator now telephoned the "business office manager" and, before consenting to discuss the complaint itself, demanded to know whether the manager had the authority to make a settlement on the hospital's behalf. Told no, he demanded to speak to someone who did. He was referred to the "manager, credit and collection," who, on being questioned, admitted that he did not have such authority, either.

☐ The Great Litigator repeated that he would not discuss the matter with someone who did not have the authority to settle the case. A few days later, he received a letter from the credit/collection fellow, reading in pertinent part:

> *This is to confirm our conversation on Tuesday . . . . As I explained to you, XXXXXXX Medical Center does not discount charges billed for services rendered . . . . We know that each department's services are reasonable and that our charges in total are reasonable, and we invite such a comparison, recognizing the quality of health care provided at XXXXXXX Medical Center.*
>
> *If you would like to review the audit of charges performed or wish to present conflicting evidence of the reasonableness of charges, I would be most appreciative to meet with you and discuss this matter further.*

☐ Note, please, the shift from hardball to medium-hardball, mainly in the last paragraph: In effect, The Great Litigator was being told, identify an unreasonable charge, and we may back off. Translation: We're ready to negotiate.

☐ And small wonder! By this time, The Great Litigator had proved that he was no paper tiger. He had taken up a lot of time of several senior executives at the hospital. According to one study at a business school, the average cost today of sending a single business letter—thinking about what to say, drafting the letter, typing it (whether by oneself or via a secretary), proofreading it, maybe redrafting and/or retyping it, making a photocopy for the files, mailing it, et cetera—exceeds $15. By now, the folks at the hospital had probably consumed more than $196 worth of time and supplies corresponding with The Great Litigator.

☐ Happy to see the olive branch, The Great Litigator nonetheless stuck to his guns. Instead of replying to the "manager, credit and collections" he wrote again to the administrator:

> *On July 27, I complained to you about an invoice dated July 9 and requested that you have someone telephone me who has authority to enter into a settlement of this matter. I was contacted subsequently by*

*XXXXXXX, manager of your business office, and XXXXXXXXXX, manager of credit and collection. Neither was able to justify to my satisfaction the fees on that invoice, and neither was willing to negotiate a settlement or to refer me to an officer at the hospital who had authority to settle.*

*I feel greatly wronged in this situation, and as a matter of principle I intend to seek legal redress of my grievances, even if doing so is far more costly to me than simply paying the bill. First, however, I want to give you one more opportunity to set this matter straight.*

*I urge you to contact me personally or through a representative— preferably a lawyer—who has both the authority and the willingness to negotiate a settlement. If I have not heard from you within ten days, I will file against the hospital and against yourself and all other pertinent officers and employees a class action lawsuit, on behalf of all patients who may have been overcharged by the hospital, seeking to enjoin you from taking procedures to collect the disputed fund or to report nonpayers of overcharges to credit-reporting agencies as delinquents and seeking also compensatory damages on behalf of all who have paid unwarranted charges and punitive damages on behalf of all who were overcharged.*

☐ Translation: I'm a crazy man, your people have pushed me close to the point-of-no-return, and I'm giving you one last chance to get off the hook; settle with me, or I'll make life miserable for you for quite some time.

☐ *Could* The Great Litigator actually bring a class action against the hospital? Well, he'd probably need a lawyer, because no court in history (as of this writing) ever permitted a nonlawyer to represent a class; but there are plenty of lawyers around, many willing to work for a percentage of whatever the jury awards, and class actions inevitably are handled on this basis. Small wonder: In class actions, the rewards have been known to go into seven, eight, and even nine digits.

☐ Would the hospital *lose* such a lawsuit? Probably not, if, as its officers insisted, all patients were being charged the same—and maybe even if *not* all patients were being charged the same. But to defend a lawsuit is extremely expensive. And there was also the prospect of some bad publicity.

☐   The Great Litigator promptly received a reply from the "associate administrator, fiscal management," reading in pertinent part:

> *I have been the chief fiscal officer of XXXXXXXXX Medical Center for the past fifteen years, and I can assure you that all patients are charged exactly the same rate, irrespective of payor. If your position is based on the fact that Medicare and Medi-Cal are cost-paying reimbursers and you feel that you want to challenge on that issue, you are free to proceed as you wish.*
>
> *Blue Cross reimburses us at our charge level; Medicare and Medi-Cal are less than cost-paying reimbursers by federal and state regulations. Before you incur legal expenses on an issue of this magnitude, you should consult with legal counsel familiar with health care regulations.*
> *Charges in each of our revenue-producing departments are based on costs of operation . . . . If you feel you have been overcharged based on specific items and our costs, I can discuss that with you; but I can assure you that all patients are charged equally.*

☐   At first glance, this reply might seem like another "go drown yourself." There's certainly plenty of bluster and condescension, as in "before you incur legal expenses on an issue of this magnitude, you should consult with legal counsel familiar with health care regulations." Translation: You're a dummy, and we've got guys who can take your head off.

☐   But the operative language is: "If you feel you have been *overcharged* based on *specific items* and our costs, I can *discuss* that with you." Discuss? Is that a little closer to "settle" than "explain," used in the earlier letter from the business office manager? In other words, is the associate administrator, fiscal management, without admitting culpability, *sending* The Great Litigator a *signal* about his amenability to settling the case?

☐   The Great Litigator telephoned the associate administrator and said, in effect, "There's a lot here in your bill that's wacky. Twenty-six bucks for a suture set? Come on, you buy those sets for 80 bucks, and all you have to do between usings is sterilize them. How do you justify $26.50 for sterilization and amortization? Why, if you used the set just three times, you'd have its cost amortized at

$26.50. And what's that $65.50 for the physician's fee? The work was done by a resident, assisted by a nurse. You don't pay both of 'em combined $200 for a shift. Are you contending that they treat an average of three patients per shift, one every three hours? They spent only a few minutes on my daughter, and there were four other patients being worked on at the same time. And that 'emergency room fee' of ninety bucks! Come on, now! Are you trying to raise money to build a new wing on the hospital? . . ."

☐ The associate administrator had justifications, of course, and he spelled out all of them. But The Great Litigator held fast and kept repeating his arguments and threatening to sue.

☐ I'll spare you additional details. After about 20 minutes on the phone, the associate administrator said, in effect, "Tell me what you think would be a fair settlement."

☐ "Fifty percent," said The Great Litigator, "minus one percent as a token to me for having to go through all this bureaucratic rigamarole before getting to speak to you."

☐ "You really want to rub our noses in it, don't you?"

☐ "No, sir, I just want to be treated fairly. Court costs would come to a heck of a lot more than nineteen dollars and sixty cents."

☐ And thus did The Great Litigator settle his dispute with a hospital that had stated repeatedly, "THERE'S NOTHING TO NEGOTIATE."

At the risk of seeming to belabor this point, I'll cite—very briefly—two more examples of The Great Litigator in action against the There's-Nothing-to-Negotiate—Offensive-Variation crowd.

☐ He bought a suit at Brooks Brothers, the well-known clothier. After a few wearings, the trousers ripped at the seam of the seat. He had them repaired and, a few days later, they ripped again. He returned the suit, requesting a replacement, but Brooks Brothers sent the original back to him, stating that there was an ink stain on the trousers and therefore the suit was nonreturnable.

☐ The Great Litigator telephoned the manager at Brooks, saying, in effect, "Look, I've bought dozens of suits from you people, and none of them ever split at the seam except this one. You people did the tailoring, and obviously the pants were cut improperly. Okay, there may be an inkstain on them, but that's irrelevant. I can wear a pair of pants with an inkstain, but I can't wear one with a split up the seat."

☐  He was told, in effect, "Go drown yourself."

☐  He could not refuse to pay, because he already had paid for the suit. He could sue, but that would be time consuming. So what he did was go to Brooks and buy another suit, identical to the damaged one. He charged it to his account, then refused to pay *that* charge, claiming that it was offset by the suit he returned.

☐  Brooks dunned, then turned over the matter to a collection agency. Eventually a lawyer sued, and The Great Litigator filed a counterclaim, alleging damages as a result of the time he had had to spend buying the new suit and attempting to arrange for replacement of the pants to the old suit. Shortly after he filed his counterclaim, he served a "notice of deposition," seeking to interrogate under oath all the officers of Brooks with whom he had discussed the matter or corresponded about it, including the chairperson of the board.

☐  The opposing lawyer filed a motion for a protective order against the depositions. The motion was denied, whereupon the opposing lawyer said to The Great Litigator, "Look, how'd you like to just keep the new suit and forget the whole thing?"

☐  The Great Litigator tells me that he considered asking to have an extra pair of pants thrown in free, but he decided against it.

Final item in this section: The Great Litigator versus The Assistant District Attorney:

☐  No, my friend was not arrested for any crime. His car was broken into by some juveniles, who were caught by the police. They asked The Great Litigator to sign a paper to the effect that it was his car. He did, then went home and forgot the whole matter.

☐  A short while later, he received a subpoena to appear as a witness at a hearing in juvenile court. He telephoned the assistant district attorney who had issued the subpoena and explained that he really could not provide any germane testimony, in that he had not seen anyone enter his car and knew only what he had been told by the police. The assistant district attorney replied that The Great Litigator could testify as to ownership of the car. The Great Litigator asked if he might not simply provide the registration and title or sign an affidavit about ownership rather than make an appearance in court. The assistant district attorney said no.

☐ The Great Litigator, as he has been known to do when people tell him to go drown himself, got testy. He said, in effect, "Look, I'd like to help you, but I've got better things to do with my time than sit around the courthouse for a case that may be continued or get plea-bargained or resolved in some other way. Why don't you just put me 'on call,' if you're going to need me, tell me and I'll get there as fast as I can."

☐ The assistant DA said, in effect, "No way."

☐ "You're being unreasonable. You really don't need me there, and you'll inconvenience me greatly. If you don't relent, I'll have to pursue this with your superiors."

☐ "Be my guest. Also, go drown yourself."

☐ The Great Litigator made a slew of phone calls to higher-ranking people in the DA's office and finally got the DA's top aide. The Great Litigator said, in effect, "What I proposed is reasonable, and it wouldn't compromise your case in any way, but that obnoxious runt who's handling this case wants to play stormtrooper and use me as his straight-man. I'm not going to stand for it. Either arrange to have me put 'on call,' or I'm going to take this thing to the newspaper and let a lot of people know how you guys inconvenience the victims of crimes. Maybe this explains why more people do not come forward to report crimes or to serve as witnesses. Are you getting my drift?"

☐ The aide said that he would take the matter up with the DA. He phoned later to say that The Great Litigator's proposal was acceptable. In a follow-up letter, a copy of which I have in my files, the assistant director of the Bureau of Special Operations of the Office of the District Attorney of the County of Los Angeles wrote to The Great Litigator:

*I have asked deputy-in-charge XXXXXXX to attempt to secure a stip-*
*ulation as to what your testimony would be, if called as a witness. If*
*agreeable to defense counsel, it would not be necessary for you to go to*
*court. Inasmuch as we will probably not be able to secure the stipula-*
*tion until the trial date, it will be necessary for you to be prepared to*
*go to court on XXXXX. I have also asked Mr. XXXXX to place you*
*'on call,' so that it is not necessary for you to be present in court, but*
*you must remain available, on forty-five minutes call, so that you will*
*be able to promptly respond. . . .*

Negotiate with the district attorney's office? Impossible, right?
Well, it's not impossible for criminals—their lawyers plea-bargain
all the time. And, as The Great Litigator proved, it's not impossible for honest citizens either, if they know enough to push the right
buttons.

## THE DOUBLE-TEAM PLOY

Many hardball negotiators send an underling to do the preliminary negotiating and then, when you think you have an agreement, the senior negotiator steps in to change things. The strategy
is akin to the con-game practiced by automobile dealers, wherein a
salesperson gives you a certain price and, when you've agreed to it,
the sales manager steps in and says, in effect, "This salesperson
didn't have the authority to give you this deal. The price he quoted
is even below the one we charge for a car with no options, let alone
one that's as loaded as this car is. He obviously miscalculated.
Now, I don't want you to be disappointed and have to walk away
from here without the car that you want, but we're just going to
have to adjust this figure a bit. . . ."

The strategy is designed, in large part, to take advantage of your
sense of investment in the negotiations and your desire to conclude
them successfully.

Sense of investment? You've probably put in quite a bit of them,
and you may have made some concessions that you did not want to
make. You don't want to lose all that, right?

Desire for a successful conclusion? Of course. You wouldn't have been negotiating otherwise. And the closer you get to an agreement, the better you feel about the fact that all this will soon be a thing of the past and you can get on with the important things in your life.

So you think you have a deal. And then your adversary in a negotiation says, "Well, this looks pretty good to me. Now all I have to do is get the boss to approve. . . ." And the boss, like the sales manager at the automobile dealership, furrows his brow and says, "There's no way I can accept this. We're going to have to make some major changes."

*You,* meanwhile, have already bargained yourself out. You've made concessions that you believe you were trading for other concessions. Your concessions are written in concrete, but the other guy's seem suddenly to be written in sand.

What the guys who are double-teaming you hope, of course, is that you will let your weariness and your desire for an agreement overcome your good judgment. And very often it happens exactly this way.

How to defend against the ploy?

First, tear a page from the book of The Great Litigator and establish at the start that your adversaries have the authority to make an agreement. It is important that you distinguish between this authority and the authority *merely to negotiate.* A great many people may be authorized to negotiate but not to *settle* the controversy.

If your adversary does not claim the authority to settle, you've got three options (1) refuse to negotiate except with someone who has that authority; (2) bring in someone else to do the preliminary negotiating for you, then deal with the other side's Big Guy only after a tentative agreement has been worked out; (3) negotiate with the Big Guy's underling but repeatedly caveat all your concessions, reserving the right to withdraw all of them if the Big Guy does not accept the agreement exactly as is.

In practice, if you're a little guy, you'll usually wind up with option three, inasmuch as your adversary will insist on using underlings to do the preliminary negotiating and you do not command a staff of your own to offset his. You could, of course, simply refuse to speak to anyone but the Big Guy; but, if you do, many Big Guys will simply say, "That's it, he's pushing us too far," and leave you to pursue your BATANA (best alternative to a negotiated settlement).

What should you do if your adversary pretends to have the authority, then acknowledges—after you've worked out the agreement—that he needs someone else's ratification? Well, it all depends on how badly you want the deal.

Unless I want the deal desperately, I generally refuse to permit the rule change. I say, in effect, "You've misled me, and that means that we are back to square one. Go to your ratifier, tell him what we've worked out, and, if he wants to change one comma, the whole deal is out the window and we've got to start again from scratch—but this time I'll talk only to him, not to you." (I reiterate, it all depends on how badly you want the deal.)

## THE PAT-AND-MIKE PLOY AND OTHER GANG-UP STRATAGEMS

Many hardballers, like wolves, run in packs. Instead of facing a single negotiator, you face a team. This is more common in big business or governmental negotiations than in little-guy/big-guy confrontations, but it is not unheard of in the latter.

The usual justification for negotiating in teams is that different people have different specialized knowledge about complex issues. In many cases, that is true enough: No one person knows enough about all the issues (in a multinational treaty, for example, or the purchase of a system comprising extremely sophisticated pieces of equipment) to handle the negotiations entirely on his or her own.

In other situations, however, the issues are fairly simple but a team shows up anyway. And if you are outnumbered, you run the risk of getting worn down sooner than your adversaries, rather like a wrestler who must singly face a tag-team or even several tag-teams.

The Pat-and-Mike approach is a favorite of policemen dealing with suspects. One cop plays Pat, the tough guy, demanding answers, threatening all sorts of dire things, perhaps even roughing up the suspect. (Yes, it's done even in these post-Miranda and post-Escobedo times.) The other cop, Mike, comes across as the nice guy, seemingly unable to understand what you've done that got Pat so angry: "Listen, I'll speak to him for you, maybe I can get him to back off a little, but if you want me to do that, you'll have to help me. Now, where were you on the evening of the nineteenth at 8:45 when Mrs. O'Leary's jewels were stolen? . . ."

The negotiator's equivalent of this routine is to have one or more obvious hardballers backed up by one or more apparent win-winners. A hardballer accuses you of trying to rip him off, threatens to sue you and maybe even bring criminal charges against you, then stalks out of the room, tossing over his shoulder something to the effect that if this controversy gets resolved amicably it'll be over his dead body. While you sit there stunned at this unprovoked attack, an ostensible win-winner chases after the hardballer, saying (well within your range of hearing), "Hey, guy, ease up a bit. I can understand why you feel ol' Manfred is trying to do a number on us, but he's really not such a bad guy. Let's hear him out fully before we decide. . . ."

Of course, the greater number of negotiators on the team, the greater the number of possible combinations of hardballers and ostensible win-winners, Pats and Mikes.

How do you deal with it?

Whenever possible, field a team at least as large as the team of your adversaries, with at least one of your specialists in every department covered by one of theirs. If that's not possible, get as close to the ideal as you can, then attempt to use time as a weapon against their greater numbers.

For example, if you've got only three guys and they have 10, refuse to separate your contingent into separate discussion groups where the other side will have them two-or-more-on-one. Instead, insist on discussing everything as a committee-of-the-whole, with all of their people present and all of yours. Given their superior numbers, such an arrangement will be costlier for them than for you; they, after all, must pay all these people who are sitting around while someone on their side is making a point to someone on yours, or vice-versa.

If you can't arrange this, stretch out the discussions for as long as you can, continuing to penalize your adversaries for their superior numbers. Take a lot of breaks, insist on a lot of caucuses for your side.

Whatever the situation, never put yourself in a position where you must negotiate continuously while your adversaries can take turns. This wears you out and leaves them relatively fresh. If they insist on working in shifts, demand very short shifts for yourself— say two or three hours at a stretch, once or twice a day. Justify your insistence, if you must, by saying that you have to bone up on the particulars of the next phase of negotiations.

## PHYSICAL FACTORS

Many hardballers do everything they can to wear you out while keeping themselves fresh, to serve their own convenience while inconveniencing you.

If the negotiations take place at my office rather than at yours, I've got a decided advantage. You've had to travel to get there, putting up with traffic and worrying about being on time, while I was able to sit comfortably back and work on something else while waiting for you to arrive. If I want a cup of coffee or a glass of water, I can simply tell my secretary to bring me one. If you want one, you have to ask *me* (and I, remember, am your adversary).

If I sit behind my desk in a big, comfortable swivel chair and you sit opposite me on a small, straight-backed chair, who is less comfortable? And who suffers the metaphoric reinforcement of the difference between the superior and inferior positions? (It is not without reason that so many courthouses look like Greek temples and must be approached via a long flight of stairs, nor is it without reason that judges sit on high benches, literally as well as metaphorically *above* the people who are pleading—apt word—before them.)

An agricultural firm whose chief executive is one of the world's all-time hardballers recently was profiled in *Advertising Age,* which revealed how the executive staged conferences between his team and the teams of ad agencies that wanted his firm's account. The hardballer and his team sat on one side of a long table, their backs to a large, high window. The other guy sat facing the window, with the sun shining into their eyes—its intensity magnified in reflections from a lake.

What to do if you find yourself in a situation of this kind? Protest—vehemently, if you can afford to—and even threaten to walk out if things aren't changed.

I've been in situations where I was given an especially uncomfortable chair or was positioned facing a window. I said, simply enough, "This chair is uncomfortable. Do you have another?" Or: "The light from that window is bothering me. Can you do something about it?"

Most hardballers, confronted with their attempt to cow/ intimidate/weary you, will back off. And if they don't, make their inhospitality an issue. ("Look, I'd hate to see these negotiations break down simply because you don't have the good manners to provide me with a comfortable chair, but that's what's going to happen unless you change things fast.")

Insofar as you can, control the territory. If the other side's lawyer serves you with a notice of deposition that specifies the locale as his office, tell him that he can take the deposition at *your* office or at the courthouse; if he wants it at his office, he'll have to file a motion for a court order to that effect—and he won't win that motion, whereupon you can seek sanctions against him for having moved frivolously.

It is not without reason that negotiations for the Vietnam peace agreement were in abeyance for more than two months while discussions were being held about the shape of the table at which the negotiations would take place. To someone who knows little about negotiating, the dispute may have seemed absurd: "Imagine these guys arguing about the shape of the table when people are out there getting killed." I agree that it was scandalous that the war continued for as long as it did and that it took so many lives. However, I can appreciate the concern of the negotiators with the shape of the table. How'd you like to represent North Vietnam during months of negotiations in which you sat at the far end of a long, rectangular table with the sun in your eyes while South Vietnam sat in the center opposite the United States, both parties being in the shade? Do you think the shape of the table and your position at it would strengthen or weaken your negotiating position?

Let me emphasize, these controversies over physical factors usually do not arise with win-win negotiators. If you and I are sincerely trying to help each other get a good deal (refer back to Chapter 14), we will bend over backward to ensure each other's comforts. I'll take you to lunch at one of the nicer restaurants I know, you'll take me to lunch at one of the nicer restaurants you know, and we'll each give the other the most comfortable chair in the office. However, not all negotiators—no matter what they may say—are of the win-win persuasion, and, when you're up against a hardballer, you have to know how to fight back.

## DEADLINE PRESSURES

Some years ago the players in the National Football League were on strike and one of my buddies, an avid fan, was grousing about not having the games on TV. He wondered aloud when, if ever, the strike would be settled.

I asked him for some information about the schedule: How many games were in the regular season, how many playoff games, when the Super Bowl would be played, et cetera. He told me, and I performed some computations. Then I informed him that the strike would be settled during the Week of X.

First he thought I was joking, but I offered to place a small wager. Then he suspected that I had read or heard about plans for a settlement, but that wasn't the case, either. Finally he accepted that I had made a bona fide judgment without benefit of "insider" information. He asked how I had made that judgment.

It was simple. I assumed that, despite their animosity toward each other, neither the players nor the owners were willing to throw the baby out with the bathwater. In other words, they could both live with cancellations of some early-season games, the losses from which were in part covered by insurance; but they would find a way to make peace in time to stage the playoffs and the Super Bowl. They would do so because (1) they realized that if *no* games were played that season, not even the playoffs and Super Bowl, they might find a year later that quite a few people had lost the football viewing habit; (2) they did not want to lose the enormous revenues that these games would provide (and that insurance would not cover).

I therefore calculated the number of regular-season games that would be necessary to produce a reasonable roster of teams for the playoffs, and I estimated that the first of these must-play games would be the one before which the strike would be resolved. I was exactly right—not because I know anything about football, but because I have made my career as a negotiator.

Deadlines are a crucial element in negotiations. If there is no *need* to resolve an issue, the tendency is to let matters slide. But if the old clock is ticking away and you must reach agreement by midnight, the closer you get to the deadline, the harder you have to work—and the more likely you are to make concessions that you would not have made earlier.

The most compelling deadlines are objective ones—in other words, independent phenomena that place limits on the negotiators, not arbitrary dates that one side or the other may establish. If the NFL teams must be on the field by October X in order to salvage the playoffs and Super Bowl, that date is sacrosanct. Having such a deadline is quite different from having the players' negotiator or the owners' negotiator say, "If you guys can't make a deal with us by October X, then the whole season is off."

Some examples of objective deadlines:

***The Expiration of a Contract.*** It is not without reason that negotiations in the auto industry become so frantic as the expiration date approaches and a strike becomes an increasingly strong possibility.

*A Date in Court.* If the trial or the hearing on a motion is scheduled for March X, the adversaries must settle by that date or face the consequences. This is a lot different from their merely *threatening* consequences. ("If you don't settle by next Tuesday, I won't be available for further discussions.") When you threaten, you *may* mean it, but then again you may not. But if the court says the trial starts on March X, there's no doubt about who means what.

*The Start or End of a Well-Established Cycle.* The Christmas selling season begins in most retail establishments around Thanksgiving. Wholesalers usually must have the goods available around the first of November. Depending on the goods—their perishability, how long they take to produce, et cetera—manufacturers and their suppliers and the suppliers' suppliers have various lead times. But whatever one's lead time, there is a date beyond which the deal cannot be made. Any negotiations about price, terms of sale, et cetera, will have as their *objective* deadline this date.

Hardballers use deadlines in a variety of ways.

Their favorite strategy is to save until last discussion of the issues that are most important to you. In other words, if they can keep you busy talking about relatively minor issues until you are staring the deadline in the eye, they may be able to get you to make extraordinary concessions on the major issues because you do not want to let the deadline pass with the negotiations unresolved.

How to counter this? Calculate how much time you'll need to negotiate the issues that are most important to you, and refuse to begin those discussions any later.

Another strategy of hardballers is to pretend that an arbitrary deadline is an objective deadline. ("My boss has said that if we can't resolve this by April X, he will assume that settlement is impossible." You must answer: "In that case, let's not waste any more time. Tell him that we refuse to negotiate on his timetable. If he would like to have us establish *mutually* an irrevocable deadline, we'll consider it, but there is no way that we are going to let him set the parameters of these discussions dictatorially.")

Actually, when objective deadlines are not present, it's a very good idea to establish mutually acceptable deadlines as *goals* of the negotiators. ("Let's agree that we'll settle all the questions about salaries before next Monday, then all the questions about fringe benefits before the following Friday.") It's also a good idea to establish arbitrary deadlines when you are threatening an adversary with action. ("If I haven't received a satisfactory explanation of this matter by May X, I will sue.")

However, it's important to understand the difference between arbitrary deadlines and objective deadlines. Hardballers will very often try to get you to treat an arbitrary deadline as if it were an objective deadline.

There's another way hardballers use deadlines to trip up adversaries: They determine an adversary's real deadline, then try to get him or her to act rashly as it approaches.

To wit:

☐ You're a lawyer who is taking my deposition. You learn that I coach Little League baseball on Tuesday nights. I'm due at the ballpark at 5:30, which means that I must leave my office at 4:30. Okay, you schedule my deposition for 2 PM, assuring me (without revealing that you know about my Little League commitment) that your questions will not take more than an hour or so to answer.

☐ The deposition begins. You question me about unimportant matters. I respond. The clock ticks away. Soon the time is 3:30, and now you get into substantive matters for the first time. The clock continues to tick away. As 4:00 approaches, I am nervously looking at my watch, because I know that we're in the middle of a rather thorny issue that probably will need another half hour. And what will you introduce after that?

☐ The closer we get to 4:30, the more apt I am to give you information that I hadn't intended; the more apt I am to acquiesce on issues where I ordinarily would take a stand; the more apt I am, in sum, to give you exactly what you want—because I want to get out of that doggone office and go to my Little League game!

Having been put in this situation more than once by hardballers, I've learned to establish rules that ensure I'll not be victimized this way again. I never schedule negotiations before an appointment unless I am confident that all matters will be resolved well before the time when I must leave.

If I cannot avoid a negotiating session that abuts an appointment, I put my adversary on notice and I give myself an extra 15 minutes: "Before we begin, let me tell you that I must leave precisely at 4:15, so, if there is any matter you want to introduce that we cannot resolve fully before that time, please save it until our next meeting." (I said 4:15 because I really had to leave at 4:30. I may let the discussion continue until 4:20 but definitely not beyond 4:25.)

If I cannot avoid scheduling a negotiating session before a major independent event, I try to locate the meeting as close as possible to the place I must be, just in case things get difficult. And I never—but *never*—let myself make concessions in the interest of wrapping things up so that I can go.

Apropos all of this, it's a good idea when negotiating against a hardballer to save the most difficult issues for last. It's much easier to win concessions on difficult issues if everyone has invested some time and energy in agreeing on minor, easily resolved points.

## THE ONE-SIDED-CONCESSION PLOY

Another favorite tactic of hardballers is to try to pin you down on a specific issue and get your concession on it before other matters are discussed. The thinking is that you will not be able to back off on this concession, no matter what happens in later stages of negotiating.

Here are a few examples of how this ploy is attempted:

☐   "Now, Ms. Butler, as I understand your position, you acknowledge that we delivered the goods on time but you refused to accept them because you found them damaged, is that right?"

☐   "Look, Sarah, from what I can see, all you can claim on

specific damages is $6,000 for loss of income between February and October. Are you claiming any more than that?"

☐ "If we come and pick up the washer and dryer, will that satisfy you?"

What I want to avoid in situations such as these is committing myself to something that undermines me with regard to other desiderata.

For example, if I agree (in the first example) that the goods were delivered on time, I'm giving up a potential bargaining point that I don't have to give up. My tendency would be to respond, "The issue here is not the timely delivery of the goods, it's the fact that they were damaged. Once we resolve the issue of their being damaged, we can talk about whether or not they were delivered on time."

Likewise, regarding loss of income (in the second example), I do not want to limit myself to the $6,000, so my tendency would be to reply, "I haven't asserted a claim for more than that, but I do not rule out that I may do so if this matter isn't resolved to my satisfaction."

Concerning the washer and dryer (third example), I'd be inclined to say, "I definitely want you to pick up the washer and dryer. I'd like to get that issue resolved before we move on to any other. What must I do to get you to come out and pick it up?"

If all of the above can be reduced to a single rule, the rule is this:

**Keep your options open; never agree irrevocably to a single point until the entire agreement has been accepted.**

# ≡17≡IT'S NOT ALWAYS EASY

## BUT IT'S USUALLY POSSIBLE

Let's face it, most of us would be very comfortable as dictators. But let's also face something else: Not too many people get the opportunity to be dictators. For those of us who have been denied that opportunity, the usual approach to getting what we want is to exchange something with someone who has what we want. Conflict arises whenever there is a difference of opinion about the exchange, and the best way to resolve the conflict is to negotiate regarding the difference of opinion. That, in the proverbial nutshell, is what this book has been about.

Old-style negotiators really are nothing more than hagglers. They take positions, argue about which position is "right," and ultimately either "split the difference" or leave the conflict unresolved. New-style negotiators pursue interest bargaining and attempt to help their adversaries get a good deal. Life is much more enjoyable when everyone wins—and it *is* possible, when negotiators are creative, for everyone to win.

If it's not possible for everyone to win, then it usually is possible for everyone to cut his losses. Consider this:

☐   Your home was burglarized. All sorts of valuables were taken. Somebody contacts you on behalf of the burglars, who are teenagers who live in the same neighborhood. The emissary offers to return all your valuables, provided that you don't prosecute the teenagers.

☐   Granted, you've been inconvenienced. But would you be willing to put the whole matter behind you and not get the kids into trouble if you could promptly regain everything you lost? You probably would.

☐   Okay, let's take it a step farther. The people who stole your valuables were not neighborhood teenagers; they were professional burglars. And their emissary offers to return *not* the whole booty but only the most valuable items, again provided that you do not prosecute.

☐   Where do you draw the line?

Extend the example as far as you like. The burglars will return only half of the most valuable items. Or only one quarter. Or only *one item*.

Where do you draw the line?

Here's another situation to consider:

☐   You and your best friend—your lover—are driving along a deserted highway. Your car gets a flat tire. You and your friend start to change it when your friend notices that something is leaking from your engine. Your friend slides underneath the car, looking for the leak, and somehow manages to dislodge the jack that was holding up the car for the tire change. Now your friend is pinned under the car and may very well die if you do not get help immediately.

☐   Alright, you set out along the deserted highway, looking for help, and you spot a telephone booth—the only sign of life for miles

and miles and miles. Doggone if it isn't the same telephone booth
we discussed in Chapter 2. Remember the illustration?

☐ You have to make an urgent telephone call. You are waiting
outside a booth that is being used by an elderly man who obviously
is in no hurry to finish his conversation. You would:

a. Expect the man to notice that you are fidgeting; when he does,
   he probably will be considerate and terminate the
   conversation.
b. Try to find another telephone.
c. Wish you were not dependent on the telephone.
d. Bang on the door to demonstrate your impatience.
e. Wait patiently; eventually the man will have to stop talking.
f. Feel guilty about your hostile feelings toward the old man; his
   phone call, after all, may be just as important to him as yours
   is to you.

☐ Well, we've got a whole new situation here, don't we, now
that your best friend is lying under the car and likely to die if you
can't summon help right away? So how do you deal with the old
man?

☐ When I've presented this example in seminars on conflict
management, I've found that responses clustered in the following
categories:

1. Ask nicely.
2. Bribe.
3. Threaten.
4. Use force.

☐ In other words, most of the members of the seminars would
first appeal to the old man's good nature. They would rap politely
on the door and explain why they need the telephone.

☐ If the old man refused to relinquish it, they would then attempt to bribe him. They would offer to pay for the use of the phone.

☐ If he still refused to relinquish it, they would threaten him—whether with ejecting him forcefully or calling the police from another phone (if one could be found) or suing him for damages if the friend under the car was seriously injured.

☐ And if the old man still refused, the members of my seminars would—almost to a person (or so they said)—forcibly eject the old man from the booth.

☐ Alright, *you* think about it and decide what you would do. In fact, don't merely think about what you would do but write it down—before you read any further.

☐ Do you have it written down?

☐ Okay, next step.

☐ Let's pretend that the occupant of the phone booth was not an old man. Let's pretend instead that it was Charles Manson . . . or Mr. T. . . . or whomever you would nominate as the modern equivalent of Attilla the Hun.

☐ Would that change your reaction?

☐ If you're looking for a "right" answer to this problem, or to the earlier one about how to react if approached by an emissary of someone who has burgled your house, I'm sorry to report that I don't have one. But the search for such answers is what creative negotiating is all about.

*Win-Win Negotiating*—that's my concept for making conflict work in which parties summon all their imaginative skills and resources to provide each other with an array of benefits that neither would realize were it not for the other.

Creative negotiating . . . synergistic negotiating.

It's a concept that I like very much.

But that's another book.

# INDEX

Alinsky, Saul, 107–108
Ambiguity, *see* Poorly defined
  responsibilities
Approach-approach, 3
Approach-avoidance, 3
Avoidance-avoidance, 3, 81

Best Alternative To A Negotiated
  Agreement (BATANA),
  202–213, 284
Blame, 15–16
Bluffing, 150–151
Bone-throwing, 256–259

Change, 55–57, 66–67
Christiansen, Bjørn, 14–15
Communication, 67, 71–73
Competition, 26–27, 34–41
Conflict, case studies, 1–3, 7–12,
  63–65, 295–298

Conflict, defined, 3, 24–27
Conflict exercise, 119–127
Conflict inventory, 7–21
Conflict resolution, 39–41, 72–73,
  95–100, 129–154
Conflict sources, 29–61, 65–69,
  130
Conflict styles, 7–21, 119–127
Control units, 111
Coser, Lewis, 25–27

Deadlines, 288–292
Destructive consequences,
  101–109. *See also* Negative
  effects
Differing interpretations, 86–
  89
Double standards, 89–92
Drives for success, recognition,
  power, 57–61, 67

Escalated conflict, 76–100, 161

Fisher, Roger, 136–144
Frank, Allan, 64–65

Groupthink, 111–117

Hostility, 102–103

Janis, Irving L., 111–117

Interest bargaining, 187–197
Issue-substitution, 259–262

Mini-max, 199–215, 217–228
Mirror image, 84–86
Misallocation of resources, 102–103
Multiple-issue conflict, 238–248, 292–293
Murray, Edward J., 25

Negative effects, 4–5. *See also* Destructive consequences
Negotiation, 136–144, 179–226, 249–293
North, Robert C., 25

Organizational conflict, 23–24, 29–61, 157–177

Parties to conflict, 69–71. *See also* Relationship, of parties to conflict
Physical factors, 286–288
Polarized positions, 92–100
Poorly defined responsibilities, 51–55, 68
Positional bargaining, 179–187
Power, 155–177, 203, 263–282
Problem-solving, 16–17
Productive consequences, 109–117

Relationship, of parties to conflict, 130–136, 142–144, 161–171. *See also* Parties to conflict

Sabotage, 103–109
Single-issue conflict, 92–100, 233–238
Sources of conflict, *see* Conflict sources

Team-negotiating, 282–286
Third-parties, 69–71
Tokening, 250–256

Undoing, 250
Unpacking, 5–6, 95–100, 229–248
Ury, William, 136–144

Values, 41–50, 66, 78, 138, 220–224